2012 JINAN DAXUE HUAQIAO DAXUE LIANGXIAO LIANZHAO
QUANGUO LIANZHAO KAOSHITI JIEJI

2012 暨南大学华侨大学两校联招 全国联招 考试题解集

主编 温宗军 副主编 张训涛 李志红

暨南大学出版社
JINAN UNIVERSITY PRESS
中国·广州

图书在版编目（CIP）数据

2012 暨南大学华侨大学两校联招、全国联招考试题解集/温宗军主编；张训涛，李志红副主编．—广州：暨南大学出版社，2013.1（2015.7 重印）
ISBN 978－7－5668－0417－4

Ⅰ.①2012…　Ⅱ.①温…②张…③李…　Ⅲ.①课程—高中—题解—升学参考资料　Ⅳ.①G632.479

中国版本图书馆 CIP 数据核字（2012）第 280771 号

出版发行：暨南大学出版社

地　址：中国广州暨南大学
电　话：总编室（8620）85221601
　　　　营销部（8620）85225284　85228291　85228292（邮购）
传　真：（8620）85221583（办公室）　85223774（营销部）
邮　编：510630
网　址：http：//www.jnupress.com　http：//press.jnu.edu.cn

排　版：广州市天河星辰文化发展部照排中心
印　刷：佛山市浩文彩色印刷有限公司

开　本：787mm×1092mm　1/16
印　张：10
字　数：251 千
版　次：2013 年 1 月第 1 版
印　次：2015 年 7 月第 2 次
印　数：3001—4500 册

定　价：33.00 元

前 言

2012年暨南大学、华侨大学招收港、澳、台、华侨、华人及其他外籍学生入学考试（简称“两校联招”）及中华人民共和国普通高等学校联合招收华侨、港澳地区、台湾省学生入学考试（简称“全国联招”）已经结束。为了帮助和指导考生有针对性地进行复习备考，我们组织了一批常年指导联招考试辅导班、具有丰富经验的教师进行了研讨，对2012年及近年的两校联招和全国联招试题进行了细致的总结、比较、分析和研究，编写了2012年的两校联招和全国联招考试真题解析集。

参加编写各科试题分析的老师主要有：袁忠群（中国语文），刘岑枫、张卓（数学），陈芳（英语），蔡贤榜（地理），姚蓓（物理），李志红（化学），何红卫（生物）。

由于作者水平有限，编写中难免出现错漏，欢迎广大师生予以指正。

编 者

2012年10月

目录

CONTENTS

■前言…………………………………………………………………… 1

■2012年暨南大学、华侨大学招收港、澳、台、华侨、华人及其他外籍学生入学考试题目

语文…………………………………………………………………… 1

数学 ………………………………………………………………… 10

英语 ………………………………………………………………… 14

地理 ………………………………………………………………… 27

物理 ………………………………………………………………… 33

化学 ………………………………………………………………… 39

生物 ………………………………………………………………… 44

■2012年中华人民共和国普通高等学校联合招收华侨、港澳地区、台湾省学生入学考试题目

语文 ………………………………………………………………… 50

数学 ………………………………………………………………… 57

英语 ………………………………………………………………… 60

地理 ………………………………………………………………… 73

物理 ………………………………………………………………… 78

化学 ………………………………………………………………… 83

■2012年暨南大学、华侨大学招收港、澳、台、华侨、华人及其他外籍学生入学考试题目答案

语文 ………………………………………………………………… 88

数学 ………………………………………………………………… 90

英语 ………………………………………………………………… 93

地理 ………………………………………………………………… 96

物理 ………………………………………………………………… 98

化学………………………………………………………………… 101

生物………………………………………………………………… 103

■2012 年中华人民共和国普通高等学校联合招收华侨、港澳地区、台湾省学生入学考试题目答案

语文…… 105
数学…… 107
英语…… 111
地理…… 113
物理…… 114
化学…… 117

■2012 年两校联招、全国联招试题比较分析

语文…… 119
数学…… 125
英语…… 130
地理…… 137
物理…… 143
化学…… 149
生物…… 154

2012年暨南大学、华侨大学招收港、澳、台、华侨、华人及其他外籍学生入学考试题目

语文

答卷时间：2小时30分

一、基础知识

（本题分选择题、非选择题两大部分。选择题的答案请填涂在答题卡上“选择题区”与题号、答案相对应的方框中；非选择题的答案则请填写在答题卡“非选择题答题区”中与题号相对应的位置上。共30分）

【选择题】

（一）单项选择题（每题2分，共20分）

1. 下列各组词语中，书写完全正确的是哪一组？

A. 具备　万事具备　缘故　无缘无故

B. 擅长　英勇擅战　变换　变幻莫测

C. 世故　人情事故　振动　震动全国

D. 直接　直截了当　原型　原形毕露

2. 下列各句中加方框的成语，哪一个使用得最为恰当？

A. 目前，中学生作文中错别字俯拾皆是，改变这种现状是当前语文教学的重要任务。

B. 他本想以次充好降低成本，没想到工程不合格，依据合同要支付巨额赔偿，真是功亏一篑。

C. 自负的他怎么也没想到，高考之后，期期艾艾盼来的竟然是专科学校的录取通知书，这对他的打击实在太大了。

D. 仅仅因为战胜了韩国队，我们就妄自菲薄地说中国足球水准已经亚洲一流了，那就太自以为是了。

3. 下列句子中，哪一句的表达完全正确？

A. 临床试验证明，采用草药防治多种疾病的效果良好，这使那些怀疑用草药防治疾病是否有效的人，改变了原来的看法。

B. 记住自己做过的错事是避免吃一堑、长一智，重蹈覆辙的前提，一个人要想少犯

错误，必须做到这一点。

C．求同和封闭的中国传统思维方式，对我们的教育产生了深远的影响。时至今日，语文阅读教学还大致是注经解经式的教学。

D．他通过社会实践活动，关于社会有了较多的了解，关于人生也有一个清澈的观照。

4．下列各句子，语言表达得体的是哪一句？

A．王海起草了一份寻物启事："昨天本人在图书馆丢失了一本《现代汉语词典》，如有拾获，请速速归还本人。"

B．人的生命，似洪水在奔流，不遇着岛屿、暗礁，难以激起美丽的浪花。

C．小明看到邻居李大爷家失火了，就急忙跑来告诉母亲："火！疯狂的大火！它吞噬了大地！它遮住了太阳！"

D．老王生性耿直，爱打抱不平，凡是看不惯的人和事，他都会鸡蛋里挑骨头，从不客气，深受大家的尊重。

5．在下面句子的画线处依次填入词语，最恰当的是哪一组？

①睡前适量的运动可以分散注意力，使紧张的精神______下来，有利于睡眠。

②翻开手稿一看，______所有的地方都用红笔改过，只有几处没有改动。

③由于摆脱了功利之争，田园山水诗人便有了一种恬静______的心境。

④这是一条公理：财富只能毁灭崇高的理想和善良的气质，倘若它只______在个人的利益上面。

A．松弛　　几乎　　淡泊　　消耗

B．松懈　　似乎　　淡薄　　消耗

C．松懈　　几乎　　淡泊　　消费

D．松弛　　似乎　　淡薄　　消费

6．在下面语段中的空白处填入句子，其中与上下文衔接最好的是哪一项？

每个夜幕深垂的晚上，山下亮起灿烂的万家灯火，山上闪出疏落的灯光。______，淡如烟，淡如雾，山也虚无，树也缥缈。

A．山上的灯把黑暗照淡了，山下的灯把黑暗照亮了

B．山上的灯把黑暗照亮了，山下的灯把黑暗照淡了

C．山下的灯把黑暗照亮了，山上的灯把黑暗照淡了

D．山下的灯把黑暗照淡了，山上的灯把黑暗照亮了

7．"质而绮，真且醇，自可传之千古；樽中酒，篱下诗，岂甘了此一生"所写的是哪位古代诗人？

A．陶潜　　B．李白　　C．杜甫　　D．陆游

8．"莫愁前路无知己，天下谁人不识君。"诗中的"君"是指下列哪一个人？

A．李白　　B．孟浩然　　C．元九　　D．董大

9．下面《归园田居》诗句中，哪一组具有比喻意义？

A．少无适俗韵，性本爱丘山。

B．羁鸟恋旧林，池鱼思故渊。

C．榆柳荫后檐，桃李罗堂前。

D. 狗吠深巷中，鸡鸣桑树颠。

10. 下列句子中标点符号使用完全正确的是哪一句？

A. 学校对面二、三十米处就是一个网吧，一些孩子考完试后来到这里“减压”，家长们颇为担忧。

B. 他说过他的报酬是多少不重要？重要的是他为大家做了什么事？

C. 联想和想象，是诗歌的艺术翅膀，借助它，诗人就能浮想联翩，“笼天地于形内，挫万物于笔端”，创造出生动的形象和感人的意境。

D. 金，原泛指一切金属，如“金就砺则利”，(《荀子·劝学》) 现在专指黄金。

(二) 判断题 (判断下列各题所表述的意思是否正确。如果正确，请在答题卡上与题号相对应的答题框选择填涂“T”；如果错误，则填涂“F”。每题 1 分，共 5 分)

11. 杂剧剧本的体例十分严整，一般由四折一楔子构成一本，少数作品也有一本分为五折或六折的，还有用两个楔子的。通常一本就是一部戏。

12. “敕造宁国府”中的“敕造”是皇帝赐与宁国府的封号。

13. 汉字在历史上出现过甲骨文、金文、篆书、隶书、楷书五种正式字体以及草书、行书等辅助字体。其中金文是指通行于西周的青铜器上的文字。

14. 明清时代，我国戏曲得到了迅速的发展，著名的作品有汤显祖《牡丹亭》、洪升《长生殿》、孔尚任《桃花扇》等。

15. 我国的旧体诗有古体近体的分别。古体诗亦称“古风”，有四言、五言、六言、七言、杂言等，如陶渊明的《归园田居》、《饮酒》；近体诗亦称“今体诗”，有律诗和绝句，如王昌龄《出塞》、王维《山居秋暝》、李白《将进酒》、杜甫《登高》等。

【非选择题】

(三) 填空题 (每空 1 分，共 5 分)

16. 知之者不如好之者，______。(《论语·雍也》)

17. 沧海月明珠有泪，______。(李商隐《锦瑟》)

18. 落红不是无情物，______。(龚自珍《己亥杂诗》)

19. “你自己荐她来，又合伙劫她去，闹得沸反盈天的，大家看了成个什么样子?”句中“沸反盈天”的意思是______。

20. “小朱说，老赵您不是做生意了吗? 什么时候您也请咱们上那儿嘬一顿，让咱们这帮刘姥姥也长回见识。”句中的“咱们这帮刘姥姥”用的修辞格是______。

二、阅读理解

(本题分选择题、非选择题两大部分。选择题的答案请填涂在答题卡上“选择题区”与题号、答案相对应的方框中；非选择题的答案则请填写在答题卡“非选择题答题区”中与题号相对应的位置上。共 50 分)

(一) 文言文阅读 (30 分)

阅读下面的文章或诗词，然后依题目要求把答案填涂或填写在答题卡上。

阅读材料一：

有蒋氏者，专其利三世矣。问之，则曰：“吾祖死于是，吾父死于是，今吾嗣为之十二年，几死者数矣。”言之，貌若甚戚者。

余悲之，且曰：“若毒之乎？余将告于莅事者，更若役，复若赋，则如何？”

蒋氏大戚，汪然出涕曰：“君将哀而生之乎？则吾斯役之不幸，未若复吾赋不幸之甚也。向吾不为斯役，则久已病矣。自吾氏三世居是乡，积于今六十岁矣，而乡邻之生日蹙，殚其地之出，竭其庐之入，号呼而转徙，饥渴而顿踣，触风雨，犯寒暑，呼嘘毒疠，往往而死者相藉也。曩与吾祖居者，今其室十无一焉；与吾父居者，今其室十无二三焉；与吾居十二年者，今其室十无四五焉。非死即徙尔，而吾以捕蛇独存。悍吏之来吾乡，叫嚣乎东西，隳突乎南北；哗然而骇者，虽鸡狗不得宁焉。吾恂恂而起，视其缶，而吾蛇尚存，则弛然而卧。谨食之，时而献焉。退而甘食其土之有，以尽吾齿。盖一岁之犯死者二焉，其余，则熙熙而乐，岂若吾乡邻之旦旦有是哉。今虽死乎此，比吾乡邻之死则已后矣，又安敢毒耶？”

阅读材料二：

陆秀夫，字君实，楚州盐城人。生三岁，□父徙家镇江。稍长，从其乡人孟先生学，孟之徒恒百余，独指秀夫曰：“此非凡儿也。”景定元年，登进士第。李庭芝镇淮南，闻其名，辟置幕中。时天下称得士多者，以淮南为第一，号“小朝廷”。

秀夫才思清丽，一时文人少能及之。性沉静，不苟求人知，每僚吏至阁，宾主交欢，秀夫独敛焉无一语。或时宴集府中，坐尊俎间，矜庄终日，未尝少有希合。至察其事，皆治，庭芝益器之，虽改官不使去己，就幕三迁至主管机宜文字。咸淳十年，庭芝制置淮东，擢参议官。德佑元年，边事急，诸僚属多亡者，惟秀夫数人不去。庭芝上其名，除司农寺丞，累擢至宗正少卿兼权起居舍人。

二年正月，以礼部侍郎使军前请和，不就而反。二王走温州，秀夫与苏刘义追从之，使人召陈宜中、张世杰等皆至，遂相与立益王于福州。进端明殿学士、签书枢密院事。宜中以秀夫久在兵间，知军务，每事谘访始行，秀夫亦悉心赞之，无不自尽。旋与议宜中不合，宜中使言者劾罢之。张世杰让宜中曰：“此何如时，动以台谏论人？”宜中皇恐，亟召秀夫还。

时君臣播越海滨，庶事疏略，杨太妃垂帘，与群臣语犹自称奴。每时节朝会，秀夫俨然正笏立，如治朝，或时在行中，凄然泣下，□朝衣拭泪，衣尽浥，左右无不悲动者。属井澳风，王以惊疾殂，群臣皆欲散去。秀夫曰：“度宗皇帝一子尚在，将焉置之？古人有以一旅一成中兴者，今百官有司皆具，士卒数万，天若未欲绝宋，此岂不可为国邪？”乃与众共立卫王。时陈宜中往占城，以与世杰不协，屡召不至。□以秀夫为左丞相，与世杰共秉政。时世杰驻兵崖山，秀夫外筹军旅，内调工役，凡有所述作，又尽出其手。虽匆遽流离中，犹日书《大学章句》以劝讲。

至元十六年二月，崖山破，秀夫走卫王舟，□世杰、刘义各断维去，秀夫度不可脱，乃杖剑驱妻子入海，即负王赴海死，年四十四。（《宋史·忠义传六》）

阅读材料三：

子夜秋歌

李白

长安一片月，万户捣衣声。

秋风吹不尽，总是玉关情。

何日平胡虏，良人罢远征。

【选择题】

（本题皆为单项选择题，每小题 3 分，共 24 分）

21. 对材料一中下列句子里加方框词语的解释，哪一项是正确的？

A. 今吾嗣为之十二年，[几]死者数矣。　　几：几次，屡次。

B. 蒋氏大戚，汪然出[涕]曰："……"　　涕：鼻涕。

C. [曩]与吾祖居者，今其室十无一焉。　　曩：从前，先前。

D. 退而甘食其土之有，以尽吾[齿]。　　齿：牙齿。

22. 材料一中的下列句子里，加方框的"若"字用作引入比较对象的介词，相当于现代汉语的"比"或"比得上"的是哪一句？

A. 言之，貌[若]甚戚者。

B. 余悲之，且曰："[若]毒之乎？"

C. 未[若]复吾赋不幸之甚也。

D. 其余则熙熙而乐，岂[若]吾乡邻之旦旦有是哉。

23. 材料一中的下列句子里，加方框的代词"之"字，哪一个用以指代捕蛇者？

A. 今吾嗣为[之]十二年，几死者数矣。

B. 余悲之，且曰："若毒[之]乎？"

C. 蒋氏大戚，汪然出涕，曰："君将哀而生[之]乎？"

D. 视其缶，而吾蛇尚存，则弛然而卧。谨食[之]，时而献焉。

24. 对材料一中"向吾不为斯役，则久已病矣"一句的翻译，下列哪一项是正确的？

A. 先前我不做这个差事，早已经困顿不堪了。

B. 先前我不做这个差事，早已经病得很严重了。

C. 我向来不做这个差事，所以早已经困顿不堪了。

D. 我向来不做这个差事，所以早已经病得很严重了。

25. 依次在材料二中的下列句子的方框处填入一个虚词，哪一项是正确的？

① □父徙家镇江。稍长，从其乡人孟先生学。

② □朝衣拭泪，衣尽浥，左右无不悲动者。

③ □以秀夫为左丞相，与世杰共秉政。

④ □世杰、刘义各断维去，秀夫度不可脱，乃杖剑驱妻子入海。

A. ①乃　②而　③其　④以

B. ①而　②乃　③其　④以

C. ①其　②以　③乃　④而

D. ①其　②乃　③而　④以

26. 对材料二的下列句子中加方框的词语的解释，哪一项是错误的？

A. 李庭芝镇淮南，闻其名，辟置幕中。　　　辟：授予（职务）。

B. 庭芝上其名，除司农寺丞。　　　　　　　除：开除；除名。

C. 张世杰让宜中曰："此何如时，动以台谏论人？"责备，指责。

D. 时君臣播越海滨，庶事疏略。　　　　　　播：播迁；流亡。

27. 对材料二中的"秀夫亦悉心赞之，无不自尽"一句的翻译，下列哪一项是正确的？

A. 陆秀夫也发自内心地赞美他，没有人不想为他而献出自己的生命。

B. 陆秀夫也全心全意地赞美他，没有人不想为他而献出自己的生命。

C. 陆秀夫也发自内心地辅佐他，没有不竭尽自己的心力的。

D. 陆秀夫也全心全意地辅佐他，没有不竭尽自己的心力的。

28. 下列对材料二的文意的理解，哪一项是错误的？

A. 陆秀夫少年时代就聪颖过人，老师都认为他将来能成大器。

B. 陆秀夫经科举考试走上仕途，从此就一直在朝廷中担任要职。

C. 陆秀夫与丞相陈宜中之间，既有过倾力合作，也曾因有矛盾而被罢官。

D. 陆秀夫先后参加过拥立南宋最后两位皇帝以挽救国家命运的行动。

【非选择题】

（本题为翻译题或简答题，每题3分，共6分）

29. 翻译材料一中的文句"悍吏之来吾乡，叫嚣乎东西，隳突乎南北；哗然而骇者，虽鸡狗不得宁焉。"

30. 材料三是以什么人的身份、口吻来传情达意的？表达了什么样的情感？

（二）现代文阅读（20分）

阅读下面的文章，然后依题目要求把答案填涂或填写在答题卡上。

①野史笔记是指私家编撰的带有历史记述性的史籍，是与官修的史书不同的另一种史书。古代有"稗官野史"的说法。稗官是采录民情民俗的小官。《汉书·艺文志》引如淳曰："细米为稗，街谈巷说，甚细碎之言也。王者欲知里巷风俗，故立稗官，使称说之。"这种闾巷风情、街谈巷议、逸闻轶事的记录，也叫"稗史"。今人所说的魏晋以来的志怪小说、轶事笔记，以及唐宋以降大量的私家笔记，多具有这种性质。这一部分图书多被人作为"小说"处理，其实其中有相当部分都是作者的所见所闻，着意编撰的并不多，只是在记述的文字上有所加工而已。

②野史笔记所涉及的内容十分广泛，刘叶秋先生曾根据笔记的内容将其大致分为三类：第一是小说故事类，像干宝《搜神记》、刘义庆《世说新语》、纪昀《阅微草堂笔记》等；第二是历史琐闻类，如刘歆《西京杂记》、刘餗《隋唐嘉话》、王士祯《池北偶谈》等；第三是考据、辨证类，如沈括《梦溪笔谈》、钱大昕《十驾斋养心录》等。若就其具体内容言，问题则复杂得多，以明清笔记为例，有记军国大事的，如屠叔方《建文朝野汇编》、李清《南渡录》等。有记社会经济生活的，如沈德符《万历野获编》、谢肇淛《五杂俎》等。有记述农业生产的，如陆容《菽园杂记》、张瀚《松窗梦语》等。有

记商业活动的，如沈榜《宛署杂记》、田汝成《西湖游览志余》、朱彝尊《日下旧闻考》等。有记手工业生产的，如顾起元《客座赘语》、沈德符《敝帚轩剩语》等。有记殊方异物的，如马欢《瀛涯胜览》、费信《星槎胜览》、张燮《东西洋考》、毛奇龄《蛮司合志》、徐松《新疆识略》等。有记各类人物的，如何乔远《名山藏》、周亮工《画人传》与《印人传》等。这些笔记往往内容兼及方方面面，杂而不纯，故往往冠有“丛谈”、“杂俎”、“琐言”、“漫钞”之类的名目。杂，正是这类书的本色。

③官修的史书，因受意识形态的制约、权力的干扰或体例的拘束，记事往往每有顾忌，不能放开，“虚美”、“隐恶”、为尊者讳的现象，已属正常。而野史笔记因为私人著述随意为之，少有忌惮，往往敢言官书所不敢言。民国初周椒青在为裘毓麟《清代轶闻》所作的序中说：“凡古人言行，其载之正史者皆山中之恒溪也，及睹其轶事与他说，则其人之性情毕露而读者之耳目为之一新，此则天外之飞瀑也。”鲁迅也曾说过：“历史上都写着中国的灵魂，指示着将来的命运，只因为涂饰太厚，废话太多，所以很不容易察出底细来。正如通过密叶投射在莓苔上面的月光，只看见点点的碎影。但如看野史和杂记，可更容易了然了，因为他们毕竟不必太摆史官的架子。”（鲁迅《华盖集·忽然想到》）“野史和杂说自然也免不了有讹传、挟恩怨，但看往事可以较分明，因为它究竟不像正史那样地装腔作势。”（鲁迅《华盖集·这个与那个》）正因如此，所以野史笔记便成了史学家研究历史非常重要的一个参考系统。唐代房玄龄等撰《晋书》，即将《语林》《世说》《幽明录》《搜神记》等野史小说资料采以为书。欧阳修撰《新五代史》，采用野史笔记，对《旧五代史》作了修订补充。清代史学家赵翼就曾利用笔记史料订正官修史书，他在《关索插枪岩歌》中写道：“呜呼！书生论古勿泥古，未必传闻皆伪史册真。”（《瓯北集》卷十九）认为正史所载未必可靠，民间传闻未必不实。王鸣盛撰《十七史商榷》，也主张实录与小说互有短长，去取之际，贵考核斟酌，不可偏执。

④野史笔记最可注意的是，它像是黑暗中的眼睛，朝野事物皆在其监视之下。有些关乎军国的大事，正史中或有忌讳，在野史中则可以大胆记述。如释文莹《续湘山野录》记宋太宗赵光义夜见宋太祖赵匡胤，“将五鼓，伺庐者寂无所闻，帝已崩矣。太宗受遗诏于柩前即位”。由此引发了“烛影斧声”千古疑案。又，关于朱元璋采用剥人皮的酷刑情况，据王圻《稗史汇编》云：“吏守贪酷，许民赴京陈诉。赃至六十四两以上者枭首示众，仍剥皮实草，以为将来之戒。于府州县卫之左特立一庙，以祀大地。为剥皮之场，名曰皮场庙。于公座傍各置剥皮实草之袋，欲使尝接于目而儆于心。人皆惴惴焉，以得免职为幸，有诈死而逃者。在京官员每入朝，必与妻子诀别。至暮无事则相庆，以为更生。至以鸩血染衣带，闻捕系之命，亟吮其血，顷刻死矣。”（卷七四《国宪门·刑法类·皮场庙》）此类记载即为正史所无。

⑤野史笔记的监督目光不止聚焦朝廷，相当多的则是关注要人、名人。名人轶事，包括隐私、丑闻，不见于正史，往往可从笔记中获得。著名学者王鸣盛以其《十七史商榷》《蛾术编》等学术著作而为学术界推重，可是野史却记下了他卑劣的为人。《啸亭续录》卷三曰：“王西庄未第时，尝馆富室家，每入宅时，必双手作搂物状。人问之，曰：‘欲将其财旺气搂入己怀也。’及仕宦后，秦诿楚諈，多所干没。人问之曰：‘先生学问富有，而乃吝不已，不畏后世之名节乎！’公曰：‘贪鄙不过一时之嘲，学问乃千古之业，余自信文名可以传世。至百年后，口碑已没，而著作长存。吾之道德文章犹在也。’故所著书

多慷慨激昂语，盖自掩贪陋也。”当然这些记载未必真实，但对达官显贵以及名人来说，确能起到监督的作用。一旦人们意识到这双黑暗中的眼睛时，其行为必然要有所注意。

【选择题】

（本题皆为单项选择题，每小题2分，共10分）

31. 下列对本文文意的理解，哪一项是错误的？

A. 第①段认为古人的“小说”，有的并非创作而是实录。

B. 第②段说“‘虚美’、‘隐恶’、为尊者讳的现象，已属正常”，这里的“为尊者讳”正是“隐恶”的表现。

C. 从第③段中引用的鲁迅的评价看，鲁迅对野史的局限性有着清醒的认识。

D. 第⑤段对野史关注要人、名人轶事（包括隐私、丑闻）的做法有所批评。

32. 本文第③段中引用了鲁迅的话“野史和杂说自然也免不了有讹传、挟恩怨，但看往事可以较分明，因为它究竟不像正史那样地装腔作势”。这段引语是个多重复句，它包含着下列哪些句法关系？

①递进关系　②转折关系　③假设关系　④因果关系

A. ①②　　B. ③④　　C. ①③　　D. ②④

33. 本文的总体结构属于下列哪一种类型？

A. 总分式　　B. 分总式　　C. 并列式　　D. 递进式

34. 第②段中提到的记载“殊方异物”的笔记，从书名看，下列哪一部内容涉及国内少数民族地区风物？

A. 马欢《瀛涯胜览》　　B. 费信《星槎胜览》

C. 毛奇龄《蛮司合志》　　D. 张燮《东西洋考》

35. 下列句子对比喻喻义的解释，哪一个是错误的？

A. 第①段中称野史为“稗史”，是以稗米的细碎比喻稗史内容的琐碎。

B. 第③段中周椒青把野史比喻成“天外飞瀑”，喻义是野史往往能给人以出人意料之外的震撼。

C. 第③段中鲁迅把正史比喻成“通过密叶投射在莓苔上面的月光”，喻义是正史经过了太多粉饰遮掩，面目已经模糊难辨了。

D. 第④、第⑤段中把野史比喻成“黑暗中的眼睛”，喻义是权贵和名人们的一言一行都在野史作者的暗中监督之下。

【非选择题】

（本题皆为简答题，共10分）

36. 文章第①段说“今人所说的魏晋以来的志怪小说、轶事笔记，以及唐宋以降大量的私家笔记，多具有这种性质”，这里说的“这种性质”指什么？（2分）

37. 第②段结尾说“王鸣盛撰《十七史商榷》，也主张实录与小说互有短长，去取之际，贵考核斟酌，不可偏执”。这里的“偏执”指什么？（2分）

38. 根据文章的内容概括野史笔记的三个特点。（6分）

三、语言文字表达

（本题全部为非选择题。请把答案填写在答题卡上“非选择题答题区”中与题号相对应的位置上。共70分）

39. 将以下消息概括为一句话新闻。不超过30字。（4分）

中新社广州2月6日电（程景伟） 2月6日是农历正月十五元宵节，2012年广府庙会在广州城隍庙前忠佑广场拉开帷幕，本届庙会将为羊城市民献上一场广府味更浓的文艺盛宴，且更突出与民众的互动。

当日的广州城隍庙及其周边人潮涌动，现场一片热闹欢乐的情景。举行广府庙会开幕式的舞台以仿制城隍庙牌坊作为背景，象征“幸福之门”，并点缀了龙柱、灯笼等迎合龙年吉祥的喜庆元素。

庙会启动仪式借用“芝麻开门”的典故，由主持人和街坊一起舞动手中风车，齐呼三声“幸福开门”，“幸福之门”便开启，随后“祥龙”上台，文艺表演顺势展开。表演节目以“龙”为线索，将广府元素贯穿其中，先是本土歌手演唱《龙的传人》等经典曲目，其间穿插少儿杂技等演出，最后以粤剧精选武戏联演压轴。

40. 在一个中学毕业晚会上，同学们准备了丰富的才艺表演节目。主持的同学要为各个节目的衔接撰写串台词（连接两个节目的台词）。他为“武术表演”和“歌曲《虞美人》（词是李煜创作的）”两个表演节目撰写了这样的串台词：

刚才几位同学表现出了男生的威武刚猛。接下来，咱们学校的“林妹妹”想向大家表演的则是女生的柔美温婉。请大家欣赏根据李煜的词改编的歌曲《虞美人》。

女声独唱《虞美人》之后的节目，是根据《孔雀东南飞》改编的舞台短剧。请模仿上述例子，为主持人写一份这两个节目之间的串台词，要求60字左右。（6分）

41. 作文

从下面的题目中任选一个，按要求写一篇作文。（60分）

题一：以《放》为题，写一篇作文。

题二：2012年春，体育界掀起了一阵“林书豪热”。一时之间，林书豪成为家喻户晓的名字。在球坛上，他带领自己的球队取得七连胜，打破多项联盟纪录。在学历上，他顶着哈佛大学的光环。然而，就在不久前，他还是个屡次被球队裁掉的试训球员。林书豪的成功被称为“林书豪现象”，并引发了各种评论。美国总统奥巴马说，林书豪的成功是“一个已经超越体育本身的伟大故事”。尼克斯队教练认为：林书豪有无穷的智慧和精神，他在比赛中善于与队友沟通，并且得到了队友的信任。有人说，林书豪的成功靠的是运气。有人则说，林书豪靠的是他坚持不懈的刻苦训练，机会只给有准备的人。也有人认为：林书豪在美国可以复制，但在中国无法粘贴。由此又引申出对中国运动员培养模式以及中国教育的反思——学业和事业、鱼与熊掌是否可以兼得？林书豪自己则表示，他的成功源于他的信仰。总之，林书豪给我们带来了很多启示。

请以“林书豪带来的启示”为话题，自拟题目，写一篇作文。

要求：①以上两题任选一题；

②除诗歌外，文体不限；

③文言文400字左右，现代文700字左右。

数　学

答卷时间：2 小时

一、选择题：本大题共 15 小题，每小题 4 分，共 60 分，每小题所列四个选项中只有一个是正确的，把你的选择按题号填入答题纸.

1. 不等式 $5-x<2$ 的解是

A. $x>1$　　B. $x\geqslant 1$　　C. $x\leqslant 3$　　D. $x>3$

2. 若关于 x 的方程 $ax=2$ 无解，则实数 a 的值为

A. 0　　B. 1　　C. 2　　D. -2

3. 若函数 $f(x)=x^2+ax+b$ 在 $x=1$ 处取得最小值 3，则

A. $a=-2$，$b=3$　　B. $a=-2$，$b=4$

C. $a=2$，$b=1$　　D. $a=-1$，$b=3$

4. 已知常数 a，$b>0$ 且都不等于 1，如果 $f(x)=a^x$ 是增函数，$g(x)=\log_b x$ 是减函数，则一定有

A. $a^2<b^2$　　B. $\log_b a>0$　　C. $3^a>3^b$　　D. $ab>1$

5. 下列函数中，定义域为全体实数的是

A. $y=\sqrt{x^2+x-2}$　　B. $y=\dfrac{1}{\lg|x-1|}$

C. $y=\tan x$　　D. $y=5^{x+2}$

6. 记 S_n 为等比数列 $\{a_n\}$ 的前 n 项和，且 $\dfrac{S_9}{S_3}=3$，则 $\dfrac{a_9}{a_3}=$

A. 3　　B. -2 或 1　　C. 4 或 1　　D. 1

7. 已知 α 是第三象限角，则 $\cos\alpha\sqrt{1-\sin^2\alpha}+\sin\alpha\sqrt{1-\cos^2\alpha}=$

A. 1　　B. -1　　C. $\cos 2\alpha$　　D. $-\cos 2\alpha$

8. 已知 $\tan x=-\dfrac{1}{2}$，则 $2\sin x\cos x=$

A. $-\dfrac{4}{5}$　　B. -3　　C. $-\dfrac{7}{5}$　　D. $-\dfrac{11}{5}$

9. 平面直线 l_1 与 l_2 相互垂直，l_1 的斜率为 $\tan\theta$（$\neq 0$），则 l_2 的斜率为

A. $\cot\theta$　　B. $\tan(\theta+\pi)$　　C. $-\tan\theta$　　D. $\tan\left(\theta+\dfrac{\pi}{2}\right)$

10. 已知向量 $\vec{a}=(1,\ -3)$，$\vec{b}=(5,\ 0)$，则 $3\vec{a}-2\vec{b}=$

A. $(7,\ -9)$　　B. $(-7,\ -9)$　　C. $(-7,\ 9)$　　D. $(7,\ 9)$

11. 已知直线 $y=kx+b$ 经过点（0，3），且与圆 $x^2+y^2+2y-3=0$ 有两个交点，则 k 的取值范围是

A. $(-\infty,\ -\sqrt{3})\cup(\sqrt{3},\ +\infty)$　　B. $(-\sqrt{3},\ \sqrt{3})$

C. $(-\infty,\ -\sqrt{3}]\cup[\sqrt{3},\ +\infty)$　　D. $[-\sqrt{3},\ \sqrt{3}]$

12. 若一条直线平行于一个平面，则垂直于这个平面的直线一定与这条直线

A. 平行　　B. 异面　　C. 垂直　　D. 相交

13. 假设在 100 件产品中，有 3 件是次品，从产品中任取 5 件，其中至少有 2 件是次品的抽法有______种

A. $C_3^2C_{97}^3$　　B. $C_3^2C_{97}^3+C_3^3C_{97}^2$

C. $C_{100}^5-C_{97}^5$　　D. $C_{100}^5-C_3^1C_{97}^4$

14. 将 4 个球随机放进 3 个空盒，则所有球都在前两个盒中，但不是全在一个盒子里的概率为

A. $\frac{80}{81}$　　B. $\frac{2}{3}$　　C. $\frac{16}{81}$　　D. $\frac{14}{81}$

15. 已知定义域为 $(-\infty,\ 0)\cup(0,\ +\infty)$ 的函数 $f(x)$ 是偶函数，并且在 $(-\infty,\ 0)$ 上为增函数，若 $f(-3)=0$，则 $\frac{f(x)}{x}<0$ 的解集为

A. $(-3,\ 0)\cup(3,\ +\infty)$　　B. $(-3,\ 0)\cup(0,\ 3)$

C. $(3,\ +\infty)$　　D. $(-\infty,\ 3)$

二、填空题：本大题共 6 小题，每小题 4 分，共 24 分，把答案按题号填入答题纸.

16. 已知 $f(\ln x)=2x+5$，则 $f(x)$ =______________.

17. 在坐标平面上，到 A（5，0）和 B（2，-6）两点距离相等的点 P 的轨迹方程是____________.

18. 已知 n 为正整数，则 $\sqrt{n+3}-\sqrt{n}$ 与 $\sqrt{n+4}-\sqrt{n+1}$ 的大小关系是____________.

19. 已知 α、β 是一个三角形的两个内角，且 $\tan\alpha$、$\tan\beta$ 是方程 $x^2-3x+2=0$ 的两个根，则 $\tan(\alpha+\beta)=$______________.

20. 不等式 $\log_{\frac{1}{3}}(2x-3)>\log_{\frac{1}{3}}(x+1)$ 的解为______________.

21. 在正方体 $ABCD-A_1B_1C_1D_1$ 中，线段 AB_1 与 BC_1 的夹角是______.

三、解答题：本大题满分 66 分. 解答题应写出文字说明、证明过程或演算步骤.

22. （本小题满分 12 分）

某蒸汽机上的飞轮直径为 1.2 m，每分钟按逆时针方向旋转 300 转，求：

（1）飞轮每秒钟转过的弧度数；

（2）轮周上的一点每秒钟经过的弧长.

23.（本小题满分 12 分）

设$\triangle ABC$的三个角A、B、C所对应的边分别为a、b、c，已知边$c=10$，又知$\frac{\cos A}{\cos B}=\frac{b}{a}=\frac{4}{3}$，求$a$、$b$.

24.（本小题满分 12 分）

如图 1 所示，已知四棱锥$P-ABCD$的底面是面积为 4 cm^2 的矩形，$PA\perp AB$，$PA\perp AD$，平面PBC和平面PCD与底面分别成$60°$和$30°$角，求四棱锥$P-ABCD$的体积.

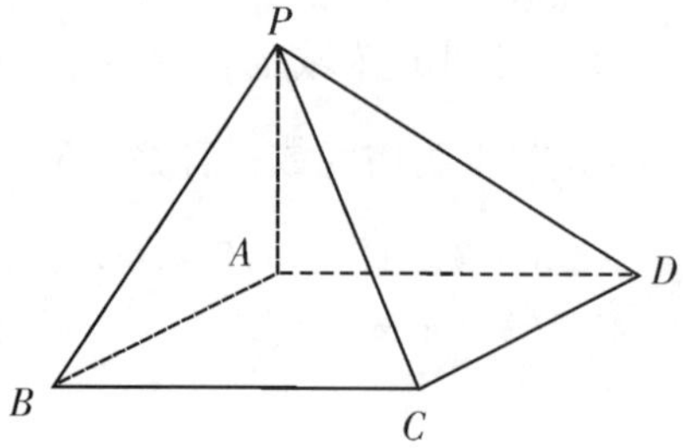

图 1

25.（本小题满分 15 分）（选考历史或地理的考生做题目Ⅰ，不必做题目Ⅱ；选考物理、化学或生物的考生做题目Ⅱ，不必做题目Ⅰ）

Ⅰ. 已知数列$\{a_n\}$中，$a_1=1$，$a_{n+1}=1-\frac{1}{4a_n}$，$b_n=\frac{2}{2a_n-1}$，其中$n\in \mathbf{N}$.

（1）求证：数列$\{b_n\}$是等差数列；

（2）求数列$\{a_n\}$的通项公式.

Ⅱ. 已知数列$\{a_n\}$的前n项和为S_n，且a_n是S_n与 2 的等差中项，在数列$\{b_n\}$中，$b_1=1$，点(b_n, b_{n+1})在直线$x-y+2=0$上.

（1）求数列$\{a_n\}$与数列$\{b_n\}$的通项公式；

（2）设$c_n=a_n\cdot b_n$，求数列$\{c_n\}$的前n项和T_n.

26.（本小题满分 15 分）（选考历史或地理的考生做题目Ⅰ，不必做题目Ⅱ；选考物理、化学或生物的考生做题目Ⅱ，不必做题目Ⅰ）

Ⅰ. 如图 2 所示，椭圆 E 经过点 A（2，3），对称轴为坐标轴，焦点 F_1、F_2 在 x 轴上，离心率 $e=\dfrac{1}{2}$.

（1）求椭圆 E 的方程；

（2）求 $\angle F_1AF_2$ 的角平分线所在直线的方程.

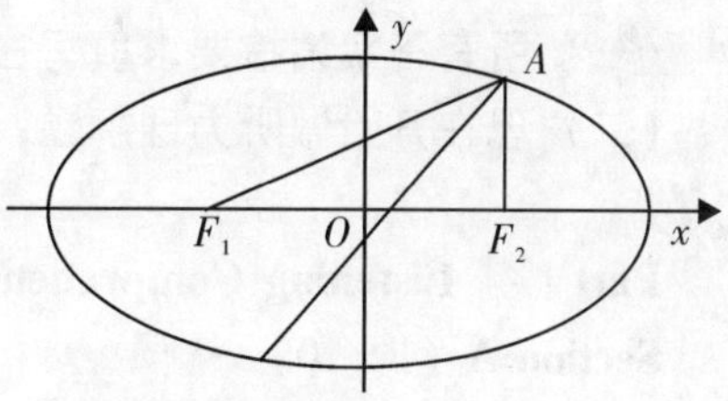

图 2

Ⅱ. 已知椭圆 C 的中心在原点，一个焦点 F（-2，0），且长轴长与短轴长的比是 $2:\sqrt{3}$.

（1）求椭圆 C 的方程；

（2）设点 M（m，0）在椭圆 C 的长轴上，点 P 是椭圆上任意一点．当 $|\overrightarrow{MP}|$ 最小时，点 P 恰好落在椭圆的右顶点，求实数 m 的取值范围.

英 语

答卷时间：2 小时

注意事项
（一）所有答案请按要求填写在答题卡上，否则无效。
（二）现在开始做听力理解题，请试听声音。

Part Ⅰ Listening Comprehension (30 points)

Section A (1×10)

Directions: *In this section you will hear* 10 *short conversations between two speakers. At the end of each conversation, a third voice will ask a question about what was said. The conversation and the question will be spoken only once. After you hear a conversation and the question about it, read the four possible answers in your test paper and choose the best one to the question you have heard.* Then, mark your answer by blackening the corresponding letter on the Answer Sheet.

1. A. Leave in 15 minutes. B. Meet Harry at the bus stop.
   C. Catch the bus at once. D. Check to see if everything is ready.
2. A. A skirt. B. A shirt.
   C. A pair of shoes. D. A coat.
3. A. Chinese B. French C. English D. German
4. A. The bad weather. B. The housing problem.
   C. The traffic problem. D. Lack of money.
5. A. At an airport. B. In Los Angeles.
   C. At a post office. D. In the man's office.
6. A. $ 64 B. $ 86 C. $ 96 D. $ 140
7. A. Tom is unable to hear well.
   B. Tom didn't say anything at the meeting.
   C. Tom doesn't listen to him.
   D. Tom went out before the meeting was over.
8. A. She doesn't care for the children's program.
   B. She regrets missing it.
   C. She has seen it before.
   D. She knows about it.
9. A. The restaurant provides good food.
   B. She enjoys her part-time job.

C. The restaurant offers cheap food.

D. There are several cooks in the restaurant.

10. A. He used to be healthy.

B. He is now away from his office.

C. He has been sick for two weeks.

D. The man may see the professor during the weekend.

Section B (2 ×10)

Directions: *In this section you will hear two short talks. Each talk will be spoken twice. After the talk you will be asked questions. When you hear a question, read the four possible answers in your test paper and choose the best answer to the question you have heard. Then, mark your answer by blackening the corresponding letter on the Answer Sheet.*

Questions 11 – 15 **are based on the passage you have just heard.**

11. A. Two. Radio and TV.

B. Four. Newspaper, magazines, books and radio.

C. Three. Education, laws, and planning for the future.

D. One. Making the air and water dirty.

12. A. Through schools.

B. Through radio, TV, and newspapers.

C. Through magazines and books.

D. All of the above.

13. A. The law lowering the speed limit for cars.

B. Laws against littering.

C. Laws against making the air and water dirty.

D. Laws helping people to save resources.

14. A. Plant trees.

B. Clean the streets.

C. Make water clean.

D. Protest against harmful products.

15. A. Atomic power and solar energy.

B. Chemical energy.

C. Light energy from the sun.

D. Electric energy produced by coal.

Questions 16 – 20 **are based on the passage you have just heard.**

16. A. When they are four years old. B. When they are five years old.

C. When they are six years old. D. When they are seven years old.

17. A. Twelve or thirteen years. B. Eleven or twelve years.

C. Thirteen or fourteen years. D. Ten or eleven years.

18. A. Public schools. B. Elementary schools.

C. Secondary schools. D. Private schools.

19. A. Half of them. B. A quarter of them.

C. One third of them. D. Two fifths of them.

20. A. He has to study hard.

B. He has to earn money for part of his college expenses.

C. He has to stop his study.

D. He has to help others.

Part Ⅱ Reading Comprehension (**40 points**)

Directions: *There are 4 passages in this part. Each passage is followed by some questions or unfinished statements. For each of them there are 4 choices marked A, B, C and D. You should decide on the best choice and mark your answer by blackening the corresponding letter on the Answer Sheet.*

Questions 21 to 25 are based on the following passage:

The Northeast is a very important part of the United States, for although it covers only about six percent of the nation's geographical area, it contains approximately one-fourth of the country's population. New York, the most popular city in the United States, and several other large cities are located in this region.

Why are these states so important? In the first place, the Northeast was one of the first sections of the country to be settled by Europeans. Busy cities developed there when most of America was still a sparsely (稀少的) settled wilderness. Many crucial events in the nation's early history took place there.

Today the Northeast is a great manufacturing and trading region. Thousands of factories produce a wide variety of goods and provide other regions of the country with items they need. Many large manufacturing firms have their central headquarters here. Some of the country's largest banks, investment agencies, and publishing houses are found in the Northeast. Several of its cities are noted for their fine museums. Some of the country's best known colleges and universities are also located in this region.

Finally the Northeast is the principal location for much of the country's international trade. In the heart of this region in New York city is the home of the United Nations.

21. What is this passage mainly about?

A. The people of the Northeast.

B. The location of the nation's capital.

C. The development of the United States.

D. The significance of the Northeast.

22. How is the Northeast described in the passage?

A. Small area, small population.

B. Small area, large population.

C. Large area, small population.

D. Large area, large population.

23. According to the passage, why is the Northeast an important part of the United States today?

A. It is visited by many tourists.

B. It was never a wilderness like the rest of the country.

C. It is both a business and cultural centre.

D. It is the home of many modern historians.

24. Which of the following statements is NOT true?

A. Many crucial events in the nation's early history took place in a sparsely settled area.

B. The Europeans who first came to the nation settled down in the Northeast.

C. Industry and business developed rapidly in this region.

D. New York is the most important financial city in this region.

25. We can infer from this passage that there are many ______ in the Northeast.

A. large banks and investment agencies

B. fine museums

C. best known colleges and universities

D. all of the above

Questions 26 to 30 are based on the following passage:

Internet shopping is a new way of shopping. Nowadays, you can shop for just about anything from your armchair. All you need is a computer which is linked to the Internet. Shopping on the Internet is becoming increasingly popular. In the United States, people spent over $ 2.5 billion on Internet shopping in 1998. This figure is expected to reach $ 11 billion by the year 2004.

People can shop for a variety of products on the Internet. Physical products include items such as books, CDs, clothes and food. These types of products are the most common purchases through the Internet. You can also buy information products such as on-line news or magazine stories, or you can download computer software through the Internet. Services such as booking airline tickets, reserving hotels or renting cars are also available on the Internet. You can also go shopping on the Internet for entertainment services and take part in on-line games.

Internet shopping offers a number of benefits for the shopper. The most important advantage is convenience. You can shop when you like as the on-line shops are open 24 hours a day and you don't have to queue with other shoppers at the checkout counters. Secondly, it is easy to find what you are looking for on the Internet. Even out-of-print books may be ordered online. Finally, it is often cheaper to buy goods through the Internet, and you can tell the shop exactly what you want.

The main disadvantage of Internet shopping is that you can't actually see the products you are buying or check their quality. Also, many people enjoy shopping in the city and miss the opportunity to talk to friends. Some people are worried about paying for goods using credit cards, so Internet companies are now finding ways to make on-line payment safe.

Internet shopping is sure to become more and more popular in the years ahead. It promises to change the way we buy all kinds of things—from tonight's dinner to a new car.

26. Which of the following is NOT true?

A. Internet shopping is a new way of shopping.

B. Internet shopping is becoming increasingly popular.

C. The advantages of Internet shopping are surely over the disadvantages of Internet shopping.

D. Internet shopping has reached $ 11 billion by the year 2004.

27. The phrase "physical products" in Paragraph 2 means ______.

A. things connected with sports

B. things useful for health care

C. things that can be seen or felt

D. things like on-line news or magazine stories

28. The most important advantage about Internet shopping is ______.

A. the speed the goods are delivered at

B. the reasonable price

C. not mentioned in this passage

D. the convenience it brings to you

29. In the passage, which of the following disadvantages of Internet shopping is NOT mentioned?

A. Customers can't actually see the products they are looking for.

B. Customers can't check the product's quantity they are buying.

C. Many people enjoy shopping in the city and miss the opportunity to talk to friends.

D. Customers can't check the qualities of their products.

30. The last paragraph is mainly about ______.

A. there being various problems with Internet

B. Internet companies' finding of a new way for payment

C. people's enjoyment of a new way of shopping

D. nothing but disappointment

Questions 31 **to** 35 **are based on the following passage:**

Mrs. Black was having a lot of trouble with her skin, so she went to her doctor about it. He could not find anything wrong with her, however, so he sent her to the local hospital for some tests. The hospital, of course, sent the results of the tests direct to Mrs. Black's doctor, and the next morning he telephoned her to give a list of the things that he thought she should not eat, as any of them might be the cause of her skin trouble.

Mrs. Black carefully wrote all the things down on a piece of paper, which she then left beside the telephone while she went out to a ladies' meeting.

When she got back home two hours later, she found her husband waiting for her. He had a big basket full of packages beside him, and when he saw her, he said, "Hullo. Dear. I have done all your shopping for you." "Done all my shopping?" she asked in surprise. "But how did you know what I wanted?" "Well, when I got home, I found your shopping list beside the telephone," answered her husband, "so I went down to the shops and bought everything you had written down."

Of course, Mrs. Black had to tell him that he had bought all the things the doctor did not allow her to eat!

31. Why did Mrs. Black go to her doctor?

A. Because she was having a lot of trouble with her skin.

B. Because she could not find anything wrong with her skin.

C. Because the doctor would tell her what things she could eat.

D. Because she wanted to have some tests in the hospital.

32. What did he find after he examined her carefully?

A. He found that her skin had been seriously hurt.

B. He found that she should be sent to hospital immediately.

C. He found the cause of her skin trouble.

D. He could not find anything wrong with her.

33. Why did the doctor telephone her the next morning?

A. Because he wanted to tell her the things she should not eat.

B. Because he wanted to inform her of the cause of her skin trouble.

C. Because he wanted to send her to the local hospital.

D. Because he wanted to give her a list of things that she should eat.

34. Where did she leave the list of the things she had written down?

A. She left it in the hospital.

B. She left it in a big basket.

C. She left it beside the telephone.

D. She left it beside her.

35. Why had he done all his wife's shopping?

A. Because he wanted to share all these things with his wife.

B. Because he had mistaken the things written down on the piece of paper for her shopping list.

C. Because these are the things his wife wanted to buy.

D. Because these are the things the doctor wanted her to eat.

Questions 36 to 40 are based on the following passage:

For many young people lucky enough to get a job after leaving school or college, the biggest shock of the transition to work is how few holidays they get.

Many would jump at the chance to take three months off—and that's exactly what happened at Virgin Atlantic, the airline run by Richard Branson. He believes the *new initiative* could help to reduce unemployment.

Faced last autumn with the recession and with its failure to acquire more flight slots out of Heathrow airport, the company was having to consider redundancies（裁员）. Mr. Branson wrote to staff saying that cutting back on jobs was "something I have never wanted to do". Instead he invited employees to take up to six months unpaid leave and to participate in a job sharing scheme.

The immediate crisis passed but the idea of a shorter working year took off. When the company later asked for 300 volunteers to take three months unpaid leave, 450 put their name forward. Mr. Branson said: "To be fair and share it around, in some cases we said that people could only take six weeks."

Most of the volunteers were cabin crew but other staff, including secretaries and pilots, took advantage of the offer as well. "And when they came back from their break ... they definitely seemed to enjoy work more," he said.

The company tends to recruit and train its own staff from scratch. As Mr. Branson said: "If you've been at college or *on the dole*, working for only nine months still makes you a lot better-off financially than you were before." He believes there is a broader social benefit to be achieved. "If you are only taking on people for nine months, that will enable others who would otherwise have no work or be living *on the dole* to have a chance too."

And he goes further. "I think this should be the basis of a pattern across the whole European Community for the first few years of working life."

36. The *new initiative* (Para. 2) refers to the __________.

A. initial reaction

B. starting point

C. new idea

D. unpaid-leave scheme

37. When Virgin Atlantic was considering redundancies, the staff were encouraged to __________.

A. leave Virgin Atlantic

B. take unpaid leave and join in a job sharing scheme

C. take a six-month holiday and attend training courses

D. acquire more flight slots out of Heathrow airport

38. The idea of a shorter working year seemed especially attractive to ______.

A. new recruits　　B. older staff

C. cabin crew D. pilots and secretaries

39. The long break turned out to have a/an ______ effect on the staff 's attitude to their work.

A. positive B. negative

C. uncertain D. arbitrary

40. The phrase *on the dole* (Para. 6) means ______ .

A. studying at college

B. being dependent on parents

C. working as a cabin crew member

D. being unemployed and receiving money from the government

Part Ⅲ Vocabulary (20 points)

Section A (10 points)

***Directions**: There are 10 incomplete sentences in this part. For each sentence there are four choices marked A, B, C and D. Choose the ONE answer that best completes the sentence. Then mark your answer by blackening the corresponding letter on the Answer Sheet.*

41. How long can the students ______ the book? They need it badly for their project report.

A. borrow B. get C. lend D. keep

42. A large number of pigs and ducks are ______ in Mr. Jeremy Smith's farm.

A. raised B. increased C. lifted D. brought

43. The government yesterday held a press conference to ______ the introduction of electric power vehicles on 1 April.

A. progress B. promote C. puzzle D. prepare

44. No one was injured because when the fire started, the fire alarm ______ immediately.

A. went up B. went away C. went down D. went off

45. When he started to develop the new product, Mr. Brown was ______ of his knowledge of target customers.

A. careful B. anxious C. confident D. active

46. Mrs. Porter has been absent from work for three days because she has to ______ her mother in hospital.

A. look at B. look up to C. look like D. look after

47. Last night it rained heavily and the cinema was almost empty. ______ people went to see the film.

A. Quite a few B. Few C. A great many D. A number of

48. How ______ can the engineers of ABC International Company finish designing the museum?

A. soon B. long C. often D. rapid

49. Our English teacher is very popular with the students because he has a good ______ of humor.

A. scene　　B. sense　　C. spot　　D. sensitivity

50. After the earthquake ______ were put up and fresh water was brought into the city.

A. shade　　B. sheets　　C. shelters　　D. shifts

Section B (**10 points**)

Directions: *There are* 10 *sentences in this part. For each sentence there are four choices marked A, B, C and D. Choose the ONE word or phrase that is closest in meaning to the underlined part. Then mark your answer by blackening the corresponding letter on the Answer Sheet.*

51. There was a sharp fall in profits because of the increasing competition and the economic recession.

A. dramatic　　B. slight　　C. slow　　D. steady

52. The manager was requested to send the latest price list to the customer as soon as possible.

A. regretted　　B. replied　　C. asked　　D. forced

53. The injured football player should be sent to hospital in no time.

A. hardly　　B. necessarily　　C. effectively　　D. immediately

54. He was disappointed to find his suggestions turned down at the monthly meeting.

A. considered　　B. rejected　　C. admitted　　D. regarded

55. The terrible noise from the airport simply drove me crazy and I finally moved to a small village.

A. made　　B. encouraged　　C. motivated　　D. persuaded

56. All the leading newspapers reported the trade talks between China and the United States.

A. current　　B. major　　C. overseas　　D. local

57. The teacher says it's not how much you read but what you read that really counts.

A. matters　　B. numbers　　C. cares　　D. proves

58. Language competence is very important in both business and social settings.

A. confidence　　B. course　　C. accuracy　　D. ability

59. He was ill so he had to stay in bed for three months, feeling as if he was isolated from the outside world.

A. cut out　　B. cut off　　C. cut up　　D. cut down

60. We were all excited that he set a new record for the 100-metre race in the Asian Games.

A. wrote　　B. won　　C. established　　D. noticed

Part Ⅳ　Grammatical Structure (10 **points**)

Directions: *There are* 10 *incomplete sentences in this part. For each sentence there are four choices marked A, B, C and D. Choose the ONE that best completes the sentence. Then mark your answer by blackening the corresponding letter on the Answer Sheet.*

61. I'm afraid that the milk is too hot for my baby ______ this moment.

A. drinks B. to drink C. for drinking D. to drink it

62. A large number of the club members ______ from south and the number ______ increasing these years.

A. is; has been B. are; has been C. is; have been D. are; have been

63. The result of the competition turned out to be very good, ______ was out of his expectation.

A. which B. it C. what D. this

64. I would rather ______ any medicine now as I have already recovered.

A. not to take B. take not C. to take not D. not take

65. The director suggested that the story ______ into a movie soon.

A. be made B. was made C. made D. is made

66. ______ is of great significance for all citizens ______ the traffic regulations.

A. This; follow B. That; follow C. There; follow D. It; to follow

67. You ought ______ the incident to the director last week.

A. to have reported B. to reporting C. to report D. to be reported

68. Let's call a meeting this Friday, ______?

A. can we B. do we C. will we D. shall we

69. We are not sure about ______ tomorrow. Could you tell me in great details?

A. what we should do B. we should do what

C. what should we do D. should we do what

70. This apartment is ______ that old one.

A. three times as big as

B. three times the size

C. as three times the size

D. three times as bigger as

Part Ⅴ Cloze (20 points)

***Directions**: There are 20 blanks in the following passage. For each blank there are 4 choices marked A, B, C and D. You should choose the ONE that best fits into the passage. Then mark your answer by blackening the corresponding letter on the Answer Sheet with a single line through the center.*

Susan Cleveland is the young president of a candy company in Chicago. Her father started the company in 1960s. He died three years ago. Now, the company belongs to Susan.

Susan, however, did not have any experience before becoming head of the company. She had just finished ___71___.

The employees became even more concerned ___72___ Susan's first months on the ___73___. Mr. Cleveland had been a strong leader. But Susan ___74___ many employees to make their own ___75___.

One employee said: "Old Mr. Cleveland always ___76___ us what to do. He kept people on a short leash. But the company did ___77___."

What does a "short leash" mean? A leash is ___78___ rope. We use a leash to ___79___ our pet dogs. The leash keeps the dog from running away ___80___ getting into trouble.

Keeping a ___81___ on a short leash means keeping him or her under ___82___ control. The person can't make many decisions for himself or herself.

Ms. Cleveland ___83___ keep her workers on a short leash. ___84___, she encourages them to get better ways to do business.

For example, her secretary proposed an idea. She said the company should give a ___85___ to the best student in the high school near its factory. The ___86___ could use the prize money to study at a university.

Ms. Cleveland ___87___ the idea. After the prize was announced, people who lived in this area of the factory began to buy ___88___ of the company's candy. Local newspapers ___89___ the competition. Business improved.

Ms. Cleveland made her secretary the company's first Director of ___90___ Relations. The former secretary was very pleased.

71.	A. office	B. holiday	C. college	D. journey
72.	A. on	B. during	C. with	D. for
73.	A. duty	B. power	C. company	D. job
74.	A. suggested	B. permitted	C. promised	D. forbade
75.	A. discovery	B. preparations	C. money	D. decision
76.	A. told	B. explained	C. wanted	D. asked
77.	A. badly	B. well	C. so	D. not
78.	A. a roll of	B. a sheet of	C. a kind of	D. a ray of
79.	A. feed	B. play with	C. talk to	D. walk
80.	A. or	B. and	C. but	D. so
81.	A. dog	B. thing	C. company	D. person
82.	A. open	B. poor	C. close	D. short
83.	A. does not	B. has to	C. never	D. would rather
84.	A. In fact	B. Instead	C. In other words	D. On the other hand
85.	A. honor	B. bill	C. reward	D. prize
86.	A. winner	B. students	C. workers	D. teachers
87.	A. promised	B. refused	C. appreciated	D. raised
88.	A. plenty	B. most	C. less	D. more
89.	A. told	B. wrote about	C. printed	D. talked
90.	A. Friendly	B. Social	C. Public	D. International

Part Ⅵ Proof Reading (10 points)

Directions: *Read each line carefully to find out the mistakes.*

1. If there is no mistake in the line, mark "√" on the right hand side.

2. If there is a redundant (多余的) word in the line, first write it off with a slanting line (\), and then write the word on the right hand side with the slanting line.

3. If there is a word missing in the line, put a missing word sign (∧) there and write the missing word on the right hand side.

4. If there is a wrong word in the line, draw a line under it and write the correct one on the right hand side.

Example:

When I have free time I go ∧ a long walk. Some	(1) for
people read ~~the~~ books or watch television while others have	(2) ~~the~~
sports. Charles and Linda Mason do all of these things as	(3) √
well as <u>climbed</u> buildings.	(4) climb

It's easier to go downhill than climb uphill; so it's	91. ______
easier to fall into bad habits than into good one.	92. ______
Bad habits do not come suddenly. They come little	93. ______
by little. Schoolboys first picked up a little in school	94. ______
and on the streets. When they cannot do them homework,	95. ______
they had copy from their schoolmates. If they see older	96. ______
boys smoking, they also want to learn to smoke. When	97. ______
they get older, the habits become more stronger and	98. ______
stronger, so that they can no longer getting rid of them.	99. ______
What necessary it is that we get rid of the bad habits at the beginning.	100. ______

Part Ⅶ Composition (20 points) (任选一题)

Directions: *Write on ONE of the following topics on the Composition Sheet. A* 200 – 250 *word limit is required.* (作文请写在作文纸上)

Ⅰ. *Write a composition of no less than* 200 *words in three paragraphs. You are given the first sentence of each paragraph and are required to develop the idea in completing the paragraph. Your part of the composition should be no less than* 200 *words, not including the words given.*

Living in School Dormitories or Living off Campus

1. Some students prefer to live on campus. There are many advantages of living in school dormitories. ____.

2. However, others would rather live off campus. They have a lot of good reasons. ____.

3. In my opinion, I will choose to live ________________.

Ⅱ. *Look at the following pictures and write a composition of no less than 200 words based on these pictures.*

This term the Students' Union (学生会) of your middle school is planning to organize the following four activities: spending a day with the children in a village; visiting the home for the aged; collecting rubbish on the beach and planting trees. You are asked to write a letter to the headmaster of your school to inform him/her of your plan and make a request for help. Your letter should include the following:

1. your purpose of writing the letter
2. introduction of the four activities
3. the benefits of the four activities
4. the possible difficulties you will meet in the four activities
5. request for help from the headmaster

地　理

答卷时间：2 小时

一、填空题（填对一空格得 1 分，全题共 20 分）

1. 亚洲和非洲都不具有的气候类型是______气候，而这种气候类型在______洲最为典型。

2. 一张地形图上，把海拔相同的各点连接起来的线，叫______。

3. 中低纬大陆东岸的洋流是______流。

4. 中国的秦岭是______水系和______水系的分水岭。

5. 中国冬季南北气温差别大是受______和______的影响。

6. 瑞士的工业多朝精细工业的方向发展，其主要原因是______。

7. 世界有三大人种，分别是______、______和______。其中，头发黑而直的人种主要分布在______、______和______、______的部分地区。

8. 日本是发达的国家，由于国内______、______，因而经济对外依赖性强，国内的工业、人口、城市高度集中在______、______沿岸的狭长地带上。

二、单项选择题（选对一题得 3 分，全题共 60 分）

1. 对英国近年经济发展有极大贡献的能源是

A. 煤炭　　B. 铀矿　　C. 石油　　D. 水能

2. 两极地区降水少的原因是

A. 在副热带高气压带控制下，降水少

B. 这个地区终年气温很低，气流下沉增温，不易成云降雨

C. 处在大陆的背风海岸，湿润气流难以到达，降水少

D. 沿岸有寒流流经，使近地面空气减温减湿，降水稀少

3. 沟通太平洋和印度洋的重要海峡是

A. 马六甲海峡　　B. 直布罗陀海峡

C. 麦哲伦海峡　　D. 台湾海峡

4. 日本将工业主要布局于沿海，其主要原因是

A. 防止地震　　B. 接近农业生产区

C. 接近劳工集中地　　D. 减少进出口的运费

5. 下列关于美国东北工业区的叙述，不正确的是

A. 这里石油资源丰富，但煤铁矿产贫乏

B. 是美国工业发展历史最早的工业区

C. 这里土地肥沃，农牧业发达

D. 这里水运条件优越

6. 当巴西热带草原正处在湿季的时候

A. 中国大部分地区高温多雨　　B. 地中海沿岸温和多雨

C. 地球正处在远日点附近　　D. 北部印度洋洋流呈顺时针方向流动

7. 地球上不同经线的长度

A. 等长　　B. 随经度的变化而变化

C. 长短不一　　D. 随海陆位置的变化而变化

8. 关于澳大利亚主要城市的叙述，不正确的是

A. 堪培拉是全国人口最多的城市

B. 悉尼是全国最大的工业中心和港口城市

C. 堪培拉是澳大利亚的首都

D. 墨尔本是全国第二大城市

9. 制糖工业属于如下哪种指向的产业

A. 技术指向　　B. 市场指向

C. 原料指向　　D. 信息指向

10. 世界四大河流域中，人口分布最稀少的是

A. 长江流域　　B. 密西西比河流域

C. 尼罗河流域　　D. 亚马孙河流域

11. 影响一地太阳辐射强度的主要因素是

A. 风力强弱　　B. 海陆差异

C. 太阳高度　　D. 气温高低

12. 距离地球最近的行星是

A. 水星　　B. 火星　　C. 金星　　D. 木星

13. 由于地球的公转，在地球上产生了

A. 物体水平运动时方向的偏转　　B. 昼夜的更替

C. 各地区地方时的差异　　D. 四季的更替

14. 每年，南极圈内有极夜现象是从以下日期开始的

A. 春分日以后　　B. 秋分日以后

C. 夏至日以后　　D. 冬至日以后

15. 太阳直射点在北回归线附近时，中国南北各地的气温

A. 相差很大，北凉南热　　B. 相差很大，北冷南凉

C. 相差不大，普遍寒冷　　D. 相差不大，普遍高温

16. 今年，天安门前举行国旗升旗仪式及国旗升起时间最早的日子应该是在

A. 十月一日　　B. 六月二十二日前后

C. 一月一日　　D. 十二月二十二日前后

17. 大气中水汽含量极少，能见度好，大气平稳，天气晴朗，对高空飞行有利的大气层是

A. 中间层　　B. 电离层

C. 平流层　　D. 散逸层

18. 北回归线通过中国多少个省区

A. 3 个　　B. 4 个　　C. 5 个　　D. 6 个

19. 以下哪项不是长江流量大的原因

A. 纬度高　　B. 流域面积广　　C. 汛期长　　D. 降水量大

20. 中国动植物资源及农作物种类极其丰富的原因是

A. 夏季雨热同期　　B. 季风气候盛行

C. 自然灾害较少　　D. 气候复杂多样

三、是非题（本题共 10 小题，每小题 2 分，共 20 分。请判断下列各题所表述的意思是否正确。如果正确，请在答题卡上将“T”涂黑，否则将“F”涂黑）

1. 通常人们所说的水资源是指水圈内的水量总体。
2. 地球公转使地球上不同经度的地方，有不同的地方时。
3. 对流层大气的热量绝大部分直接来自太阳辐射。
4. 在北半球，由于一年之中太阳辐射在 6 月份最强，因而这里气温最高的月份是出现在 6 月份。
5. 以雨水补给为主的河流，其径流量主要是随气温变化而变化。
6. 环大西洋和地中海地区是世界上的主要地震带。
7. 石钟乳及石笋主要是由水流的冲刷作用所形成的。
8. 在中国，气候和地势是决定自然地理环境差异的两个基本因素。
9. 由于北冰洋的水汽的进入，中国准噶尔盆地的降水比塔里木盆地稍多。
10. 中国 1 000 毫米等降水量线所通过的地区同 1 月 0℃等温线所通过的地区大体一致。

四、读图及连线题（共 30 分，本题共 3 小题，填对每一空及连对一线得 1 分）

1. 读图并填空（11 分）：

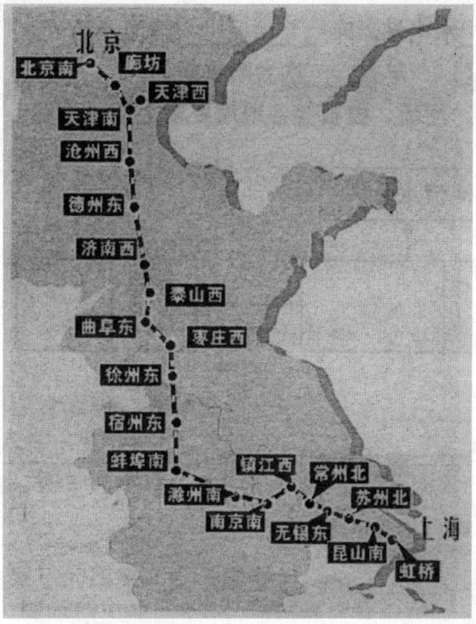

从上图可见，京沪高速铁路全线纵贯北京、天津、上海三大直辖市和四个省，这四个省分别是__a__省、__b__省、__c__省和__d__省，其简称依次是_e_、_f_、_g_、_h_。请填写出其中三个省的省会：__i__市、__j__市和__k__市。

2. 用直线将下列地区与其对应的气候特征连接起来（4 分）：

①地中海沿岸	A. 全年多雨
②赤道地带	B. 全年少雨
③大陆东岸（30°N ~ 40°N）的中国北方地区	C. 夏季多雨
④大陆西岸（回归线附近）的非洲北部地区	D. 冬季多雨

3. 下图是四地气温曲线和降水柱状图，读图并完成下列要求（15 分）：

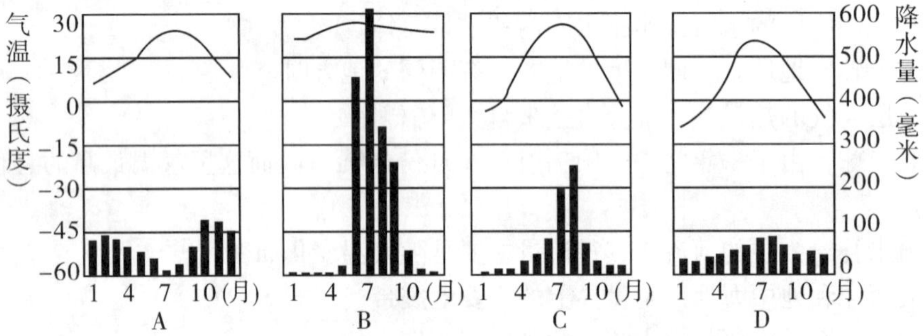

（1）四地气温比较，年较差最小的是______地，年较差较大的两地是______地和______地。

（2）由 A 地气温与降水配合看，高温时期降水______，低温时期降水______。因此，其降水属于______多雨区，这种气候类型为______，分布在__________。

（3）由 C 地气温与降水配合看，降水特点是______季多雨，______季少雨。这种气候类型为______，主要分布在______。

（4）D 地气温年较差较______，全年各月降水量较______，这种气候类型为______。

五、综合题（共 20 分。本题共 3 小题，请选做其中 2 题。3 题全做的只取前 2 题判卷。每小题 10 分）

1. 读图 1 并完成下列要求及答题（第一、二个问题各 3 分，第三、四个问题各 2 分）：

（1）画出地形图中 PP 线的地形剖面示意图。

（2）图中所表示的地形是五种地形（山地、高原、丘陵、平原和盆地）中的哪一种？您判断的理由是什么？

（3）河流大致的流向是______；图上 A、B 两点的距离是 1 厘米，地面实际距离是______米。

（4）这条河流水量丰富稳定，计划修建一个小水电站，仅就地形考虑，比较 C、D 和 E 三处，您认为将堤坝建在何处其工程量较小？理由是什么？

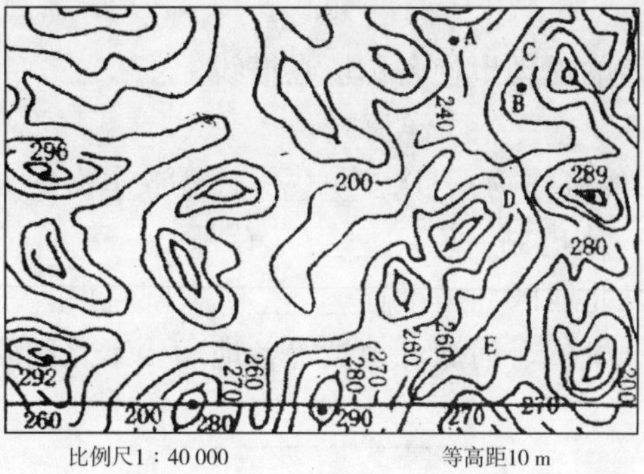

图 1

2. 图 2 三张图片分别表示三种地形，看图回答（第一个问题 4 分，第二、三个问题各 3 分）：

（1）A 是______地形；它的成因是______。

（2）B 地形的名称是______；它与图 A 在形成地区上的差别是______。

（3）C 景观的名称是______；此地形分布于______地区；其形成原因是______。

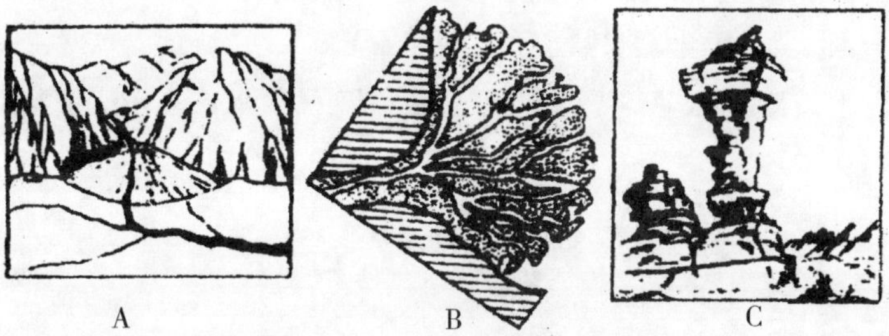

图 2

3. 读图 3，完成下列要求（第一个问题 4 分，第二、三个问题各 3 分）：

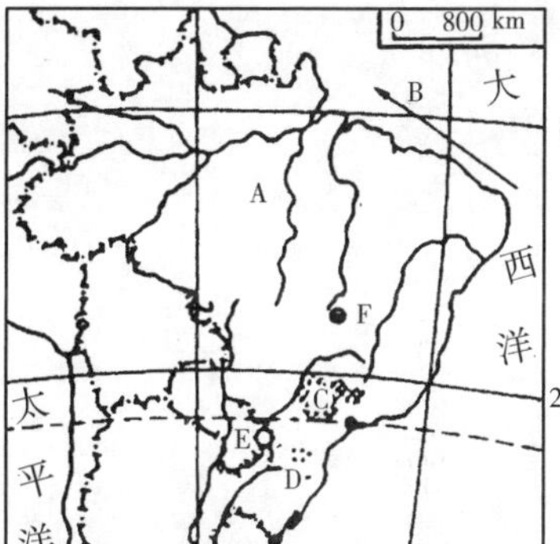

图 3

（1）将图中代号所代表的地理事物名称填在横线上：

A. ______（国家），B. ______（洋流），

C. ______（主要热带经济作物），D. ______（经济作物），

E. 与邻国合建的______水电站，F. ______（首都）。

（2）A 国在南回归线以北地区，一年有______次太阳直射。

（3）完成该国的位置、气候、河流、植被等各地理要素之间联系图。

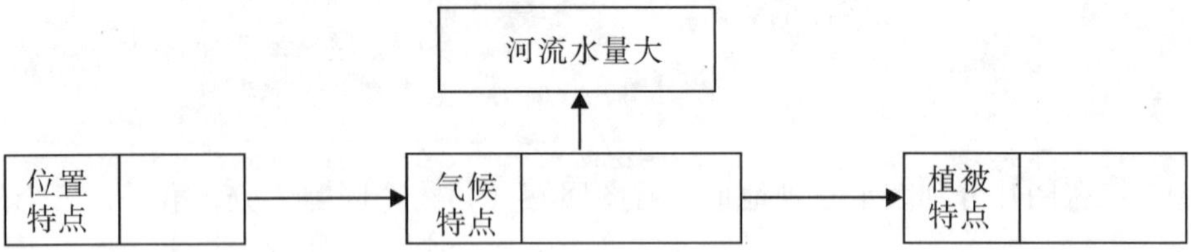

物 理

答卷时间：2 小时

一、选择题（60 分）

以下各小题中只有一个答案是正确的，把你认为正确的答案分别填入答题卡对应的表格中．每小题选对的给 4 分，多选、错选或不选的不给分．

1. 甲乙两汽车从同一车站出发，甲先出发，乙后出发，当乙车追上甲车时，两车运动相同的物理量是

A. 加速度　　B. 速度　　C. 位移　　D. 时间

2. 下列有关弹力（elastic force）的叙述，正确的是

A. 两个靠在一起的物体一定有弹力的相互作用

B. 两个相互接触的物体若发生了弹性形变就一定有弹力的相互作用

C. 两个没有接触的物体之间可能有弹力的相互作用

D. 弹簧只有在伸长时才有弹力

3. 两个质量相等的物体静止在光滑水平面上，现分别对这两个物体施加大小相等的水平恒力，作用时间相同，则

A. 两个物体受到的冲量一定相等

B. 两个物体的末动量大小一定相等

C. 两个物体的末动量一定相等

D. 两个物体的动量增量一定相等

4. 如图所示，由于地球的自转，地球表面上 P、Q 两点均绕地球自转轴做匀速率圆周运动，对于这两点的运动，下列说法正确的是

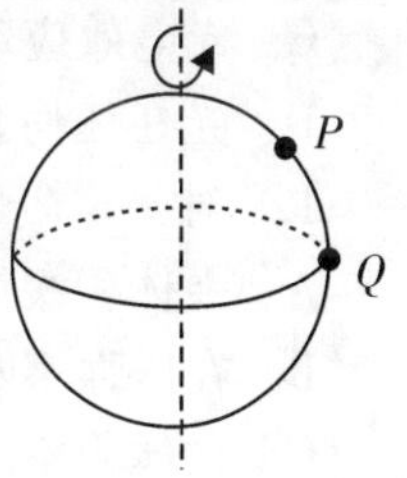

A. P、Q 两点的角速度大小相等

B. P、Q 两点的线速度大小相等

C. P 点的角速度比 Q 点的角速度大

D. P 点的线速度比 Q 点的线速度大

5. 做简谐运动的质点，在通过最大位移处时，具有最小值的物理量是

A. 速度　　B. 回复力　　C. 加速度　　D. 振幅

6. 设发电站向用户输电的输出功率为 P，输出电压为 U，输电线的电阻为 R，则用户获得的功率是

A. P　　B. $(P/U)^2R$　　C. $R-U^2/R$　　D. $P-(P/U)^2R$

7. 雷雨天当带电云层靠近高大建筑物时，由于静电感应，建筑物顶端会聚集电荷，避雷针通过一根导线连接到大地上而避免雷击．若你想知道导线中的电流方向，进而判断云层所带电荷的正负，安全可行的方法是

A. 在导线中接入电流表

B. 在导线中接入电压表

C. 在导线中接入小灯泡

D. 在导线旁放一些可自由转动的小磁针

8. 右图是显像管的示意图，没有磁场时，显像管内电子束打在荧光屏正中的 O 点，加磁场后电子束打在荧光屏 O 点上方的 P 点，则所加磁场的方向可能是

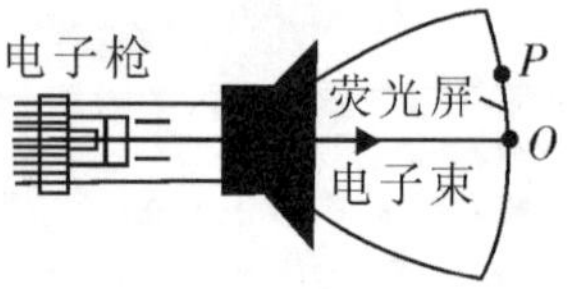

A. 垂直于纸面向内　　B. 垂直于纸面向外

C. 平行于纸面向上　　D. 平行于纸面向下

9. 下列关于电场强度的说法，正确的是

A. 电场强度的大小与检验电荷的电量成反比

B. 电场强度的方向与检验电荷的正负有关

C. 电场线越密集的地方电场强度越大

D. 进入电场中的电荷的受力方向就是电场强度的方向

10. 一理想变压器原、副线圈（the primary，secondary coil）的匝数比为 $n_1:n_2=2:1$，原线圈两端接一正弦交变电流，其电压 u 随时间 t 变化的规律如图所示，则副线圈两端电压的有效值和频率分别为

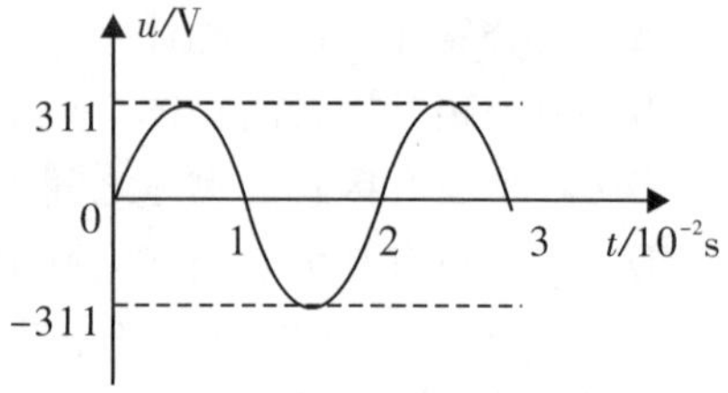

A. 110 V，50 Hz　　B. 110 V，0. 5 Hz

C. 220 V，50 Hz　　D. 220 V，0. 5 Hz

11. 下列说法中正确的是

A. 小孔成像说明光具有波动性

B. 光的衍射现象说明光具有粒子性

C. 光电效应现象说明了光具有粒子性

D. 光在任何介质中的速度都相同

12. 对一定质量的气体，下列说法正确的是

A. 在体积缓慢地不断增大的过程中，气体一定对外界做功

B. 在压强不断增大的过程中，外界一定对气体做功

C. 在体积不断被压缩的过程中，内能一定增加

D. 在与外界没有发生热量交换的过程中，内能一定不变

13. 放射性同位素（radioisotope）可做示踪原子（tracer），在医学上可以用于确定肿瘤位置等用途．医生将放射性同位素作为示踪原子注入病人体内，当示踪原子到达病变的器官后，便可以通过拍摄示踪原子发出的辐射从而得到器官的影像．今有四种不同的放射性同位素 R、P、Q、S，它们的半衰期（half-life）分别为十年、半年、38 天和 2 天，则我们应考虑选用作为示踪原子的同位素是

A. R　　B. P　　C. Q　　D. S

14. 卢瑟福根据 α 粒子散射实验提出了原子的结构模型．如图所示，虚线表示原子核所形成的电场的等势面，实线表示一个 α 粒子的运动轨迹．在 α 粒子从 a 点运动到 b 点再运动到 c 点的过程中，下列说法正确的是

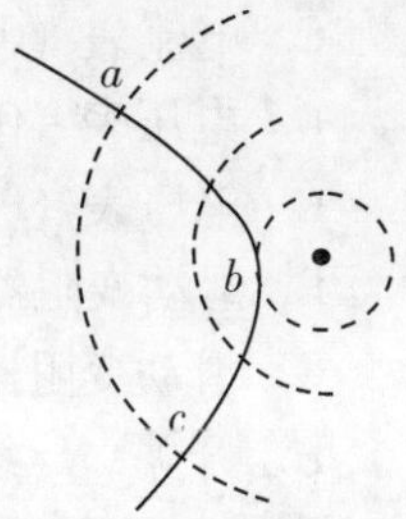

A. 动能先增大，后减小

B. 电势能先减小，后增大

C. 电场力先做负功，后做正功，总功为零

D. 加速度先变小，后变大

15. 氢原子的能级图如图所示，一群氢原子处于量子数 $n=4$ 的能级状态，则

A. 氢原子可能辐射3种频率的光子

B. 氢原子可能辐射4种频率的光子

C. 氢原子可能辐射5种频率的光子

D. 氢原子可能辐射6种频率的光子

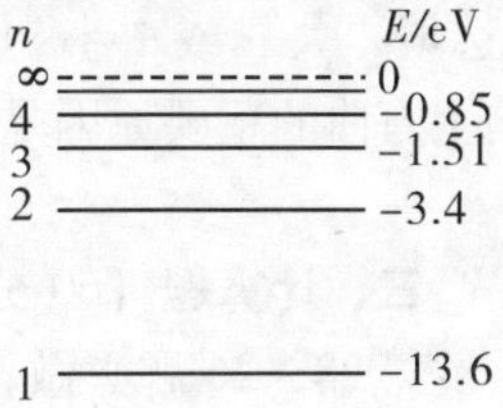

二、填空题（30分）

在以下各小题横线上填入（写在答题卡上）你认为正确的答案（其中16~20题每空3分）.

16. 用10 N的水平推力可使所受重力为25 N的物体在水平地面上匀速滑动，则该物体与地面间的滑动摩擦系数（coefficient of sliding friction）为______.

17. 一个弹簧振子的振幅是2 cm，这个振子在1 s内通过的路程是80 cm，则这个振子的周期是______ s.

18. 一电容器的电容为 C，用电动势为 E 的电池组给它充电，则此电容器在充电完成后带的电量是______.

19. 在真空中，电磁波的传播速度______光速 c（请填"大于"、"等于"或"小于"）.

20. 近几年来，朝鲜的"核危机"引起了全世界的瞩目，其焦点问题就是朝鲜核电站采用的是轻水堆还是重水堆．因为重水堆核电站在发电的同时还可以产生供研究核武器用的钚239（$^{239}_{94}\mathrm{Pu}$），这种$^{239}_{94}\mathrm{Pu}$可由铀239（$^{239}_{92}\mathrm{U}$）经过______次β衰变产生.

21. （6分）某电磁式打点计时器是使用频率为50 Hz的交流电源供电的．某次实验用该打点器连续打了一系列点的纸带如图所示，由此可以判断，这段纸带的运动属于______（填"匀速"或"匀变速"）直线运动，纸带上 AB 段运动的时间 $t=$ ______ s, AB 段的平均速度是______ m/s .

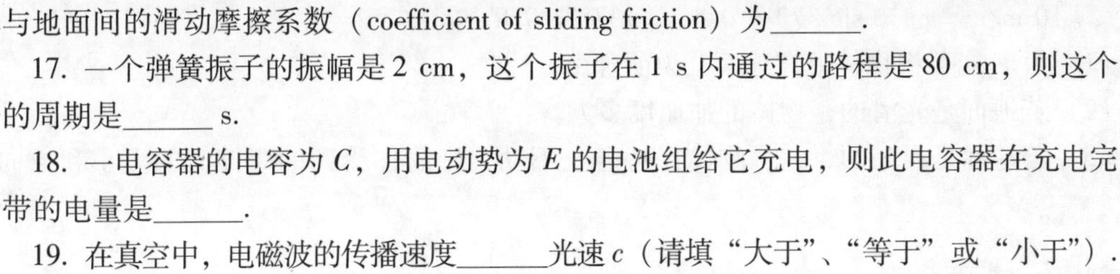

22. （9分）在做"用电压表和电流表测电阻"的实验中，若待测电阻丝的电阻约为5 Ω，要求测量结果尽量精确，备有以下器材：

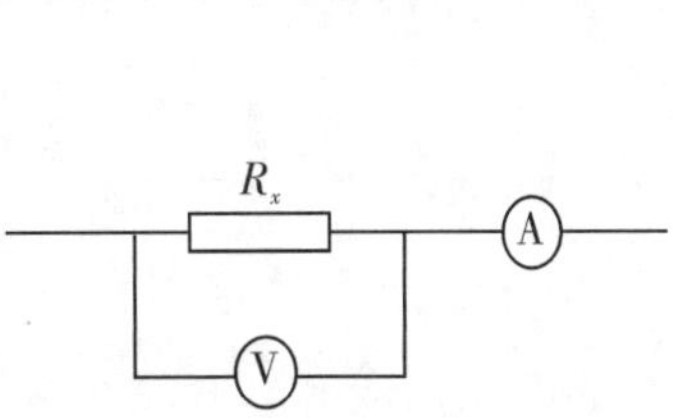

(a)

A. 电池组（3 V、内阻1 Ω）

B. 电流表（0~3 A，内阻0.012 5 Ω）

C. 电流表（0 ~ 0.6 A，内阻 0.125 Ω）
D. 电压表（0 ~ 3 V，内阻 4 kΩ）
E. 电压表（0 ~ 15 V，内阻 15 kΩ）
F. 滑动变阻器（0 ~ 20 Ω，允许最大电流 1 A）
G. 滑动变阻器（0 ~ 2 000 Ω，允许最大电流 0.3 A）
H. 开关、导线

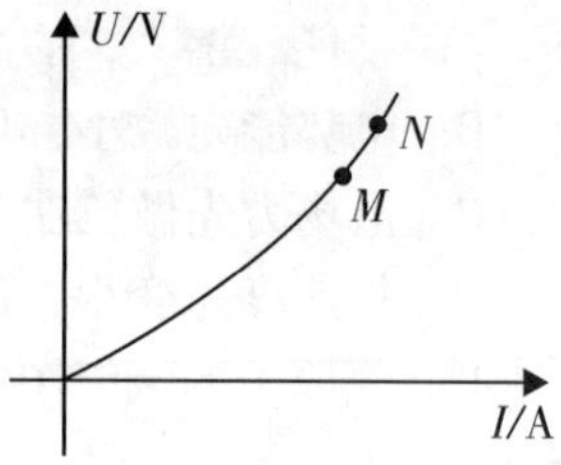

(b)

（1）上述器材中应选用的是______（填编号）；

（2）某同学采用了图（a）所示的部分电路测量电阻，则测量值比真实值偏______（选填“大”或“小”）．根据测量数据得到的伏安特性曲线如图（b）所示，图中 MN 段向上弯曲的主要原因是______．

三、计算题（60 分）

第 23 ~ 26 题必做，第 27 ~ 28 题选做一题．

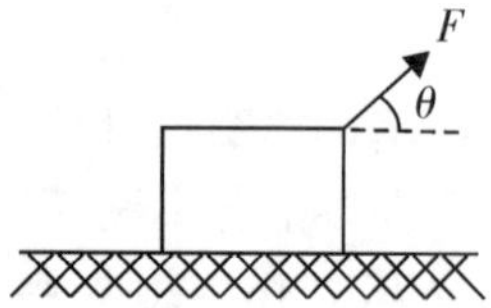

23．（12 分）如图所示，一物体质量 $m = 10$ kg，放在水平地面上．现对物体施加一个与水平面成 $\theta = 37°$ 角、大小为 80 N 的拉力 F 的作用．取重力加速度 $g = 10\ \text{m/s}^2$，已知 $\sin 37° = 0.6$，$\cos 37° = 0.8$，问：

（1）力 F 能否将物体提离地面？说明理由．

（2）若地面是光滑的，物体的加速度多大？

（3）若地面是粗糙的，并且物体保持静止不动，则物体受到的摩擦力的大小和方向如何？

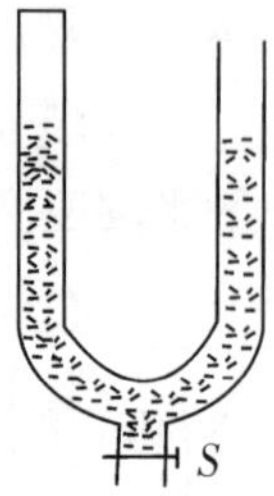

24．（12 分）如图所示，一端封闭的 U 形玻璃管竖直放置，左管中被水银封闭有 20 cm 高的空气柱，右管开口，两管水银面等高．现将阀门 S 打开，流出部分水银（设水银柱足够长），使封闭端水银面下降 18 cm，则开口端水银面下降多少？设此过程中气体温度保持不变，大气压强 $p_0 = 76$ cmHg．

25.（12 分）如图所示，一根长为 L 的轻质细线，一端固定在 O 点，另一端拴一质量为 m、带电量为 q 的小球（可视为点电荷），处于水平向右的匀强电场中．先将小球拉至 A 点，使细线绷直并与电场强度方向平行，然后释放小球，则其由静止开始向下摆动，到达 B 点时速度恰好为零，此时细线转过 60°角．

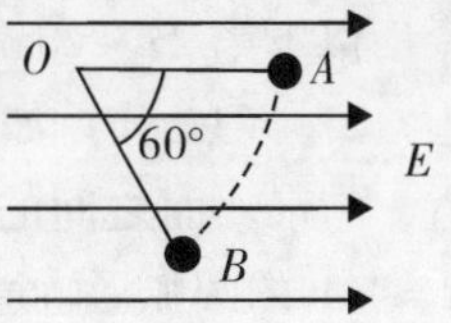

（1）小球带正电荷还是负电荷？

（2）小球从 A 点到 B 点的过程中，重力势能减少了多少？

（3）求 A、B 两点的电势差 U_{AB}；

（4）匀强电场的场强大小是多少？

26.（12 分）如图所示，折射率 $n=1.5$ 的玻璃砖的上下表面是平行的，厚度 $d=1$ cm，置于真空中．一束细光束射到玻璃砖上表面的入射角 $i=45°$，光线一部分从上表面反射回真空中，形成光线Ⅰ；另一部分折射入玻璃砖，在玻璃砖下表面发生反射，又在上表面折射后射入真空中，形成光线Ⅱ．光线Ⅰ与光线Ⅱ的距离 l 为多少？

以下第 27 ~28 题选做一题.

27.（12 分）如图所示，*ABCD* 是处于同一竖直平面内的光滑轨道. 其中 *AB* 为斜面轨道，与水平面之间的夹角 $\theta = 53°$，*BCD* 为半径 $R = 4$ m 的圆弧形轨道，这两段轨道相切于 *B* 点，*B* 点与 *D* 点在同一水平面上. 一质量 $m = 1$ kg 的物体在 *A* 点由静止开始沿轨道滑下，经过 *B*、*C* 点后从 *D* 点斜抛出轨道，最后落到地面上的 *S* 点时的速度大小为 8 m/s. 设物体从 *D* 点抛出前所受的空气阻力可忽略不计，但抛出后所受的空气阻力不可忽略. 已知 *A*、*B* 点距地面的高度分别为 $H = 10$ m 和 $h = 5$ m，取重力加速度 $g = 10\ \text{m/s}^2$，$\cos 53° = 0.6$. 求：

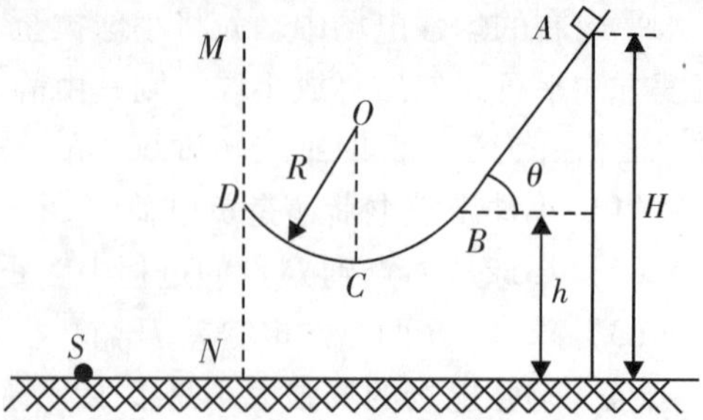

（1）物体经过 *B* 点时的速度大小；

（2）物体经过圆弧轨道最低处 *C* 点时对轨道的压力；

（3）物体从 *D* 点抛出至落到 *S* 点的过程中空气阻力所做的功.

28.（12 分）如图所示，两相距 $L = 0.20$ m、足够长的平行光滑金属直导轨竖直放置，并且处在垂直于导轨平面向内的匀强磁场中，磁感应强度 $B = 0.50$ T. 两导轨间接有导体棒 *MN*，电源和开关 S_1、S_2. *MN* 与导轨接触良好，且可自由滑动，其电阻 $R = 1.5\ \Omega$，电源电动势 $E = 3.0$ V. 导轨电阻和电源内阻均可忽略不计，取重力加速度 $g = 10\ \text{m/s}^2$.

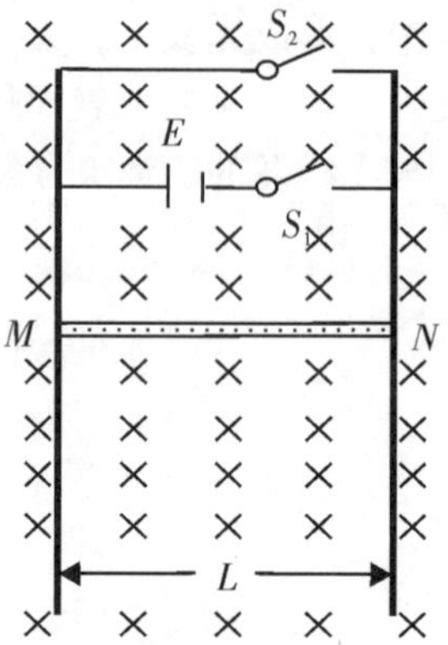

（1）当开关 S_1 闭合、S_2 断开时，导体棒恰好能够保持静止不动，求导体棒所受安培力的大小；

（2）若将 S_1 断开、S_2 闭合，导体棒由静止开始运动，求导体棒能够达到的最大速度是多少？

（3）按第（2）问的条件，当导体棒的加速度 $a = 5.0\ \text{m/s}^2$ 时，求导体棒所产生的感应电动势的大小.

化　学

答卷时间：2 小时

H：1　C：12　O：16　Cl：35.5　Na：23　N：14　S：32　Mg：24　Al：27

Ba：137　P：31　K：39　Fe：56　Ca：40　Cu：64　Mn：55

一、选择题（每题只有一个正确答案，每小题 3 分，共 60 分）

1. 实验室中运用 2008 年诺贝尔化学奖的研究成果，可依据生物发光现象检测超微量钙的存在。这里的“钙”是指

A. 原子　　B. 元素　　C. 分子　　D. 离子

2. 汽车安全气囊内的物质能在碰撞后 10 s 内迅速反应，生成一种空气中含量最多的气体，该气体是

A. 氧气　　B. 二氧化碳　　C. 氮气　　D. 稀有气体

3. 下列各组物质中化学键的类型相同的是

A. HCl　$MgCl_2$　NH_4Cl　　B. H_2O　Na_2O　CO_2

C. $CaCl_2$　$NaOH$　H_2O　　D. NH_3　H_2O　CO_2

4. 将下列物质加入适量的水中充分搅拌，能够得到溶液的是

A. 面粉　　B. 白糖　　C. 牛奶　　D. 植物油

5. 下列防腐措施中，利用原电池反应使主要金属得到保护的是

A. 用氧化剂使金属表面生成致密稳定的氧化物保护膜

B. 在金属中加入一些铬或镍制成合金

C. 在轮船的壳体水线以下部分装上锌锭

D. 在地下输油的铸铁管上接直流电源的负极

6. 关于下列水溶液的说法正确的是

A. HCl 溶液中无 OH^-

B. 氢氧化钠溶液中无 H^+

C. NaCl 溶液中既无 OH^- 也无 H^+

D. 常温下，任何物质水溶液中都有 H^+ 和 OH^-，且 $K_w = 10^{-14}$

7. 在下列反应中，HCl 作氧化剂的是

A. $NaOH + HCl = NaCl + H_2O$

B. $Zn + 2HCl = ZnCl_2 + H_2\uparrow$

C. $MnO_2 + 4HCl(浓) \xlongequal{\triangle} MnCl_2 + 2H_2O + Cl_2\uparrow$

D. $CuO + 2HCl = CuCl_2 + H_2O$

8. 下列化合物中，只有在水溶液中才能导电的电解质是

A. NaCl　　B. CH_3CH_2OH　　C. HCl　　D. KOH

9. 将4 mol A气体和2 mol B气体在2 L的容器中混合并在一定条件下发生如下反应 2A（气）+B（气）══2C（气）。若经2 s后测得C的浓度为0.6 $mol \cdot L^{-1}$，现有下列几种说法：

①用物质A表示的反应的平均速率为0.3 $mol \cdot L^{-1} \cdot s^{-1}$

②用物质B表示的反应的平均速率为0.6 $mol \cdot L^{-1} \cdot s^{-1}$

③2 s时物质A的转化率为70%

④2 s时物质B的浓度为0.7 $mol \cdot L^{-1}$

其中正确的是

A. ①③　　B. ①④　　C. ②③　　D. ③④

10. 压强变化不会使下列化学反应的平衡发生移动的是

A. H_2（g）$+I_2$（g）$\rightleftharpoons$2 HI（g）

B. $3H_2$（g）$+N_2$（g）$\rightleftharpoons 2NH_3$（g）

C. $2SO_2$（g）$+O_2$（g）$\rightleftharpoons 2SO_3$（g）

D. C（s）$+CO_2$（g）$\rightleftharpoons$2CO（g）

11. 有一种气体的质量是14.2 g，体积是4.48 L（STP），该气体的摩尔质量是

A. 28.4　　B. 28.4 $g \cdot mol^{-1}$　　C. 71　　D. 71 $g \cdot mol^{-1}$

12. 元素性质存在周期性变化的本质原因是

A. 元素原子相对原子质量周期性变化的结果

B. 元素原子核外电子排布周期性变化的结果

C. 元素的原子序数递增的结果

D. 元素金属性和非金属性周期性变化的结果

13. 学生用化学知识解决生活中的问题，下列做法不合理的是

A. 用食醋除去暖水瓶中的薄层水垢（主要成分为$CaCO_3$）

B. 用热的纯碱溶液洗涤餐具上的油污

C. 往米汤中加食盐，检验食盐中是否含碘酸钾（KIO_3）

D. 用灼烧并闻气味的方法区别纯棉织物和纯羊毛织物

14. 下列各组物质中，用分液漏斗无法将其分开的是

A. 四氯化碳和水　　B. 溴乙烷和水　　C. 硝基苯和水　　D. 苯和苯酚

15. 下列有机物互为同系物的是

A. 乙烷和乙烯　　B. 苯和溴苯　　C. 乙醇和乙醛　　D. 丙酸和乙酸

16. 下列说法正确的是

A. 葡萄糖、麦芽糖的分子式都是$C_{12}H_{22}O_{11}$，二者互为同分异构体

B. 甘油既可以用于制造护肤品，也可以用于制造炸药

C. 蛋白质、油脂、淀粉、纤维素均属于高分子化合物

D. 乙酸乙酯和食用植物油均可水解生成乙醇

17. 下列关于有机化合物的说法完全正确的是

A. 只有在生物体内才能合成的物质

B. 有机物都含有碳元素

C. 有机化合物都能燃烧

D. 含有碳元素的物质都是有机物

18. 两种气态烃组成的混合物 0. 1 mol 完全燃烧得 0. 16 mol 二氧化碳和 3. 6 g 水。下列说法正确的是

A. 一定有甲烷　　B. 一定是甲烷和乙烯

C. 一定有乙烷　　D. 一定有乙炔

19. 只用一种试剂就可以把 4 种无色稀溶液：乙醇、苯酚、$AgNO_3$ 溶液、KOH 溶液一一区分的是

A. 自来水　　B. 稀硫酸　　C. $BaCl_2$ 溶液　　D. $FeCl_3$ 溶液

20. 下列有机物发生的反应属于酯化反应的是

A. 乙醇与浓硫酸混合加热到 170 ℃

B. 乙烯使溴的四氯化碳溶液退色

C. 溴乙烷与氢氧化钠的水溶液共热

D. 乙醇、乙酸与浓硫酸混合加热

二、填空题（每空 1 分，共 28 分）

1. 写出下列溶液中溶质的化学式：

（1）食盐水______；

（2）碘酒______；

（3）碳酸钙溶于适量的稀盐酸______；

（4）锌与过量的稀硫酸混合______、______。

2. 右图是 A、B、C 三种物质的溶解度曲线，试填空回答：

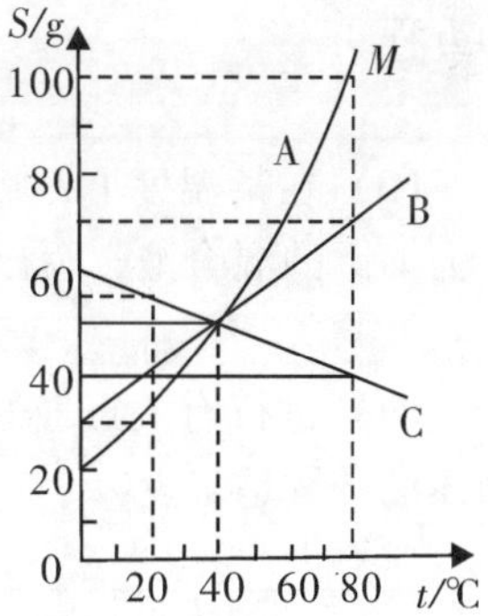

（1）80 ℃时，A、B、C 三种物质的溶解度由大到小的顺序为______。

（2）在______ ℃时，A、B、C 三种物质的溶解度相等，其数值为______ g。

（3）M 点表示在______℃时，在______ g 水中最多能溶解______ g 的 A 物质。

（4）将 80 ℃时 A、B、C 三种物质的饱和溶液温度降低到 20 ℃，变成不饱和溶液的是______。

3. 有甲基、苯基、羟基、羧基四种基团，在它们两两组合形成的化合物中，写出具有以下性质的物质的结构简式：

（1）能使石蕊试液变色的是______和______。

（2）能与溴水发生取代反应的是______。

（3）催化氧化后产物能与新制氢氧化铜发生氧化还原反应的是______。

（4）能与氯化铁溶液发生显色反应的是______。

（5）不同情况下与氢氧化钠反应能生成两种盐的是______。

4. 有A、B、C、D、E五种有机物，各取1 mol在空气中完全燃烧都生成2 mol的CO_2（二氧化碳）。A与浓H_2SO_4（硫酸）反应生成C，C与H_2（氢气）加成生成D，B氧化生成E，B还原生成A，则A、B、C、D、E名称分别是A ________，B ________，C ______，D ______，E ______。结构简式分别是A ______，B ______ ，C ______，D ______，E ______。

三、问答题（共32分）

1. （本题8分）一定温度下，将一定质量的冰醋酸加水稀释，溶液的导电能力变化如右图所示，

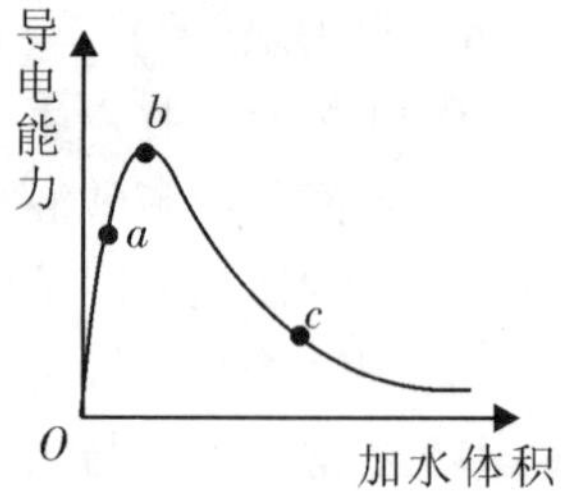

（1）*O*点导电能力为0的理由是什么？

（2）*a*、*b*、*c*三点溶液的c（H^+）由小到大的顺序是什么？

（3）*a*、*b*、*c*三点醋酸的电离度最大的是哪个点，为什么？

（4）要使*c*点c（Ac^-）增大，c（H^+）减少，可采取什么措施？

2. （本题10分）实验室里通常用MnO_2与浓盐酸反应制取氯气，其反应的化学方程式为：MnO_2+4HCl（浓）$\xlongequal{}MnCl_2+Cl_2\uparrow+2H_2O$

（1）在该反应中，如有1 mol Cl_2生成，被氧化的HCl的物质的量是多少？

（2）将制得的氯气通入冷的熟石灰［$Ca(OH)_2$］中即可制得漂白粉，写出反应的化学方程式。

（3）在某温度下，将Cl_2通入NaOH溶液中，反应得到含有ClO^-与ClO_3^-物质的量之比为1∶1的混合液，写出反应的化学方程式。

（4）进行有关氯气的性质实验时，需2.24 L的氯气（标准状况），理论上需要MnO_2固体的质量是多少？

（5）曾经有报纸报道了多起卫生间清洗时，因混合使用“洁厕灵”（主要成分是盐酸）与“84消毒液”（主要成分是NaClO）发生氯气中毒的事件。试根据你的化学知识分析，原因是什么？（用离子方程式表示）

3. （本题8分）按右图所示操作，充分反应后：

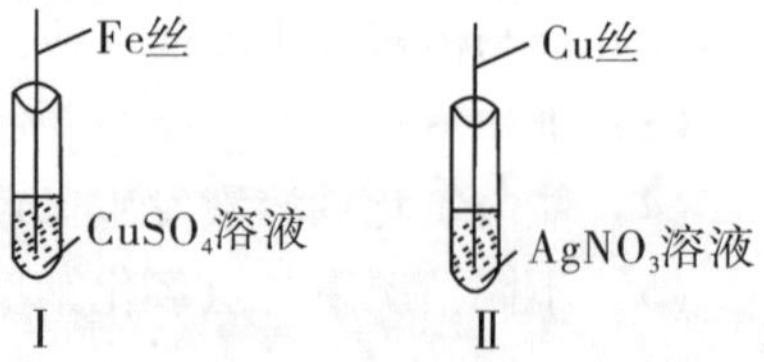

（1）描述Ⅰ中铁丝上观察到的现象。

（2）写出Ⅰ中发生反应的化学方程式。

（3）写出Ⅱ中发生反应的化学方程式。

____

（4）结合Ⅰ、Ⅱ实验现象可知，Fe、Cu、Ag 的还原性顺序是什么？

____

4.（本题 6 分）

（1）实验室经常使用到玻璃磨口仪器，有时会遇到磨口活塞打不开的情况，如果是凡士林等油状物质粘住活塞，请问如何处理？

____

（2）配制一定摩尔浓度的氢氧化钠溶液，为什么要待溶液冷却后再注入容量瓶中？

____

（3）烧杯里的溶液注入容量瓶后，为什么要用少量水洗涤两次，并把洗液注入容量瓶中？

____

四、计算题（从以下 3 题中任选 2 题，每题 15 分，共 30 分）

1. 向 8 g 某二价金属的氧化物固体中加入稀硫酸，使其恰好完全溶解，已知所消耗稀硫酸的体积为 100 mL，在所得溶液中插入铂电极进行电解，通电一定时间后，在一个电极上收集到 224 mL（标准状况）氧气，在另一个电极上析出该金属 1.28 g。

（1）根据计算确定金属氧化物的名称。

（2）计算通电后剩余的混合溶液中，硫酸的物质的量浓度（溶液体积按 100 mL 计算）。

2. 把铝、铁混合物 1.1 g 溶于 200 mL 5 $mol \cdot L^{-1}$ 盐酸中，反应后盐酸的浓度变为 4.6 $mol \cdot L^{-1}$（溶液体积变化忽略不计）。求：

（1）反应中消耗 HCl 的物质的量。

（2）该混合物中铝、铁的物质的量。

3. 在容积为 1 L 的密闭容器中，充入 1 mol N_2 和 4 mol H_2，一定条件下反应 $N_2 + 3H_2 \rightleftharpoons 2NH_3$ 达到平衡，此时 N_2 和 H_2 的物质的量之比恰好为 1∶5。试回答下列问题：

（1）该平衡混合气体中 NH_3 的体积百分数是多少？

（2）平衡时，H_2 的转化率为多少？

生 物

答卷时间：2 小时

一、选择题（每小题 2 分，共 60 分，每小题只有一个正确答案）

1. 人唾液中的淀粉酶能把食物中的淀粉分解成(　　)，所以人们细嚼米饭或馒头时，会觉得有甜味。

A. 麦芽糖　　B. 蔗糖　　C. 葡萄糖　　D. 果糖

2. 成年人的小肠一般长约(　　)。

A. 2 ~ 3 m　　B. 3 ~ 4 m　　C. 5 ~ 6 m　　D. 7 ~ 8 m

3. 碳在生物群落与无机环境之间的循环以(　　)的形式进行。

A. 一氧化碳　　B. 二氧化碳　　C. 葡萄糖　　D. 蔗糖

4. T 细胞在人体的(　　)内发育成淋巴细胞。

A. 胸腺　　B. 骨髓　　C. 血液　　D. 体液

5. 一个体重约为 70 kg 的人，如把全身的(　　)首尾连接起来可以绕地球一周。

A. 毛细血管　　B. 动脉　　C. 静脉　　D. 淋巴管

6. (　　)是人体排出水的最主要途径。

A. 皮肤的排出量　　B. 肺的排出量　　C. 大肠的排出量　　D. 肾脏排尿

7. 以玉米为主食的人群，特别是儿童应额外补充(　　)。

A. 赖氨酸　　B. 苯丙氨酸　　C. 甘氨酸　　D. 丙氨酸

8. 病毒的直径一般在(　　)之间。

A. 10 ~ 300 nm　　B. 6 ~ 10 μm　　C. 0.5 ~ 5 μm　　D. 10 ~ 15 μm

9. (　　)细胞中具有真正的细胞核。

A. 细菌　　B. 放线菌　　C. 真菌　　D. 病毒

10. 有些人在乘车时会感到眩晕和恶心。人耳中与此现象相关的身体平衡感受器是(　　)。

A. 耳蜗　　B. 前庭器　　C. 鼓膜　　D. 听小骨

11. 人免疫系统中大量合成并分泌抗体的细胞是(　　)。

A. 巨噬细胞　　B. T 淋巴细胞　　C. 致敏 T 细胞　　D. 浆细胞

12. (　　)约占细胞总膜面积的一半，是真核细胞中最多的膜。

A. 内质网膜　　B. 叶绿体膜　　C. 核膜　　D. 细胞膜

13. 基因突变在生物进化中起重要作用，下列表述错误的是(　　)。

A. A 基因突变为 a 基因，a 基因还可能再突变为 A 基因

B. A 基因可突变为 A1、A2、A3……它们为一组复等位基因

C. 基因突变大部分是有害的

D. 基因突变不改变种群的基因频率

14. (　　)是新陈代谢的所需能量的直接来源。

A. ATP　　B. 糖类　　C. 脂类　　D. 蛋白质

15. 植物的大多数干物质来自于(　　)。

A. 土壤中的矿物质　　B. 土壤中的碳

C. 大气中的碳　　D. 土壤水分中的氧

16. 马的体细胞染色体数为 64，如果一个马细胞进行减数分裂，所产生配子的染色体数是(　　)。

A. 16　　B. 32　　C. 64　　D. 128

17. 合成蛋白质的遗传信息必须从细胞核转移到细胞质中，将遗传信息转移到细胞质中的是(　　)。

A. 核糖体　　B. DNA　　C. RNA　　D. 氨基酸

18. 细胞内 tRNA 的作用之一是(　　)。

A. 为 mRNA 制备基因　　B. 将碱基转变成氨基酸

C. 为核糖体制备 mRNA　　D. 运送氨基酸到核糖体上

19. 单性生殖是一种无性生殖。进行这种生殖时，成年植物体直接由卵细胞生长而来，在此过程中不存在(　　)。

A. 有丝分裂　　B. 受精　　C. 翻译　　D. 转录

20. 男人中患红绿色盲的概率约为 7.0%，而女人中的患病率仅约为 0.4%，这种数据表明红绿色盲是一种(　　)。

A. 基因在 Y 染色体上的显性性状　　B. 基因在 X 染色体上的显性性状

C. 基因在 Y 染色体上的隐性性状　　D. 基因在 X 染色体上的隐性性状

21. 悬挂耳垂基因 e 和非悬挂耳垂基因 E 是一对等位基因，E 为显性，e 为隐性。基因型为 Ee 的女人同基因型为 ee 的男人生悬挂耳垂孩子的概率是(　　)。

A. 0%　　B. 25%　　C. 50%　　D. 75%

22. 人的性母细胞在进行减数分裂过程中，最不可能出现的是(　　)。

A. 产生基因组合完全相同的配子　　B. 非等位基因间的重组

C. 同源染色体的交换　　D. 染色体数减半

23. 下述(　　)表示一个正常女人的核型。

A. XXY　　B. XX　　C. XO　　D. XXX

24. 两条 DNA 片段如下图所示。

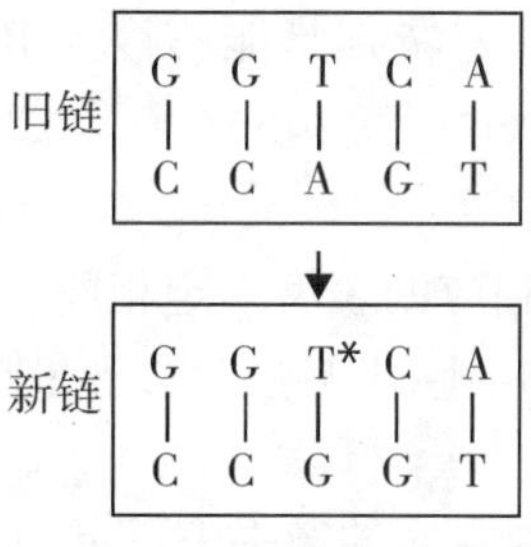

在旧链中，胸腺嘧啶（T）是正常的，这个 T 在新链中被一个异常的 T^* 所代替，异常的 T^* 与鸟嘌呤（G）配对而不是与腺嘌呤（A）配对，这种变化是一种(　　)。

A. 细胞分化　　B. 蛋白质合成　　C. 突变　　D. 有丝分裂

25. 在生态系统中，大约只有(　　)的能量能够流动到下一个营养级。

A. 1% ~9%　　B. 10% ~20%　　C. 21% ~29%　　D. 30% ~39%

26. 具有 $3n$ 染色体数的是（　　）。

A. 胚乳　　B. 胚　　C. 胚柄　　D. 子房

27. 许多植物的表面均具有一些蜡质的覆盖物。这些覆盖物是不透水的，因此可以减少水分损失。这些蜡质的覆盖物属于下列有机分子中的（　　）。

A. 碳水化合物　　B. 脂类　　C. 核酸　　D. 蛋白质

28. 日常生活中有“春兰秋菊”之说，造成这种差异的生态因素主要为(　　)。

A. 温度和水分　　B. 光照和温度　　C. 水分和光照　　D. 温度和土壤

29. 在下列生物学研究中，所选择的技术（或方法）不恰当的是(　　)。

A. 利用纸层析法分离叶绿体中的色素

B. 利用同位素示踪法研究 DNA 复制

C. 利用 γ 射线诱变育种

D. 利用光学显微镜观察细胞膜磷脂双分子层

30. 下列选项中，所采用的灭菌或除菌方法错误的为(　　)。

A. 抗生素溶液用高压蒸汽灭菌

B. 玻璃器皿用干热灭菌

C. 皮肤用 70% 乙醇消毒

D. 染菌桌面用 1% 来苏尔液消毒

二、判断题（下列表述，正确的请填涂“T”，错误的请填涂“F”。每小题 2 分，共 20 分）

1. 人体内成熟的红细胞和血小板都有细胞核。（　　）
2. 人体的血压一般是指体循环的动脉血压。（　　）
3. 扁桃体是人体内最大的淋巴器官。（　　）
4. 淋巴循环的特点是双向运行。（　　）
5. 在人体的血液中，二氧化碳主要结合成碳酸氢盐的形式而被运输到肺。（　　）
6. 血清中不含有纤维蛋白原。（　　）
7. HIV 能够攻击人体的免疫系统，特别是能够侵入 B 细胞，使 B 细胞大量死亡，导致患者丧失免疫功能。（　　）
8. 病毒可以在培养基上繁殖。（　　）
9. 两个基因型相同的个体，其相应的表型一定相同。（　　）
10. 细胞中结合水的含量会影响细胞代谢强度，含量越大，新陈代谢越旺盛。（　　）

三、本大题共 8 小题，请将答案写在答题卡上（共 70 分）

1. （8 分）在南瓜中，果实的白色（W）对黄色（w）为显性，果实的盘状（D）对球状（d）为显性。如这两对基因是自由组合的，那么，请问下列杂交所得子代的基因型和表型的种类和比例如何?

（1）WWDD × wwdd　　（2）Wwdd × WwDd

（3）WwDd × wwdd　　（4）Wwdd × wwDd

2. （10 分）遗传信息表达所涉及的生物大分子主要是核酸和蛋白质。

（1）核酸有 DNA 和 RNA 两种，它们的全称分别是(　　)和(　　)，DNA 由许多(　　)相互连接而成，RNA 由许多(　　)相互连接而成。

（2）蛋白质的基本组成单位是(　　)。这些基本组成单位的种类约有(　　)种。

（3）下图为中心法则的示意图。

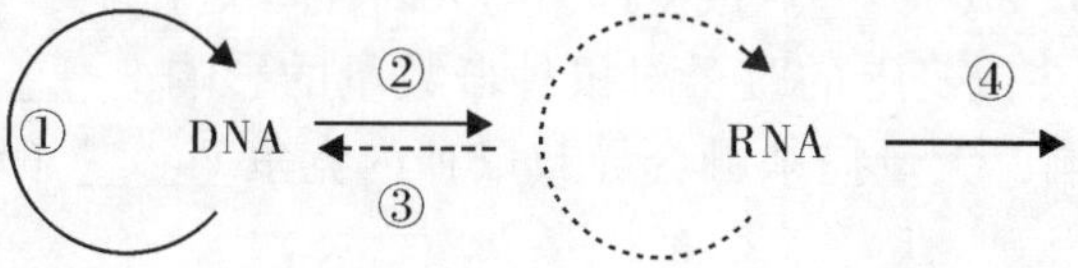

请说明图中遗传信息传递过程的名称：

①表示(　　)，②表示(　　)，③表示(　　)，④表示(　　)。

3. （12 分）番茄茎的颜色由一对等位基因 R 和 r 控制。现有紫茎 A、紫茎 B 和绿茎 C 三株番茄，经相互杂交，结果如下：

第一组：紫茎 A × 紫茎 B→紫茎

第二组：紫茎 B × 绿茎 C→紫茎

第三组：紫茎 A × 绿茎 C→紫茎、绿茎

根据上述结果，请分析回答：

（1）番茄茎的(　　)色为显性性状。

（2）紫茎 A、紫茎 B 和绿茎 C 的基因型依次为(　　)、(　　)、(　　)。

（3）第二组杂交后所得紫茎番茄，经减数分裂产生的配子种类有(　　)种，比例为(　　)。

4. （6 分）下图是某动物的一个细胞在精子形成过程中的两个时期的模式图，据图回答下列问题：

（1）A 图表示(　　)精母细胞；B 图表示(　　)精母细胞。

（2）就染色体组的倍性而言，A 细胞是(　　)倍体。

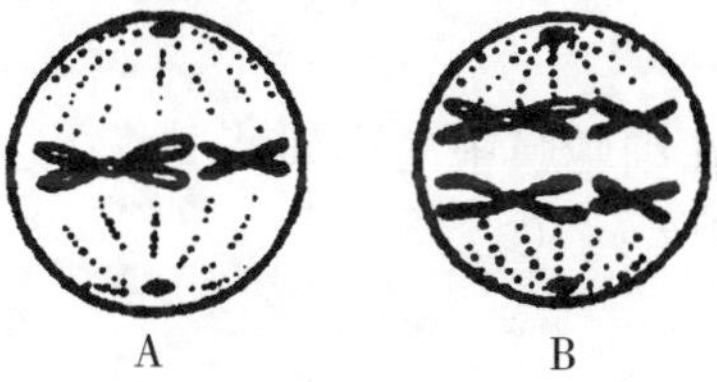

5. （8 分）某岛屿居民与该岛上的植物、兔、鼠、鼬和鹰构成的食物网如下图所示。某个时期，当地居民大量捕杀鼬，导致岛上鼠种群暴发，随后由鼠疫杆菌引起的鼠疫通过

跳蚤使人感染。

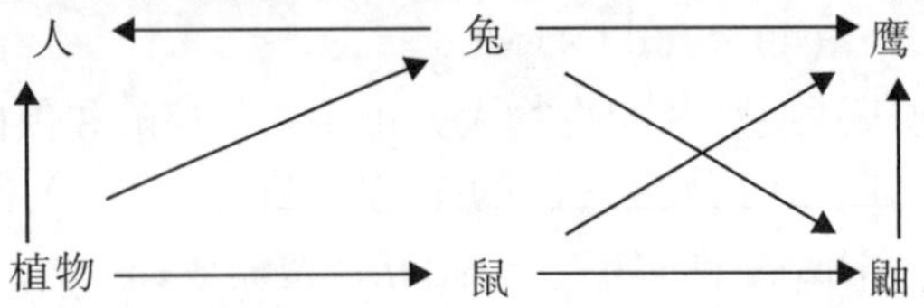

（1）该食物网中，植物中的能量能通过(　　)条食物链传递给鹰，鹰所处的营养级为(　　)；兔与人的种间关系为(　　)。鼠疫杆菌与人的种间关系为(　　)。

（2）通常情况下，寄生在鼠身上的跳蚤对鼠种群数量的影响______（大于、小于、等于）鼬对鼠种群数量的影响；大量捕杀鼬会导致鼠种内竞争______（增强、不变、减弱）。

（3）生长在该岛上的真菌属于生态系统的______（生产者、消费者、分解者），其体内储存的能量______（能、不能）传递给植物。

6.（12分）下图为物质出入细胞膜的示意图，请据图回答下列问题。

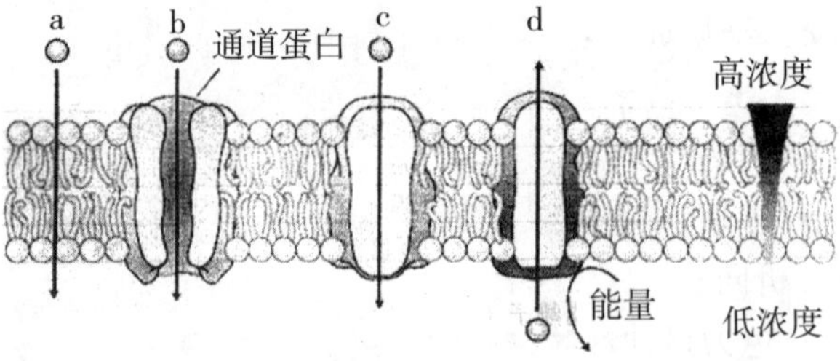

（1）在a至d的4种过程中，代表自由扩散的为（　　），代表协助扩散的为（　　），代表主动运输的为（　　）。

（2）假如甲、乙两种物质分别依赖自由扩散和协助扩散方式进入细胞。如果以人工合成的磷脂双层膜代替细胞膜，并维持其他条件不变，则(　　)。

A. 甲物质的运输速度加快

B. 乙物质的运输速度加快

C. 甲物质的运输速度降低

D. 乙物质的运输速度降低

（3）右图所示为磷脂分子在细胞膜中的排列情况。在这种排列中，最有可能在哪里发现水分子？(　　)

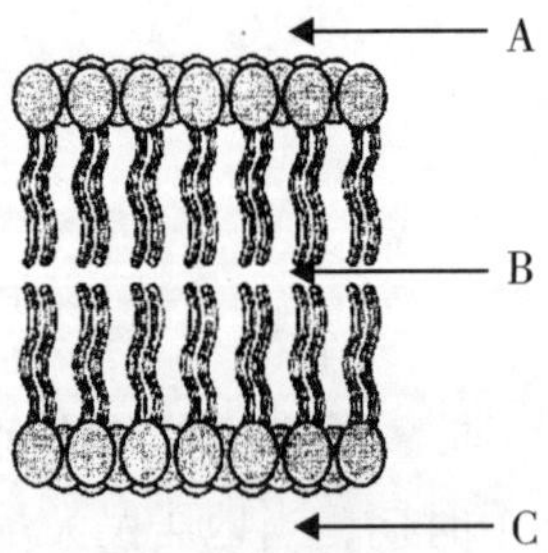

A. A

B. B

C. C

D. A和C

7. （8分）环境污染物多聚联苯难以降解。研究发现联苯降解菌细胞内的联苯水解酶是降解多聚联苯的关键酶。

（1）下列培养基中能用来有效分离联苯降解菌的为(　　)。

A培养基（$g \cdot L^{-1}$）：某生长因子2.0，$(NH_4)_2SO_4$ 2.0，K_2HPO_4 3.0，$MgSO_4$ 1.0，pH 7.4，多聚联苯50 mL。

B培养基（$g \cdot L^{-1}$）：牛肉膏10.0，蛋白胨20.0，葡萄糖20.0，NaCl 5.0，pH 7.4。

C培养基（$g \cdot L^{-1}$）：某生长因子2.0，淀粉20.0，NH_4NO_3 2.5，$MgCl_2$ 0.5，K_2HPO_4 3.0，多聚联苯50 mL，pH 7.4。

（2）进一步研究发现，不同金属离子对联苯水解酶的活性有一定影响，结果见下表：

	相对活性（%）
对照组	100
加入Mn^{2+}	126
加入Mo^{2+}	79

依据表中结果可以看出，金属离子(　　)对该酶的活性有一定的促进作用。

（3）酶是活细胞产生的一类具有生物催化作用的有机物。酶与一般催化剂一样，能降低化学反应所需的(　　)，使反应速度加快。反应完成时，酶本身的化学性质(　　)变化。

（4）绝大多数酶是(　　)，有的酶是(　　)。

（5）酶的(　　)是指任何一种酶只作用于一种底物，或一类分子结构相似的底物，促使底物进行一定的化学反应，产生一定的反应产物。

8. （6分）一学生在显微镜下观察不同类型的细胞，他观察到的3个细胞如下：

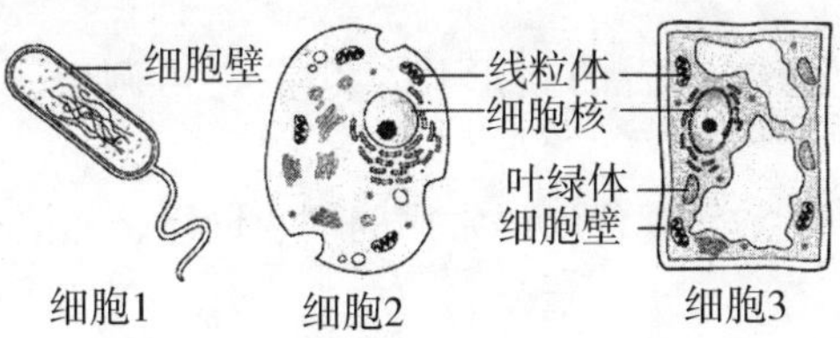

（1）细胞(　　)为植物细胞。判断的依据之一为：此细胞有能够合成$C_6H_{12}O_6$的(　　)。

（2）细胞(　　)是一个原核细胞。

（3）丙酮酸彻底氧化分解为水和二氧化碳是在(　　)中完成的。

（4）植物细胞壁的化学成分主要是(　　)和(　　)。

2012年中华人民共和国普通高等学校联合招收华侨、港澳地区、台湾省学生入学考试题目

语　文

第一部分

本部分为选择题，有18小题，每小题3分，共54分。在每小题给出的四个选项中，只有一项是符合题目要求的。

一、语文基础知识（30分）

1. 下列各句中，加点的虚词使用正确的一句是

A. 凤凰乡不过才巴掌大的一个小地方，倒也算得上山清水又秀，人杰地又灵。

B. 爱是她油画创作中的一个主题，而且她也在描绘美的同时美化了自己的生活。

C. 离别故乡那天，白发苍苍的母亲把我的行李仔细清点，送我到十里外的汽车站。

D. 千千万万的农民自从进城务工以来，他们的生活正在发生了很大的改变。

2. 依次填入下面横线处的词语，恰当的一组是

①经过长时间的筛选比较，当地______至今的瓜果蔬菜品种，不仅营养价值高，而且十分容易种植。

②为了应对中国加入WTO以后的新形势，红星公司调整了产业结构，提高了生产______。

③词典中所收的条目，______现代汉语常用的词、词组、熟语和成语等，共约五万六千多条。

A. 传播　效益　囊括　　　　B. 留传　效能　包括

C. 传播　效能　囊括　　　　D. 留传　效益　包括

3. 下列句子中，加点的成语使用恰当的一句是

A. 张主任搞技术革新样样在行，对产品销售也满腹经纶，是个非常难得的人才。

B. 刘老师虽说已经退休，但他却年富力强，思路敏捷，精力充沛，简直像一个小伙子。

C. 有关自己的身世，他从来都没有说过，即使别人有时问起来，他也总是讳莫如深。

D. 李导演妙手回春，把潘金莲从传统小说中的荡妇形象，改成追求个性解放的新女性。

4. 下列各句中，没有语病的一句是

A. 他现在学习成绩不错，但是能否考上大学，关键还在于要改进学习方法，提高审题解题的能力。

B. 单口相声《珍珠翡翠白玉汤》讲了这样一个故事：九五之尊的皇上用厨房泔水大宴群臣，当然他自己也喝。

C. 这个养猪场经营不善，存栏的生猪从五年前的 5 600 头变成现在的 800 头，数量减少了四五倍。

D. 夏夜，大家围坐在小院中讲故事，说见闻，拉家常，听着蟋蟀浅唱和小狗欢跳，其乐融融。

5. 下列各句中，语意明确的一句是

A. 父母上班之前，嘱咐他照顾好家里，可是双亲一出门，他就丢下残疾的弟弟和妹妹去看电影了。

B. 电视台法制栏目讲述了一个流氓团伙伏法前三年中横行乡里，为非作歹，引起了社会公愤。

C. 有些人利用监管漏洞，故意把水搅浑，牟取暴利，有关部门必须采取有效措施，维护市场秩序。

D. 以前村民们要理发，只能等每个月来一次的剃头匠，可是今年这里居然有了一家妇女理发店。

6. 下列各句中，标点符号使用不正确的一句是

A. 2006 年 8 月 24 日，一个权威的组织——国际天文学联合会投票决定，将冥王星排除在九大行星之外，把它归到“矮行星”的圈子里。

B. 一个朋友告诉我，装修房子的品位，最主要体现在两处：餐厅和卫生间。尤其是餐厅，地方不大，却最难，一点都不能马虎。

C.《华盛顿邮报》报道，这个男婴 23 日上午 9 时 46 分（北京时间 21 时 46 分）在锡布利医院出生，取名为塞缪尔·戴维·切尼。

D.“真的，我是听到了”，小赵说，“当时有两个路人在聊天。一个说，《大宅门》里的白景琦演得可好啦。另一个说，是啊，确实演得很传神。”

7. 下列各句中，没有使用排比或比拟修辞手法的一句是

A. 科研人员研究出一种“神奇”药水，这种药水在人体内能够透过细菌的细胞壁，使细菌死亡，并提高人体的免疫力。

B. 随着一股冷空气的靠近，傍晚前后本市的西北部地区上空会“长出”许多对流云团，一旦条件成熟，阵雨就会再次光临。

C. 那汗水发酵的肥沃土地，那绿环翠绕的潺潺小河，那炊烟袅袅的秀丽村庄……故乡，我永远割不断的爱，断不了的思念！

D. 年轻本就不怕失败，小将们上缴“学费”就是为了将来能够飞得更高，成长需要过程，也需要代价，输球并不可怕。

8. 下列有关文学常识的表述，不正确的一项是

A.《左传》为鲁国史官左丘明著，是编年体史书，将历史人物的形象塑造得真实丰满，有血有肉。

B.《项脊轩志》以清淡朴素的笔法写身边琐事，以口头语说家常事，亲切动人。作者归有光被认为是“桐城派”的代表人物。

C. 冰心是五四新文学运动中涌现的著名女作家，她的《往事》《寄小读者》等作品，被誉为具有典范意义的“美文”。

D. 马克·吐温和欧·亨利都擅长写讽刺小说。马克·吐温的《竞选州长》和欧·亨利的《警察与赞美诗》等都深受读者的喜爱。

9. 下列有关中国文化常识的表述，不正确的一项是

A. 古人纪月，除了用序数，还有一些特殊的称谓，如把每个季节中的三个月份冠以“伯”、“仲”、“季”，以表示顺序。

B. 古代名与字的运用，一般的习惯是：在谦称、上对下、长对幼时用名；在尊称、下对上或平辈相称时用字。

C. 甲骨文是我国已发现的最古老的成熟文字，它刻在龟甲兽骨上，又称“契文”、“卜辞”或“殷墟文字”。

D. 戏曲是中国传统的戏剧形式，行当包括生、旦、净、末、丑，表演上有唱、做、念、打等形式。

10. 对下面这首唐诗的赏析，不恰当的一项是

山中问答　李白

问余何意栖碧山，笑而不答心自闲。
桃花流水窅然[注]去，别有天地非人间。

【注】窅（yǎo）然：深远的样子。

A. 首句以提问起句，突出题旨，而第二句妙在“不答”，造成悬念，引人入胜。

B.“桃花流水”句与李煜的“流水落花春去也”一样，表现出一种落寞的情调。

C.“别有天地”句不仅是说碧山的清幽，也在说诗人悠闲的心境。

D. 全诗结构灵活，有叙述，有描绘，有议论；笔法有虚有实，意趣盎然。

二、白话文阅读（一）（12 分）

阅读下面的文字，完成 11 ~ 14 题。

鸟的导航能力一直令我们迷惑不解。早在 18 世纪时，人们就发现，栖息于北极圈内的北极燕鸥秋天会飞到一万多公里外的南半球去过冬。由于路途遥远，飞行期间要作多次停留，还要跨越好几个不同的气候季节带，面对如此遥远复杂的飞行路线，即使是最优秀的飞行员也会望而却步，那么鸟类究竟是用什么方式来导航的呢？

直到 20 世纪 50 年代，鸟类学家才发现，鸟类在飞行时把太阳作为定向物。科学家们在实验室里把一只八哥关入笼中，并设置了一个类似太阳的光源，这个光源完全按照太阳的旋转方向和速度运动。结果发现，这只八哥会有规律地从放置在不同角度位置上的器皿里叼食，大约每小时转 15 度，这与太阳从东方地平线升起后每小时转 15 度的运动速度是一致的。人们还发现，夜间飞行的鸟类则是根据月亮和星星来定向的，某些鸟类甚至能记住一些星星的位置。

但是，利用日月星辰来定向肯定不是唯一的方法。如果在阴天和没有月光的夜晚，鸟类又如何确定飞行方向呢？进一步的研究发现，鸟类的定向能力综合了多种手段，其中最

主要的是通过地球磁场来确定自己的位置。地球磁场在不同的位置，其磁力的强弱和方向是不同的，这种差别就形成了一个个地磁路标，鸟类把这些地磁路标作为自己的导航依据。科学家在候鸟的必经地模拟了一个虚假的地球磁场，结果路经此地的夜莺竟根据人造磁场改变了飞行方向。鸟类在天气晴朗的白天主要根据阳光来辨别方向，在阴天则根据地球磁场来定向，那么，在日出和日落这段时间呢？研究者发现，某些鸟类能根据偏振光定向，知更鸟就是采取这种方式导航的。某些鸟类能根据其发达的嗅觉进行导航，鸽子就能根据不同风向传来的不同气味辨别飞行方向。

科学家通过对候鸟飞行觅食的观察发现，成年候鸟，尤其是年龄较大的成年候鸟有较好的记忆能力。成年候鸟在飞行途中如果发现某地食物充足，这个地点就会给它留下强烈的印象，并形成记忆，这种记忆在其脑中至少会保留一年，这样它们在以后的迁徙中就会适当地调整飞行路线，飞向该地点觅食。观察表明，年轻候鸟缺乏这种记忆能力，它们不会有目的地飞向觅食点；而燕子的这种记忆能力最强，超过了其他候鸟。

11．下列对鸟类“导航方式”的表述，不正确的一项是

A．在天气晴朗的白天，鸟类主要是根据太阳来辨别方向的。

B．在阴天和没有月光的夜晚，鸟类可以利用地球磁场来导航。

C．在夜间，鸟类可以根据偏振光来确定方向，例如知更鸟和夜莺。

D．鸽子有发达的嗅觉，能根据不同风向传来的不同气味辨别方向。

12．下列对文中画线部分的理解，不正确的一项是

A．科学家在实验室里设置了一个光源，这个光源完全按照太阳的旋转方向和旋转速度进行运动。

B．科学家仿照太阳的旋转方向和旋转速度，在实验室里设置了一个光源，并让这个光源仿照太阳进行运动。

C．八哥从每小时转动 15 度的器皿中叼食，与太阳从东方地平线升起后每小时转 15 度的运动速度是一致的。

D．八哥每小时转换 15 度从器皿中叼食，与太阳从东方地平线升起后每小时转 15 度的运动速度是一致的。

13．下列表述，不符合原文意思的一项是

A．北极燕鸥在秋天时能飞到一万多公里外的南半球去过冬，其辨别方向的本领远远超过最优秀的飞行员。

B．某些鸟类具有准确识记一些星星的位置的本领，所以在晴朗的夜晚能够根据天空的星星来定向。

C．地球磁场在不同的地区表现出不同强弱的磁力和不同的方向，所以鸟类能够通过地球磁场来确定飞行方向。

D．成年候鸟一旦在飞行途中发现某个食物充足的地方，就会在脑中留下记忆，以后就经常去那里觅食。

14．根据原文的信息，下列推断不正确的一项是

A．栖息于北极圈内的北极燕鸥一到秋天就要飞到地球的南半球去过冬，可见其在耐寒方面不及北极熊。

B: 夜莺能通过地球磁场来确定位置，但它根本分辨不出地球磁场的真假，即使人造的磁场也能使其改变飞行方向。

C. 对候鸟觅食飞行的观察表明，成年候鸟具有很强的记忆能力，而且较老的候鸟往往记忆能力也较强。

D. 在记忆能力方面，燕子的水平超过了其他候鸟，即使是年轻燕子的记忆能力也远远超过年老的其他候鸟。

三、文言文阅读（12 分）

阅读下面的文言文，完成 15 ~ 18 题。

梁彦光字修芝，安定乌氏人也。少有至性，其父每谓所亲曰："此儿有风骨，当兴吾宗。"七岁时，父遇笃疾，医云饵五石可愈。时求紫石英不得，彦光忧瘁不知所为。忽□园中见一物，彦光所不识，怪□持归，即紫石英也。亲属咸异□，以为至孝所感。及高祖受禅，□为岐州刺史，甚有惠政，嘉禾连理，出于州境。开皇二年，上幸岐州，悦其能；未几，又赐钱五万。后数岁，转相州刺史。<u>彦光前在岐州，其俗颇质，以静镇之，</u>合境大化，奏课连最，为天下第一。及居相部，如岐州法。邺都杂俗，人多变诈，为之作歌，称其不能理化。上闻而谴之，竟坐免。岁余，拜赵州刺史，彦光言于上曰："请复为相州，改弦易调，庶有以变其风俗，上答隆恩。"上从之，复为相州刺史。豪猾者闻彦光自请而来，莫不嗤笑。彦光下车，发擿奸隐，有若神明，于是狡猾之徒莫不潜窜，合境大骇。彦光欲革其弊，<u>乃用秩俸之物，招致山东大儒，</u>每乡立学，非圣哲之书不得教授。常以季月招集之，亲临策试。于是人皆克励，风俗大改。有滏阳人焦通，性酗酒，事亲礼阙，为从弟所讼。彦光弗之罪，将至州学，令观于孔子庙。于时庙中有韩伯瑜母杖不痛，哀母力弱，对母悲泣之像。通遂感悟，既悲且愧，若无自容。彦光训谕而遣之。后改过励行，卒为善士。以德化人，皆此类也。吏人感悦，略无争讼。后数岁，卒官，时年六十。

（节选自《隋书·梁彦光传》）

15. 依次填入下列各句方框中的字，正确的一项是

①忽□园中见一物，彦光所不识。 ②怪□持归，即紫石英也。

③亲属咸异□，以为至孝所感。 ④及高祖受禅，□为岐州刺史。

A. ①于 ②而 ③之 ④以

B. ①从 ②以 ③也 ④乃

C. ①从 ②而 ③也 ④以

D. ①于 ②以 ③之 ④乃

16. 对下列各句中加点的词的解释，不正确的一项是

A. 七岁时，父遇笃疾。 笃疾：危重疾病。

B. 彦光忧瘁不知所为。 忧瘁：忧伤劳累。

C. 甚有惠政，嘉禾连理。 惠政：优惠待遇。

D. 合境大化，奏课连最。 合境：整个区域。

17. "上闻而谴之，竟坐免。"这个复句的类型是

A. 连贯复句 B. 假设复句 C. 递进复句 D. 因果复句

18. 下列叙述和分析，不符合原文意思的一项是

A. 梁彦光自幼深受其父赏识，其父生病需药饵而不得，彦光偶然中得到，人们认为

是他的孝行所致。

B. 梁彦光在岐州刺史任上政绩卓著，皇上极为欣赏；任相州刺史时，却因人多变诈遭遇挫折而免职。

C. 梁彦光自请复任相州刺史，到任之后强力打击不法行径，主张教授圣贤之书，致使境内风俗大改。

D. 梁彦光注重以德化人，焦通事亲不孝，彦光让他观看韩伯瑜不孝的画像，终于使他改过。

第二部分

本部分为非选择题，有 7 小题，共 96 分。

四、文言文翻译、默写（13 分）

19. 把第一部分文言文阅读材料中画横线的句子翻译成现代汉语。(10 分)

(1) 彦光前在岐州，其俗颇质，以静镇之。

(2) 乃用秩俸之物，招致山东大儒。

20. 补出下列名句的空缺部分。(3 分)

(1) ＿＿＿＿＿，勿施于人。(《论语 · 卫灵公》)

(2) 无边落木萧萧下，＿＿＿＿＿。(杜甫《登高》)

(3) 青，＿＿＿＿＿；冰，水为之而寒于水。(《荀子 · 劝学》)

五、白话文阅读（二）(23 分)

阅读下面的文字，完成 21 ~ 24 题。

冬　天　　朱自清

说起冬天，忽然想到豆腐。是一“小洋锅”（铝锅）白煮豆腐，热腾腾的。水滚着，像好些鱼眼睛，一小块一小块豆腐养在里面，嫩而滑，仿佛反穿的白狐大衣。锅在“洋炉子”（煤油不打气炉）上，和炉子都熏得乌黑乌黑，越显出豆腐的白。这是晚上，屋子老了，虽点着“洋灯”①也还是阴暗。围着桌子坐的是父亲跟我们哥儿三个。“洋炉子”太高了，父亲得常常站起来，微微地仰着脸，觑着眼睛，从氤氲的热气里伸进筷子，夹起豆腐，一一地放在我们的酱油碟里。我们有时也自己动手，但炉子实在太高了，总还是坐享其成的多。这并不是吃饭，只是玩儿。父亲说晚上冷，吃了大家暖和些。我们都喜欢这种白水豆腐；一上桌就眼巴巴望着那锅，等着那热气，等着热气里从父亲筷子上掉下来的豆腐。

又是冬天，记得是阴历十一月十六晚上，跟 S 君 P 君在西湖里坐小划子。S 君刚到杭州教书，事先来信说：“我们要游西湖，不管它是冬天。”那晚月色真好，现在想起来还像照在身上。本来前一晚上是“月当头”；也许十一月的月亮真有些特别吧。那时九点多了，湖上似乎只有我们一只划子。有点风，月光照着软软的水波；当间那一溜儿反光，像新研②的银子。湖上的山只剩下淡淡的影子。山下偶尔有一两星灯火。S 君口占两句诗道：

"数星灯火认渔村，淡墨轻描远黛痕。"我们都不大说话，只有均匀的桨声。我渐渐地快睡着了。P君"喂"了一下，才抬起眼皮，看见他在微笑。船夫问要不要上净寺去；是阿弥陀佛生日，那边蛮热闹的。到了寺里，殿上灯烛辉煌，满是佛婆念佛的声音，好像醒了一场梦。这已是十多年前的事了。S君还常常通着信，P君听说转变了好几次，前年是在一个特税局里收特税了，以后便没有消息。

在台州过了一个冬天，一家四口子。台州是个山城，可以说在一个大谷里。只有一条二里长的大街。别的路上白天简直不大见人；晚上一片漆黑。偶尔人家窗户里透出一点灯光，还有走路的拿着的火把；但那是少极了。我们住在山脚下。有的是山上松林里的风声，跟天上一只两只的鸟影。夏末到那里，春初便走，却好像老在过着冬天似的；可是即便真冬天也并不冷。我们住在楼上，书房临着大路；路上有人说话，可以清清楚楚地听见。但因为走路的人太少了，间或有点说话的声音，听起来还只当远风送来的，想不到就在窗外。我们是外路人，除上学校去之外，常只在家里坐着。妻也惯了那寂寞，只和我们爷儿们守着。外边虽老是冬天，家里却老是春天。有一回我上街去，回来的时候，楼下厨房的大方窗开着，并排地挨着她们母子三个；三张脸都带着天真微笑地向着我。似乎台州空空的，只有我们四人；天地空空的，也只有我们四人。那时是民国十年，妻刚从家里出来，满自在。现在她死了快四年了，我却还老记着她那微笑的影子。

无论怎么冷，大风大雪，想到这些，我心上总是温暖的。

【注】①洋灯：煤油灯。②研：碾磨。

21. 第一自然段中，作者极力要铺染的是什么样的气氛？为什么要这样铺染？(5分)

22. 作者是通过几个什么样的画面来写"冬天"的？(6分)

23. 作者很善于运用比喻来增添文章的情趣，请你从文中找出两处比喻并加以简析。(6分)

24. 本文题目为"冬天"，你认为作者所要表现的主题是什么？又是如何表现的？(6分)

六、写作（60分）

25. 请从下列两个题目中任选一题，写一篇不少于600字的文章。把所选的题目写在作文纸上。(60分)

当代人的追求

我盼望的那一天

数　学

一、选择题：本大题共 12 小题；每小题 5 分. 在每小题给出的四个选项中，只有一项是符合题目要求的.

1. 设集合 M 含有 10 个元素，那么 M 的真子集中，至少含有 8 个元素的共有

A. 56 个　　B. 55 个　　C. 46 个　　D. 45 个

2. 函数 $f(x)=2^x+\ln(2x+1)$ 在 $x=0$ 处的导数 $f'(0)=$

A. $2+\ln2$　　B. $1+\ln2$　　C. 2　　D. 3

3. 已知直线 $ax+2y=4$ 的倾斜角为 $135°$，则 $a=$

A. -2　　B. -1　　C. 1　　D. 2

4. $\lim\limits_{n\to\infty}\sum\limits_{k=1}^{n}\frac{1}{k(k+2)}=$

A. 0　　B. $\frac{1}{2}$　　C. $\frac{3}{4}$　　D. 1

5. 设 a_1，a_2，…，a_9 成等差数列，若 $\sum\limits_{k=1}^{9}a_k=0$，$\sum\limits_{k=1}^{9}a_k^2=15$，且 $a_1<a_2$，则 $a_9=$

A. 2　　B. $\frac{3}{2}$　　C. 1　　D. $\frac{3}{4}$

6. 设复数 z 满足 $1+2z+4z^2+8z^3=0$，则 $|z|=$

A. 2　　B. 1　　C. $\frac{1}{2}$　　D. $\frac{1}{4}$

7. 9 个人站成一排，从中任选 3 人，则这 3 人中任意 2 人都不相邻的概率为

A. $\frac{7}{12}$　　B. $\frac{5}{12}$　　C. $\frac{4}{9}$　　D. $\frac{5}{9}$

8. 离心率为 2 的双曲线的焦点到渐近线的距离等于 3，则该双曲线的焦距为

A. 3　　B. $2\sqrt{3}$　　C. 6　　D. $4\sqrt{3}$

9. 设椭圆 $\frac{x^2}{18}+\frac{y^2}{9}=1$ 的左、右焦点为 F_1、F_2，点 $P(x_0,y_0)$ 在椭圆上，且 $|PF_1|=2|PF_2|$，则 $x_0=$

A. 2　　B. 3　　C. $2\sqrt{3}$　　D. $3\sqrt{2}$

10. 在正三棱锥 $P-ABC$ 中，若侧棱与底面成 $30°$ 角，则侧面与底面所成的二面角 $\alpha=$

A. $\arctan\frac{\sqrt{3}}{2}$　　B. $\arctan\frac{2\sqrt{3}}{3}$　　C. $\arcsin\frac{\sqrt{3}}{2}$　　D. $\arcsin\frac{1}{2}$

11. 设 $\omega>0$，函数 $f(x)=\sin\omega x\cos\omega x$ 在区间 $\left[-\frac{\pi}{6},\frac{\pi}{3}\right]$ 单调增加，则 ω 的最大值为

A. $\frac{3}{2}$　　B. $\frac{5}{4}$　　C. $\frac{4}{3}$　　D. $\frac{3}{4}$

12. 设 $a+b+c=0$，$a^2+b^2+c^2=1$，则 $a^4+b^4+c^4=$

A. $\frac{3}{4}$　　B. $\frac{2}{3}$　　C. $\frac{1}{2}$　　D. $\frac{1}{3}$

二、填空题：本大题共 6 小题；每小题 5 分.

13. 某企业从甲、乙、丙三地招聘一批员工，其中 39 人招自甲地，91 人招自乙地，余者招自丙地. 为了解他们对企业发展的意见和建议，采用分层抽样的方法，从这批员工中抽取 56 人进行调研. 如果被抽取的这些人中来自丙地的共有 16 人，那么，这批新招的员工共有______人.

14. 直线 $x+2y=1$ 关于点 M（1，2）对称的直线的方程为______.

15. 若正四棱柱的对角线长为 3，则其侧面积的最大值是______.

16. 在空间直角坐标系中，经过点 P（1，1，1）和 Q（-1，0，2）且与直线 $\begin{cases}3x-2y+2=0\\ y-3z+5=0\end{cases}$ 平行的平面方程为______.

17. 用 x^2+x 除多项式 x^5+3x^3+4x-3 得到的余式为______.

18. 设圆锥轴截面的顶角为 θ，$\cos\theta=-\frac{7}{25}$，则该圆锥侧面展开图扇形的圆心角 $\alpha=$______.

三、解答题：本大题共 4 小题；每小题 15 分. 解答应写出文字说明、证明过程或演算步骤.

19. 在 $\triangle ABC$ 中，设内角 A、B、C 所对边长分别为 a、b、c. 已知 $(\tan A+1)(\tan B+1)=2$，$\cos 2B+\sin^2 C=1+\sin^2 A$，$a=2$. 求角 C、边长 b 和 $\triangle ABC$ 的面积.

20. 设等比数列 $\{a_n\}$ 的首项 $a_1 = a > 0$，公比 $q = \frac{1}{2}$. 数列 $\{b_n\}$ 的前 n 项和 $S_n = n^2 + 3n$.

（Ⅰ）求 $\{a_n\}$ 和 $\{b_n\}$ 的通项；

（Ⅱ）是否存在正数 p 和 r 使 $b_n + \log_P a_n = r$ 对任意正整数 n 都成立？若存在，求 p 和 r；若不存在，说明理由.

21. 已知直线 l 与抛物线 $y^2 = 4x$ 相交于 A、B 两点，且与圆 $(x-1)^2 + y^2 = 1$ 相切.

（Ⅰ）求直线 l 在 x 轴上截距 c 的取值范围；

（Ⅱ）设 F 是抛物线的焦点，$\overrightarrow{FA} \cdot \overrightarrow{FB} = 0$，求直线 l 的方程.

22. 设函数 $f(x) = ax^3 + bx^2 + cx\ (a \neq 0)$ 是增函数，$g(x) = f(x + x_0) - f(x_0)$，且对任意 $x_0 \geqslant -\frac{1}{2}$，$g(x)$ 都不是奇函数. 证明 $M = \frac{3a + 2b + c}{2b - 3a} > 0$，并求 M 的最小值.

英　语

Matriculation English Test（MET12）

本试卷分第一卷（选择题）和第二卷（非选择题）两部分。

注意事项：

1. 答卷前，考生务必将自己的姓名、准考证号填写在答题卡上。
2. 将答案涂写在答题卡上，写在本试卷上无效。
3. 考试结束后，将本试卷和答题卡一并交回。

第一卷

Ⅰ．听力（共 20 小题，每小题 1.5 分；满分 30 分）

听完录音后，从各题所给的四个选项中选出能回答所提问题的最佳选项。所有录音材料均仅读一遍。

例：（录音）Man：I wonder why the office is still not open.

Woman：But it's not yet eight. In fact，it's only a quarter to eight.

When does the office open?

A. At 8：30.　B. At 8：15.　C. At 8：00.　D. At 7：45.

答案是 C。

听第 1 段材料，回答第 1 小题

1. Where are the two speakers?

A. In a hospital.　B. In a classroom.　C. In a cinema.　D. In a restaurant.

听第 2 段材料，回答第 2 小题

2. What gift has Mike got for his birthday?

A. A book.　B. A CD player.　C. A picture.　D. A radio.

听第 3 段材料，回答第 3 小题

3. What does the man want to do?

A. To take back his seat.　B. To change for a better seat.

C. To be near the front door.　D. To sit together with the girl.

听第4段材料，回答第4、5小题

4. Who might Mr. Smith be to the woman?

A. Her boss. B. Her secretary C. Her father. D. Her husband.

5. What will Jane do after the conversation?

A. Join another team. B. Take time off from work.

C. Apologize to the class. D. Try to finish work soon.

听第5段材料，回答第6、7小题

6. When does the man usually have breakfast every day?

A. At 5: 00 a. m. B. At 6: 00 a. m.

C. At 6: 40 a. m. D. At 7: 00 a. m.

7. How long does it take the man to walk to the train station?

A. 10 minutes. B. 15 minutes.

C. 20 minutes. D. 30 minutes.

听第6段材料，回答第8至10小题

8. How did the man probably find out about Dr. Warner?

A. From a friend. B. By driving past the clinic.

C. By watching TV. D. From a website.

9. What does the man do around four in the afternoon?

A. He has classes. B. He goes to work.

C. He takes care of his kids. D. He drives his kids to school.

10. When will the man see the doctor?

A. At 11: 00 a. m. Friday. B. At 10: 00 a. m. Thursday.

C. At 9: 00 a. m. Friday. D. At 8: 30 a. m. Thursday.

听第7段材料，回答第11至13小题

11. Why is Peter going to Germany this summer?

A. To learn German. B. To meet his old friends.

C. To go to a Math Camp. D. To teach English.

12. What does Mary suggest Peter do when meeting people for the first time?

A. Arrive on time. B. Greet them in German.

C. Shake hands with them. D. Call them by their first name.

13. What's better for Peter to do before leaving for Germany?

A. To join a Math club. B. To call up Ms. Schmitt.

C. To make a German friend. D. To take a short German course.

听第 8 段材料，回答第 14 至 16 小题

14. Where are they planning to go in the morning?

A. To an art Museum.
B. To the Science Museum.
C. To an Indian shop.
D. To the beach.

15. Why does the man want to visit the zoo?

A. It is very cheap.
B. He can buy some gifts.
C. It is close to the museum.
D. He can see some unusual animals.

16. What do the speakers decide to do in the afternoon?

A. Go to the beach.
B. Read the city guide.
C. Look for a restaurant.
D. Cash traveler's checks.

听第 9 段材料，回答第 17 至 20 小题

17. What's the talk mainly about?

A. The speaker's tea drinking habits.
B. Differences between tea and coffee.
C. Why black tea tastes better.
D. How to make a cup of tea.

18. Why did the speaker's brother think it's strange to bring tea to China?

A. English tea has a strange taste.
B. China produces lots of tea.
C. It's very heavy to carry.
D. The brother doesn't like tea.

19. What does the speaker think of green tea now?

A. It has a good taste.
B. It is more popular than black tea.
C. It takes time to make.
D. It is pretty expensive.

20. What is the speaker's opinion about drinking tea?

A. It's not as popular as coffee.
B. More research is necessary.
C. It's cheaper than coffee.
D. It's good for health.

Ⅱ. 英语运用（共 35 小题，每小题 1 分；满分 35 分）

A）单项填空（共 15 小题）

从 A、B、C、D 四个选项中，选出可以填入空白处的最佳答案。

21. —Did you close the door?

—Yes, Mum. I remember ______ it.

A. to close B. close C. closing D. closed

22. The doctor told me to take the medicine three times ______ day and stay in ______ bed, and then I would be better soon.

A. a; the B. /; a C. the; a D. a; /

23. Every year he takes a month off work to go climbing in the great ______.

A. nature B. wild C. outdoors D. weather

24. —How do you think about this novel?

— Well, the writer ______ have spent more time and effort to make it better.

A. must B. will C. might D. should

25. The clock ______ ten as we went into the church for the wedding.

A. strikes B. struck C. was striking D. has stricken

26. The baby is crying. Will you please ______ him while I'm preparing the milk?

A. look into B. look up C. look for D. look after

27. That printer is giving Mr. Smith so much trouble that he has decided to go to the service center ______.

A. to repair B. to be repaired

C. to have it repaired D. to have it repair

28. —What did the gentleman say to you?

—It's too noisy and I've hardly got ______ he has told me.

A. that B. what C. which D. who

29. The computer system will not permit one ______ without the correct password.

A. enters B. entering C. enter D. to enter

30. Can you lend me the book ______ the other day?

A. you talked B. you talked about it

C. you talked with D. you talked about

31. You can't get a job ______ you've got experience in doing this job.

A. unless B. since C. if D. but

32. —We'll do what we can ______ English well this term.

—I'm so glad to hear that. Not just English though.

A. study B. to study C. be studied D. studying

33. —How can I get to the village quickly?

—It will take you at least one hour, ______ way you travel.

A. whenever B. whatever C. whichever D. wherever

34. Sarah demanded that Jack ______ the books he borrowed from her.

A. return B. returned C. returning D. to return

35. —How did you get to know Tom?

—I first met him in Paris ______ I lived in the early nineties, and then we became friends.

A. when B. which C. what D. where

B）完形填空（共 20 小题）

阅读下面短文，掌握其大意，然后从 36 至 55 各题所给的四个选项中选出一个最佳答案。

There is a special day of the year at the beginning of October. It's for us to __36__ the little yellow smiley face we all know and love. It is __37__ a circle with two dots in the middle to represent（表示）eyes, and a half circle for the mouth. The smiley is __38__ today. How many times do you __39__ a smiley in your text messages? How often do you quickly draw a smiley with your __40__ on a bathroom mirror? Believe me, __41__ tiny children can do this. The happy little face is now __42__ of the most popular images on __43__. If we could all follow this little face, what a(n) __44__ world this would be!

Bet you didn't know the smiley was the __45__ of an American artist, Harvey Ball, in 1963. In 1971, two businessmen __46__ it in a campaign（促销活动）to sell funny products, They produced coffee cups, T-shirts and stickers and __47__ smiley was worldwide. The Smiley is registered（注册）in over 100 __48__ outside the U. S. for many different products and __49__. Harvey Ball wanted to use his idea for a good __50__. He decided the first Friday in October each year would be *World Smiley Day*. The theme（主题）for this __51__ is: "Do an act of kindness; help one person smile." The *World Smile Organization* __52__ that each one of us can __53__ a difference in this world. *World Smiley Day* is the day when everyone's __54__ can make the world a better place. It's a __55__ this day isn't every day of the year.

36. A. see B. draw C. have D. celebrate
37. A. as B. yet C. just D. about
38. A. everywhere B. somewhere C. nowhere D. anywhere
39. A. form B. place C. show D. take
40. A. hair B. eyes C. finger D. heart
41. A. only B. very C. even D. no
42. A. first B. any C. each D. one
43. A. the line B. the earth C. the face D. the wall
44. A. interesting B. wonderful C. strange D. big
45. A. draw B. decision C. desire D. design
46. A. stole B. took C. used D. made
47. A. suddenly B. probably C. fortunately D. especially
48. A. offices B. documents C. cities D. countries
49. A. factories B. information C. services D. workers
50. A. cause B. thing C. result D. effect
51. A. year B. world C. day D. American
52. A. refused B. blamed C. regretted D. believed
53. A. bring B. change C. make D. gain
54. A. act B. messages C. face D. products
55. A. surprise B. shame C. story D. problem

Ⅲ. 阅读理解（共 20 小题，每小题 2.5 分；满分 50 分）

阅读下列短文，并做每篇后面的题目。从四个选项中，选出能回答所提问题或完成所给句子的最佳答案。

A

Vancouver, B. C. —For six months, Ted Schredd and Deanna Kopel cycled around North America to show others a way to help the environment. "Nobody wants to breathe dirty air—but for the air to change. people have to stop driving cars," says Ted. "If more people start riding bikes, the air will be cleaner."

Ted started his trip alone. He had $ 160 in his pocket and plans to cycle around North America. He left his hometown of Vancouver, and when he arrived in San Diego he got the chance to make some extra money for the rest of his 13, 000 km trip. A cyclist he met asked him to speak at an environmental meeting in Texas. Within a few hours, Ted was on a plane to the meeting and a big surprise.

When he met Deanna at the meeting, they talked for six hours straight. It was love at first sight. The next day, he called her to ask if she wanted to finish the trip with him. She said yes, sold everything in her flat, gave her notice at work, and was on the road with Ted three weeks later.

Deanna found Ted's timetable difficult because he got up early in the morning. Deanna was a nurse and usually worked at night. "All of a sudden, I was up at six when I wanted to sleep until noon," said Deanna.

As the couple cycled to Florida and up to Montreal and then back to Vancouver, every day was an adventure. They got free meals in restaurants, and slept in people's yards. When they ran out of money, people gave them extra cash. Sometimes people gave away $ 50 or $ 100.

And like all good stories this one has a happy ending. On the way back to Vancouver, they stopped in Edmonton to visit Ted's relatives. During the visit, they got married. People tied tin cans and a "Just Married" sign to the back of their bikes.

They now want to write a book about their trip. "We want people to know that you can protect our earth and still have fun," Schredd said.

56. What did Ted Schredd believe to be a way to protect the environment?

A. Driving less. B. Breathing clean air.

C. Saving waste tin cans. D. Staying healthy by cycling.

57. Why did Ted speak at an environmental meeting?

A. He could get a big surprise.

B. He was in the city of the meeting.

C. He hoped to find someone to join him.

D. He wanted more people to know about his opinion.

58. What difficulty did Deanna meet after starting the trip with Ted?

A. Getting free meals in restaurants.

B. Sleeping in people's yards.

C. Getting up very early.

D. Missing her friends.

59. In what way does the story have a happy ending for Ted and Deanna?

A. They got married during their trip.

B. They got together with their relatives.

C. They became very famous in America.

D. They wrote a book about their experience.

B

Computer Engineer Barbie doll（芭比娃娃）comes with pink glasses and a tiny Bluetooth. Well, that's what women computer engineers did to gain more support for their field because their positions have been worse and worse in the last twenty years. When Mattel Inc., Barbie's maker, asked the public to decide on Barbie's next job, 96% of the women computer engineers all wanted Barbie to be a computer engineer, according to the *Wall Street Journal* on Friday.

The women hoped the doll would raise the position of their chosen career（职业）and get more women interested in this job.

If you want further information about why computer engineering—one of the fastest growing professions, is not attracting girls, check this out: Last year, 67% of all boys chose computer science as a "very good" or "good" career, but only 9% of girls considered it as "very good" and 17% as "good", according to a report by New Image for Computing.

Twenty years ago, women were awarded twice as many computer science degrees as they were in 2008. Of course, there are more fields open to women today, but that only explains part of the reason this well-paid, fast-growing field is losing women.

"Though we can't be certain of the cause of this situation, research suggests several likely possibilities," says Catherine Ashcraft, senior researcher at the University of Colorado. "Many of these are related to the image of computer science and the lack of women role models. Girls get some messages from all sorts of places—the Internet, TV, parents, teachers, pop stars, and other famous figures—that computer science isn't really 'something girls do'."

Other research suggests that young people in general, and especially girls, often don't know exactly what a computer-science career means. "They have a much clearer image of what it means to be a doctor or a lawyer, for example," Ms. Ashcraft said.

There are also several key reasons why women leave computing careers once they have begun them. These include lack of role models or others' support, as well as inequality in the workplace that might affect women's values and their performance, which make them get tired of such work.

60. why do women computer engineers want Barbie Doll to be like them?

A. They want to improve their image.

B. They think Barbie should be smart.

C. They all like the doll very much.

D. They support Mattel Inc.

61. What is the percentage of boys who considered "computer engineering" as a satisfactory job last year?

A. 9%. B. 17%. C. 67%. D. 96%.

62. According to Catherine Ashcraft, what might be the main reason for fewer women in computer engineering?

A. Today girls can have more career choices.

B. Women computer engineers are not usually well-paid.

C. People know little about this profession.

D. It's hard to get a computer science degree in college.

63. What's the main idea of the last paragraph?

A. Why women leave the computer career.

B. How women want to be models for others.

C. The advantages of a computing career.

D. The position of women in computing profession.

64. What type of writing is this article?

A. A news report.

B. A children's story.

C. A part of a book.

D. A job introduction.

C

This is the season when millions of parents go into toy stores, looking for the latest game or toys to give to the little ones they love. Interest and educational uses often top a parent's wish list, and low price is always attractive, but safety should be No. 1. A research report says that about 230,000 toy-related accidents are treated in hospital every year. The Consumer Products Safety Commission (CPSC) provides some shopping tips to follow:

Pay attention to the age on the box. There's a reason why some *Lego* pieces and *Hungry Hippos* are not right for children under 3. They contain small parts that kids like to put in their mouths, making them at high risk. Watch out for toys with small buttons as well.

Test out noisemakers. Some musical instruments, or loud playthings give out 90 decibels (分贝) of sound—that's as loud as heavy rock. Hold it close to your ear (as many kids do), and it's more like 120 decibels, enough to hurt your hearing. Listen to the toy in the store and if it's too loud for you, find something quieter.

Pass on "weapons". Toy guns, Frisbees, or anything that flies or shoots can lead to serious eye injuries, even blindness. Give up these types of toys for younger kids; for older ones, make sure they have soft tips or other protective points.

Be sure to get ride-on protection. Bikes, skateboards and other riding toys might cause more injuries than any other toys. Proper-fitting helmets（头盔）and pads（护垫）are a must.

Check for low-quality products. The CPSC keeps an up-to-date list of unsatisfactory toys. Visit http://www.cpsc.gov.

65. Which of the following should be considered as the most important when parents buy toys?

A. Safety. B. Interest. C. Education. D. Price.

66. Which type of toy might cause eye injuries to children?

A. The guitar. B. Toy guns. C. Lego. D. Skateboards.

67. Where can you find information about low-quality toys?

A. From research reports. B. From CPSC newspaper.

C. From other parents. D. From the official website.

D

Just as a picture is worth a thousand words, our faces can express a wealth of information. The ability to give subtle（微妙的）feelings with a simple raised eyebrow may be innate. Charles Darwin was one of the first to declare this theory in his book *The Expression of the Emotions in Man and Animals*, in which he wrote: "The young and the old of widely different races, both with man and animals, express the same state of mind by the same movements."

Recent work supports Darwin's theory that smiles, making faces and other facial expressions are hardwired—commonly seen in social groups. For example, studies show that babies, including those who are blind or have underdeveloped brains, use facial expressions to tell their parents how they feel. Babies use their faces to communicate（交际）even before they are old enough to understand the meaning of their own expressions. Because humans depend on one another for life, facial expressions may have developed as effective ways to show feelings and wants.

By studying faces, researchers have matched small changes in the positioning of the mouth, eyes and others to changes in the six basic human feelings—happiness, surprise, dislikes, sadness, anger and fear. Scientists want to use this information to develop computer technology that examines facial movements to help decide whether people are telling the truth.

However, facial expressions do not just give us away; they may also allow us to experience our own feelings more fully. This process is still not well understood, but it is possible that forcing your face to express happiness, sadness or anger may help you feel those emotions. What's more, new research using MRI（核磁共振成像）shows that facial expressions not only show what people are feeling, they can change how you behave, too. For example, studies have shown that when people are making an angry face, they'll have less activity in the part of their brain which is related with decision-making ability, and they will not do their job very successfully.

68. What does the underlined word "innate" in Paragraph 1 most probably mean?

A. fixed beforehand B. not natural

C. very different D. born with people

69. What can babies do with their facial expressions?

A. To show that they understand.

B. To depend on one another.

C. To express how they feel.

D. To learn to speak.

70. Why do scientists match facial expressions with the six basic human feelings?

A. To make facial expressions on computer.

B. To help to decide whether people are lying.

C. To find out why people are happy or sad.

D. To gain more understanding about people's feelings.

71. What's the main idea of this article?

A. The uses of facial expressions.

B. The six basic feelings of humans.

C. How we react to facial expressions.

D. Differences between humans and animals.

E

Wonderful Museums in Cyprus

The Leventis Municipal Museum

It shows the history of the city of Nicosia from prehistory to the present time, covers several traditional buildings on Hippocrates Street No. 15 – 17.

The idea of creating a museum memorizing the history of Nicosia was that of the former city leader, Lellos Demetriades. The Museum was planned in 1984 and finished in 1989. Two years later, the Leventis Museum was honored with the *European Museum of the Year Award*. The Museum aims to contribute to the protection of Nicosia's history.

Opening hours: Tuesday – Sunday: 10: 00 – 16: 30

Closed: Monday and public holidays

Entrance: Free. The Museum provides equipment for visitors with disabilities.

The Steni Museum of Village Life

The Museum shows the history of Steni Village from its foundation to the end of World War II. Sewing, tools and equipment, handkerchief, kitchenware, pots and jars, traditional clothing are some of the exhibitions of this amazing museum.

Open: All year round

Monday to Sunday—October 1 to March 31: 10am – 4pm

Monday to Sunday—April 1 to September 30: 10am – 6pm

Free Entrance

Marion-Arsinoe Archaeological Museum

The Museum of Marion-Arsinoe is located in Polis Chrysochous. The exhibits are from the ancient city of Marion, renamed Arsinoe in the 3rd century BC.

Address: 26 Makarios III Avenue, Polis, Paphos

Opening hours:

Tuesday, Wednesday & Friday 8am – 3pm, Thursday 8am – 5pm, Saturday 9am – 3pm, Monday, Sunday: closed

Entrance Fee: €1, 75

Maa-Palaeokastro Museum

The small museum is located within the Maa-Palaeokastro site. Built in 1989, the museum's unusual design is the work of architect Andrea Bruno.

The museum houses a small collection of objects, mainly copies, as well as some educational information on the site.

Open daily: 8: 30am – 5pm (November – March), 8: 30am – 6pm (April – October). All year round.

Entrance Fee: €1, 75

72. Which Museum offers equipment for disabled visitors?

A. The Leventis Municipal Museum.

B. The Steni Museum of Village Life.

C. Marion-Arsinoe Archaeological Museum.

D. Maa-Palaeokastro Museum.

73. When did Leventis Museum receive the *European Museum of the Year Award*?

A. 1984. B. 1989. C. 1991. D. 1994.

74. What can you see in the Steni Museum of Village Life?

A. Famous paintings.

B. Things used in daily life.

C. The education of the villagers.

D. The story of the village leader.

75. Which Museum can you visit at 8: 00am on Wednesday?

A. The Leventis Municipal Museum.

B. The Steni Museum of Village Life.

C. Marion-Arsinoe Archaeological Museum.

D. Maa-Palaeokastro Museum.

第二卷

Ⅳ. 短文改错（共 15 小题，每小题 1 分；满分 15 分）

此题要求你对一段文章改错。先对每一行作出判断是对还是错。如果是对的，在该行右边横线上画一个钩（√）；如果有错误（每行不会多于一个错误），则按情况改错如下：

此行多一个词：把多余的词用斜线（\）划掉，在该行右边横线上写出该词，也用斜线划掉。

此行缺一个词：在缺词处加一个漏字符号（∧），在该行右边横线上写出该加的词。

此行错一个词：在错的词下画一横线，在该行右边横线上写出改正后的词。

注意：原行没有错的不要改。

例：

When I have free time I go ∧ a long walk. Some (a) for

people read ~~the~~ books or watch television while (b) ~~the~~

others have sports. Charles and Linda Mason do all (c) √

of these things as well as <u>climbed</u> buildings. (d) climbing; climb

Dear Sally,

It feels such a long time since last time I see you. 76. ____

So far my summer in Xiamen been great! I spent all 77. ____

my weekends at the beach. I am getting a nice tan（晒黑） 78. ____

and you can not longer say I am paler than you. 79. ____

I've been playing lots of beach volleyballs, and just this 80. ____

passed weekend I got the first place in a match! 81. ____

On weekdays I work in a club which I teach kids 82. ____

to draw. Although the pay isn't high, but I love the job 83. ____

very much, because I like draw and I love kids a lot. 84. ____

I hope the summer's been going good for you too. 85. ____

There has only one month left in the summer vacation 86. ____

and after that it's time to school. Would you like 87. ____

to meet up some time before school starting? 88. ____

I want to share with your the photos I've taken. 89. ____

I'll give you call when I return home. See you soon! 90. ____

Love,

Mary

Ⅴ. 书面表达（共 1 题，满分 20 分）

假设你是李华，与几位同学一起成立了一个英语俱乐部。为了号召同学们积极报名参加，你需在校刊“英语园地”上写一篇英文“致同学信”。信中包括以下要点：

· 举办“英语俱乐部”的目的
· 将开展哪些活动
· 如何加入（如联系方式、所需条件等）

注意：1. 词数 100 个左右；
　　　2. 可适当增减细节，以使行文连贯。

地　理

一、选择题：本大题共20小题，每小题3分。在每小题给出的四个选项中，只有一项是符合题目要求的。

读图1，完成1~2题。

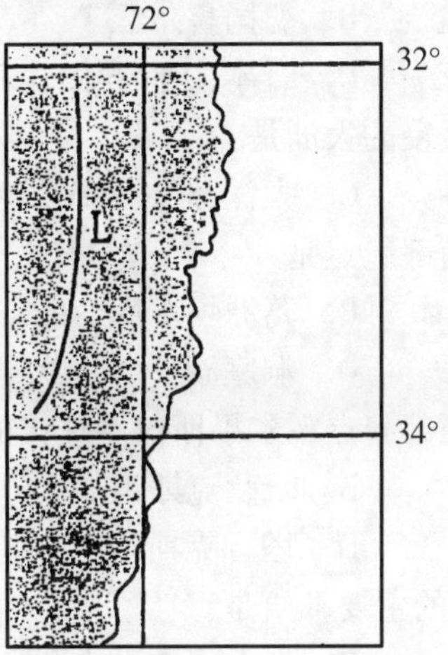

图1

1. 图中洋流L为

A. 自北向南流的暖流　　B. 自南向北流的暖流

C. 自北向南流的寒流　　D. 自南向北流的寒流

2. 图中海洋沿岸地区的气候类型为

A. 温带海洋性气候　　B. 地中海气候

C. 亚热带季风气候　　D. 热带沙漠气候

读图2，完成3~4题。

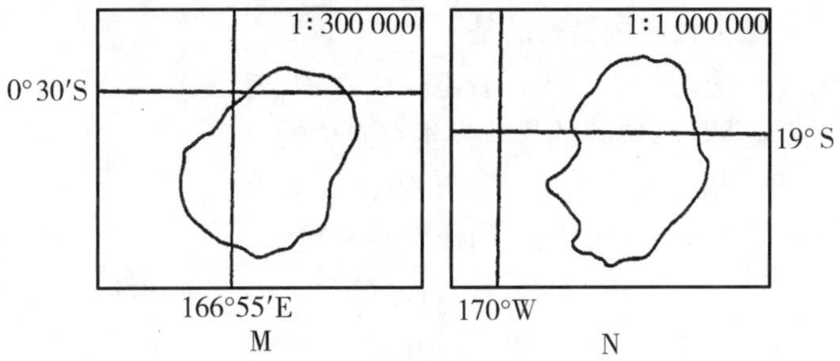

图2

3. M岛位于N岛的

A. 东北方　　B. 东南方

C. 西北方　　D. 西南方

4. 与N岛相比，M岛

A. 更靠近澳大利亚，面积较大　B. 更靠近澳大利亚，面积较小

C. 更靠近智利，面积较大　D. 更靠近智利，面积较小

5. 下列地区中，农业地域类型为大牧场放牧业的是

A. 阿根廷潘帕斯草原　B. 美国中部大平原

C. 非洲刚果盆地　D. 欧洲波德平原

6. 在下列工业区中，燃料、原料主要依赖国际市场的是

A. 美国东北部工业区　B. 德国鲁尔区

C. 英国中部工业区　D. 日本太平洋沿岸工业区

7. 目前，人口自然增长最缓慢的大洲是

A. 欧洲　B. 北美洲　C. 大洋洲　D. 南美洲

8. 我国南水北调中线工程南部起点是

A. 三峡水库　B. 葛洲坝水库

C. 丹江口水库　D. 洞庭湖

9. 我国西气东输二线工程西部起点霍尔果斯口岸连接的邻国是

A. 俄罗斯　B. 哈萨克斯坦

C. 吉尔吉斯斯坦　D. 塔吉克斯坦

10. 松花江春汛（桃花汛）的主要补给是

A. 大气降水　B. 高山冰雪融水

C. 冬季积雪融水　D. 地下水

11. 下列高原中，由板块挤压形成的是

A. 青藏高原　B. 巴西高原

C. 东非高原　D. 黄土高原

12. 全球削减碳排放应对的环境问题主要是

A. 臭氧层空洞　B. 酸雨

C. 土地退化　D. 全球变暖

13. 云南省昆明市附近地区成为我国鲜切花重要生产和出口基地的优势自然条件是

A. 气候　B. 地下水　C. 土壤　D. 地形

14. 下列城市中，夏至日白昼最长的是

A. 新加坡　B. 悉尼　C. 香港　D. 东京

15. “杨柳岸，晓风残月”描述的景象发生在农历的

A. 初三四　B. 初七八　C. 十五六　D. 廿七八

16. 导致我国北方冬季大风暴雪天气的锋面系统是

A. 暖锋　B. 快行冷锋

C. 慢行冷锋　D. 准静止锋

17. 我国四大盆地中，位于地势第一级阶梯的是

A. 塔里木盆地　B. 准噶尔盆地

C. 柴达木盆地　D. 四川盆地

18. 下列海洋中，属于我国内海的是

A. 南海　　B. 东海　　C. 黄海　　D. 渤海

19. 斑马、长颈鹿主要生活在

A. 热带雨林带　　B. 热带季雨林带

C. 热带草原带　　D. 热带荒漠带

20. 非洲流量最大、水能资源最丰富的大河是

A. 尼罗河　　B. 刚果河　　C. 尼日尔河　　D. 赞比西河

二、填充题：本题共 20 个空格，每填对一空得 1 分，共 20 分。请将答案填写在答题卡相应空格内。

21. 影响工业区位选择的主导因素各不相同。一般而言，制糖厂宜接近______，普通家具制造厂宜接近______，炼铝厂宜接近______，普通服装制造厂考虑的主要区位因素是______，精密仪表厂考虑的主要区位因素是______。

22. 在世界重要的海峡和运河中，扼守波斯湾的是______海峡，由地中海进入大西洋的是______海峡，由地中海进入印度洋需途经______运河，自美国东海岸至美国西海岸，最近的海上航线经过______运河，自卡拉奇至新加坡，最近的海上航线经过______海峡。

23. 导致大气增温的温室气体主要有______和______。人类活动产生温室气体的主要途径有使用______能源等。导致酸雨的是人类生产和生活排放的______。臭氧层“空洞”会使到达地表的______增多。

24. 依据板块构造学说，地中海位于______板块和______板块之间的______型板块边界上，面积将逐渐______，其沿岸多火山地震的地区主要分布在______板块上。

三、读图、填图题：每项 2 分，共 40 分。请将答案填写在答题卡相应空格内。

25. 读图 3 回答：

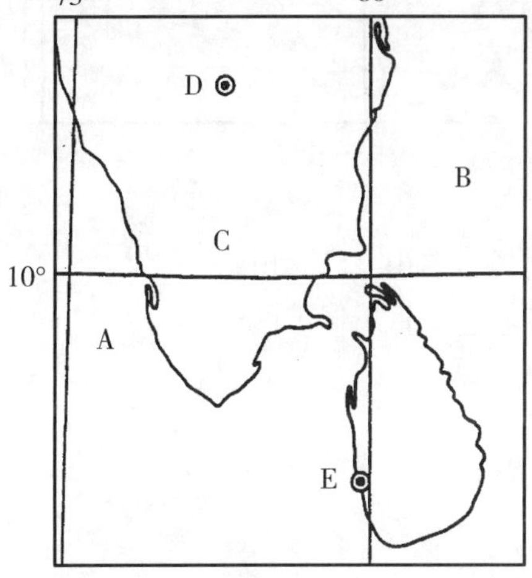

图 3

（1）图中水域 A 是______海，B 是______湾。

(2) C是______半岛；D是所在国著名的高新技术产业中心______；E是首都兼港口城市______。

26. 图4示意“大气热力作用联系”。回答：

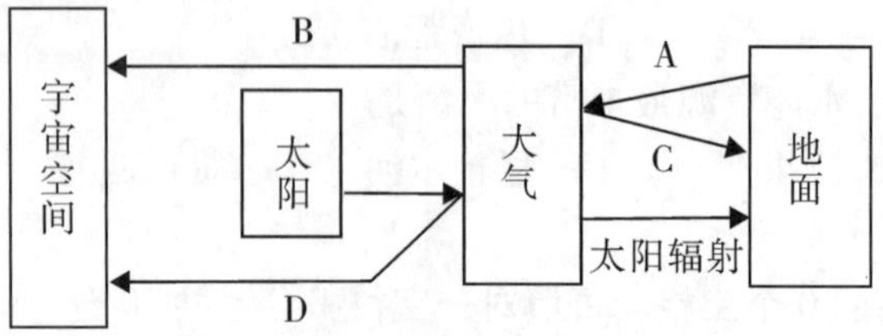

图4

(1) A表示______辐射，B表示______辐射，C表示______辐射；

(2) D表示大气的______作用，C的存在表明大气具有______作用。

27. 读图5回答：

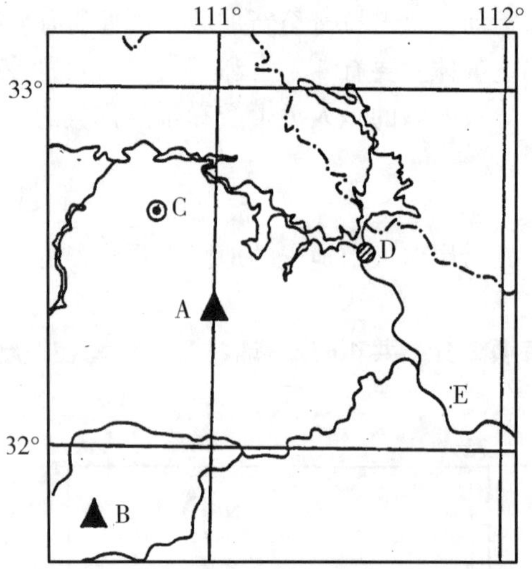

图5

(1) A是世界遗产、著名道教名山______山；

(2) B是著名自然保护区______自然保护区；

(3) C是著名汽车城______市；

(4) D是______水利枢纽；

(5) E是长江支流______江。

28．读图 6，将图中字母填在相应空格内：

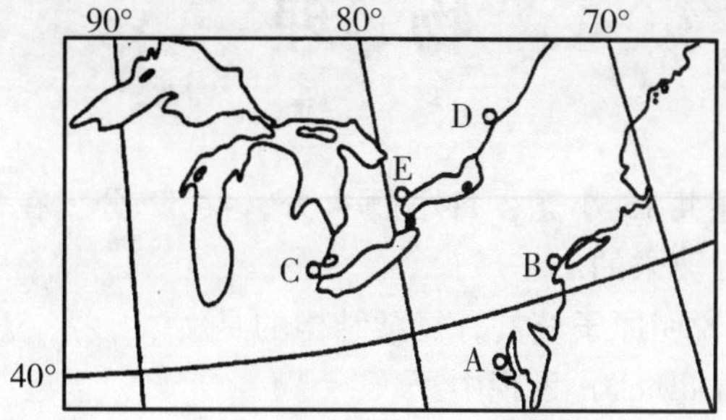

图 6

（1）______是著名的汽车城底特律；

（2）______是美国最大城市、金融中心纽约；

（3）______是美国首都华盛顿；

（4）______是加拿大最大城市多伦多；

（5）______是加拿大首都渥太华。

四、综合题（共 30 分）

29．比较发达国家和发展中国家城市化的差异。（15 分）

30．图 7 中甲地 1 月平均气温高于乙地。比较并说明甲、乙城市地理位置的异同。分析甲地 1 月平均气温高于乙地的原因。（15 分）

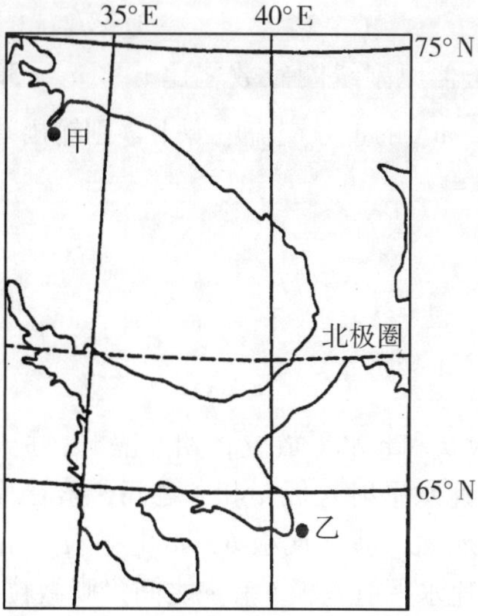

图 7

物　理

一、选择题：本大题共13小题，每小题4分，共52分．在每小题给出的四个选项中，只有一项是符合题目要求的．

1．在下列事件中，说明原子核具有复杂结构的是

A．查德威克（J. Chadwick）发现中子

B．卢瑟福（E. Rutherford）的α粒子散射实验

C．伦琴（W. Röntgen）发现X射线

D．赫兹（H. Hertz）发现光电效应

2．如图所示，一支上端封闭、粗细均匀的试管插在盛有水银的器皿中，试管中水银柱的上方封有一定量的气体．保持试管的高度不变，向器皿中缓慢地再倒入一些水银，若环境温度保持不变，则

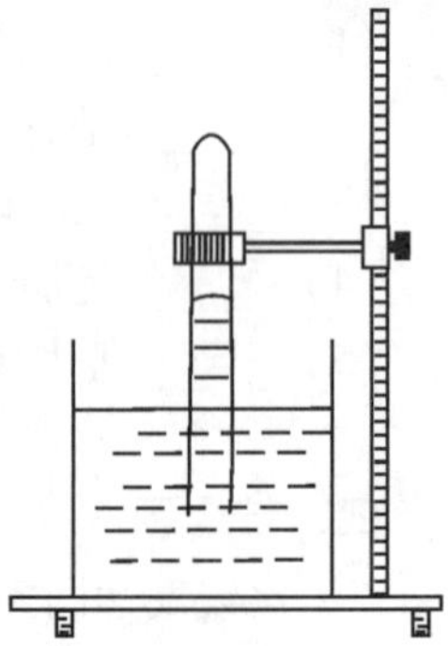

A．管内气体的长度保持不变，压强保持不变

B．管内气体的长度增大，压强减小

C．管内气体的长度减小，压强减小

D．管内气体的长度减小，压强增大

3．一物体做自由落体运动，在前λ秒内下落的距离与λ到（$\lambda+1$）秒内下落的距离相等，则λ为

A．$\sqrt{2}-1$　　B．$\sqrt{2}$　　C．2　　D．$\sqrt{2}+1$

4．如图所示，一理想变压器原副线圈匝数之比$n_1:n_2=30:1$，输入端接在电流最大值为$30\sqrt{2}$ mA的正弦交流电源上，则输出端电流表的示数为

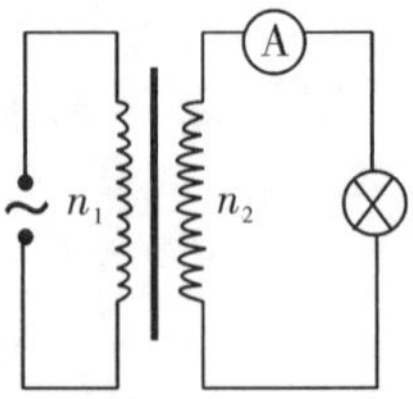

A．$900\sqrt{2}$ mA

B．900 mA

C．$\sqrt{2}$ mA

D．1 mA

5．如图所示，两块金属板a和c水平放置，相互隔开；板a和c接在电池上．闭合开关，一带电微粒P以某一初速水平射入板a和c之间，落在板c上的Q点．断开开关，平行地插入薄金属板b，带电微粒P在同样的入射位置、以同样的初速水平射入板b和c之间，则微粒

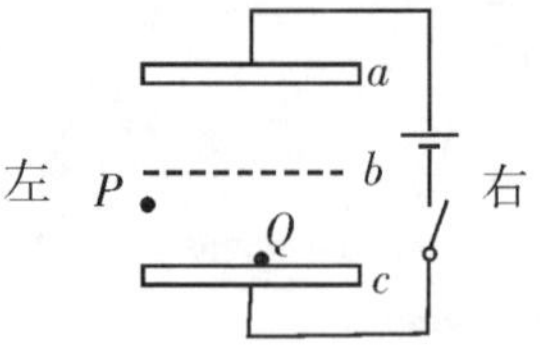

A．落在c板上Q点的左侧

B．落在c板上Q点的右侧

C．落在c板上的Q点

D．沿直线飞出

6. 如图所示，在一半径为 r 的圆形区域中存在一匀强磁场，磁感应强度大小随时间而变化. 若有一半径为 R（$R>r$）的导体圆环，导体环的环心是磁场区域的对称中心，则环中感应电动势的大小

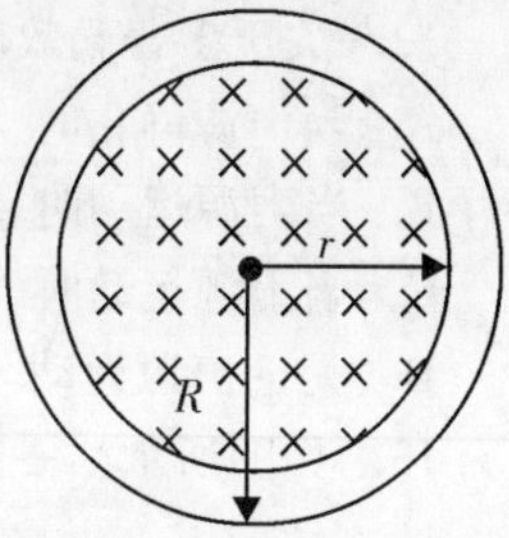

A. 与磁感应强度的大小成正比

B. 与磁感应强度的大小随时间的变化率无关

C. 与 R^2 成正比

D. 与 r^2 成正比

7. 如图所示，红光 a 与蓝光 b 斜射入一长方玻璃砖，入射前两束光线平行且间距为 d，所对应的两条出射光线分别记为 a'与 b'。则

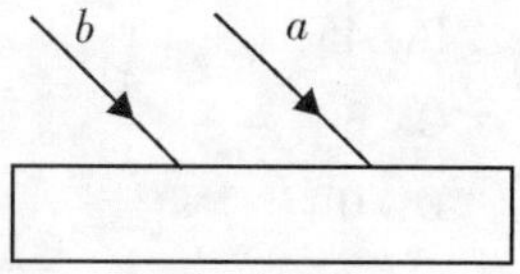

A. a'与 b'仍平行，距离仍为 d

B. a'与 b'仍平行，距离大于 d

C. a'与 b'仍平行，距离小于 d

D. a'与 b'不平行

8. 如图所示，水平地面上固定一质量为 M 的支架，其顶端用细线拴有一质量为 m 的摆球. 现将摆球拉至水平位置后释放，小球在竖直平面内来回摆动. 重力加速度为 g. 在摆球到达最低点时，支架对地面压力的大小为

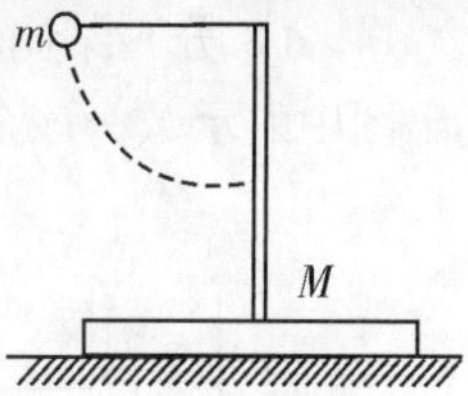

A. $(m+M)g$

B. $(2m+M)g$

C. $(3m+M)g$

D. $(4m+M)g$

9. 一静止的放射性原子核在匀强磁场中发生衰变，形成两个相互外切的圆形径迹，它们的半径之比为 41∶1. 已知子核的质量数大于 200，则下列说法可能正确的是

A. 母核的原子序数为 39

B. 衰变后的粒子做圆周运动的周期相同

C. 衰变后的粒子一个做逆时针方向的圆周运动，另一个做顺时针方向的圆周运动

D. 衰变后的粒子都做同方向的圆周运动

10. 氢原子光谱中的巴耳末（Balmer）线系对应于电子从能级 $n'\geqslant 3$ 到能级 $n=2$ 的跃迁. 将巴耳末线系的光谱线按波长从大到小的顺序排列，前三条谱线的波长依次记为 λ_1、λ_2 和 λ_3，则 $\lambda_1:\lambda_2:\lambda_3$ 等于

A. 189: 140: 125　　B. 756: 675: 500

C. 25: 16: 9　　D. 400: 225: 144

11. 如图所示，一固定斜面高 h，用大小为 F、沿斜面向上的恒力恰好能将质量为 m 的物块沿斜面向上移动. 假设物块与斜面之间的动摩擦系数增大一倍，且用大小为 $2F$、沿斜面向下的恒力使此物块从静止开始沿斜面由顶端向下滑动，重力加速度大小为 g，则物块滑至斜面底端时的动能为

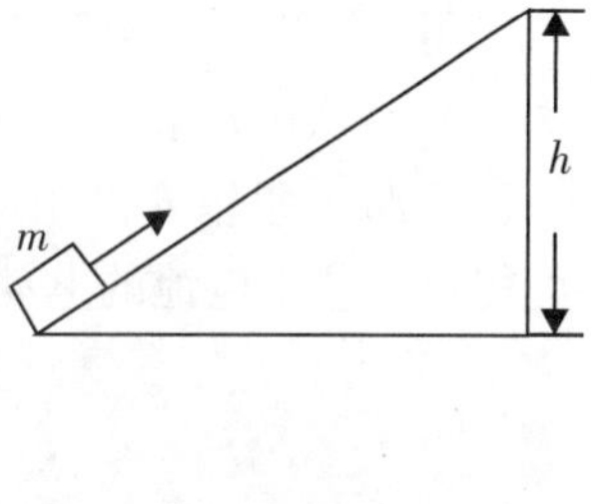

A. $2mgh$　　B. $3mgh$　　C. $2Fh$　　D. $3Fh$

12．关于多普勒效应，下列说法正确的是

A．当声源静止时，运动的观测者接收到的声波的频率与声源振动的频率不同

B．当声源运动时，声源后方媒质中的声波的波长变短

C．当声源运动时，声源前方媒质中的声波的波长变长

D．无论声源运动与否，声音在媒质中的波长不会改变

13．如图所示，一固定斜面倾角为60°，一物块置于斜面上，物块与斜面之间的动摩擦系数$\mu=\frac{\sqrt{3}}{3}$．用一外力F作用于物块，为了使物块在斜面上匀速下滑，而且力F的值最小，则力F的方向与斜面方向的夹角α应为

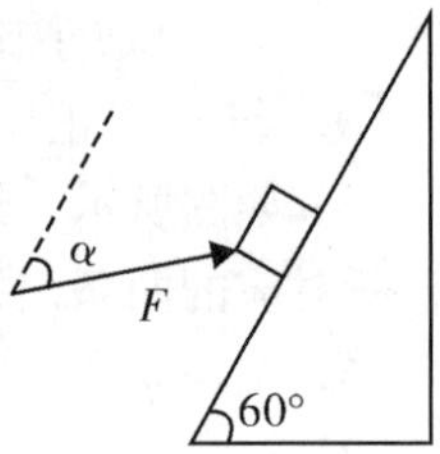

A．60°

B．45°

C．30°

D．0°

二、实验题：本大题共 2 小题，共 24 分．按题目要求作答．

14．（8 分）某同学用游标卡尺和螺旋测微器分别测量一薄的金属圆片的直径和厚度，读出图中的示数，该金属圆片的直径的测量值为__①__cm，厚度的测量值为__②__mm.

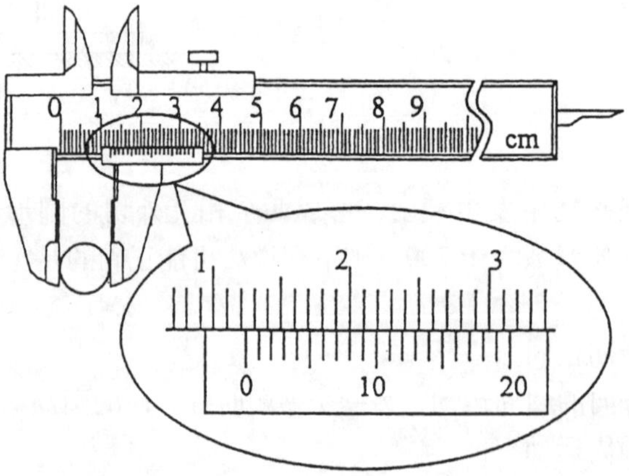

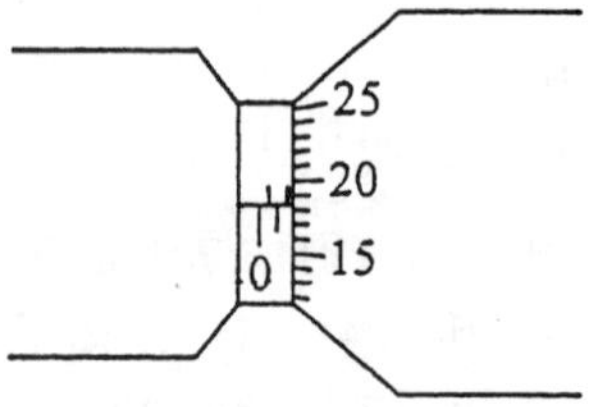

15．（16 分）为了测量干电池的电动势和内阻，提供下列器材：两节完全一样的干电池（每节干电池电动势约为 1.5 V，内阻约为 0.5 Ω）；直流电流表（量程适当，内阻$R_A=0.5\Omega$）；电阻箱（阻值范围 0 ~ 999.9 Ω）；导线；开关．现用两节干电池串联作为电源，采用如图 1 所示电路进行测定．

（1）某次电流表的读数如图 2 所示，由图读得，电流$I=$__①__mA.

（2）将电阻箱R的阻值分别置于两个不同的值，得到两组数据R_1、I_1和R_2、I_2，由此可得每一节干电池的电动势为__②__，内阻的阻值为__③__.

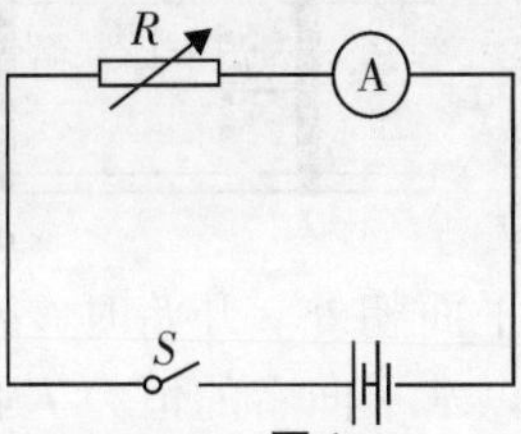

图 1

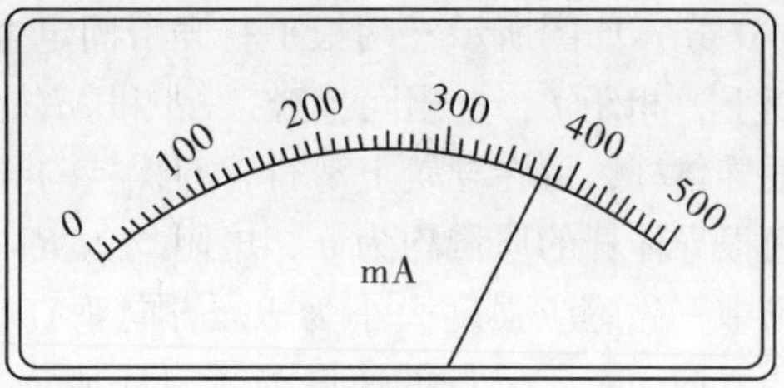

图 2

三、计算题：本大题共 4 小题，共 74 分．解答时应写出必要的文字说明、方程式和主要演算步骤．只写出最后答案，不能得分．有数值计算的题，答案中必须明确写出数值和单位．

16．（16 分）如图所示，一艘海轮从船上天线 D 向海岸边的信号接收器 A 发送电磁波信号．信号接收器和船上天线的海拔高度分别为 $AB = H$ 和 $DC = h$．船上天线某时刻发出一个电磁脉冲信号，接收器接收到一个较强和一个较弱的脉冲，前者是直接到达的信号，后者是经海平面反射的信号．两个脉冲信号的时间间隔为 τ，电磁波的传播速度为 c．求船上天线发出此信号时海轮与海岸的距离 L．

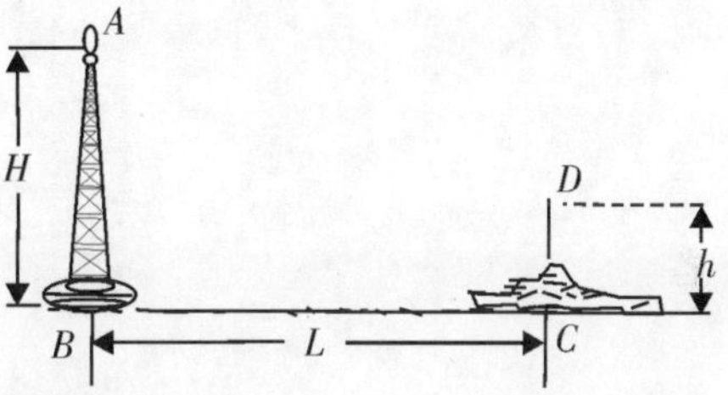

17．（18 分）如图所示，一气体温度计由装有水银的 U 形玻璃管连接两个浸没在水中的导热的气体泡室 A 和 B 构成．当 A 和 B 室周围都是冰水混合物（温度为 273 K）时，U 形玻璃管中的水银柱等高．当 B 室周围保持为冰水混合物，A 室置于沸腾的水中时，水银柱的高度差为 120 mmHg．仍保持 B 室周围是冰水混合物，逐渐降低 A 室周围的水温，求水银柱的高度差降为 90 mmHg 时 A 室周围的水温．已知两泡室的体积均可视为不变，U 形玻璃管的体积可忽略不计．

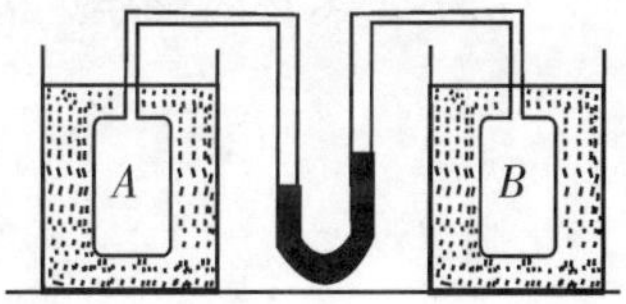

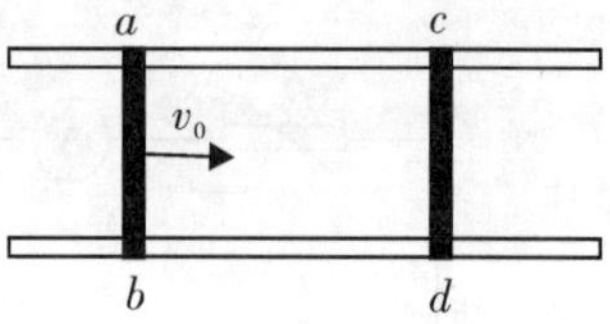

18. （20 分）如图所示，两根平行光滑固定金属导轨位于同一水平面上，相距 L，电阻可忽略. ab 和 cd 是导轨上面横放着的两根导体杆，可在导轨上滑行，并保持与导轨垂直且接触良好；两根导体杆的质量均为 m，电阻均为 R；整个装置位于匀强磁场中，磁感应强度大小为 B，方向垂直于导轨所在平面朝外. 开始时，ab 杆的速度为 v_0，方向向右，cd 杆的速度为零. 从某一时刻开始，以水平向右的恒力 F 作用在导体杆 ab 上，在经过一段时间 t 后的瞬间，测得 ab 杆的瞬时速度为 v_1，求导体杆 ab 和 cd 在此瞬时的加速度的大小.

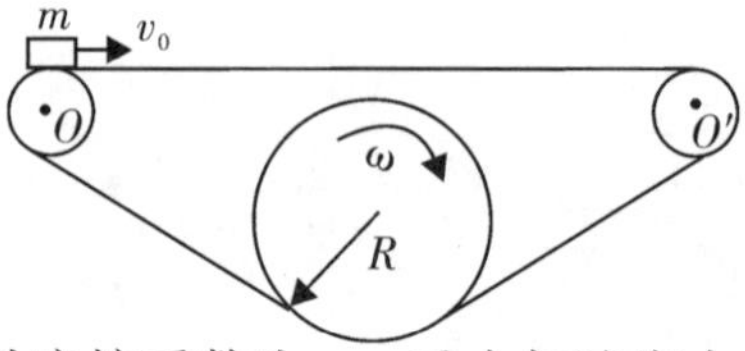

19. （20 分）如图所示，一传送带绕过定滑轮 O 和 O'，由半径为 R、以恒定角速度 ω 按顺时针转动的驱动轮带动，两滑轮轴 O 和 O'之间的距离为 L. 现将一质量为 m、水平速度为 v_0（v_0 不大于传送带的线速度）的货物轻放于传送带水平部分左端. 若此货物与传送带之间的动摩擦系数为 μ，重力加速度大小为 g，求将货物从传送带水平部分左端传送到右端的时间.

化 学

可能用到的原子量 H 1 C 12 N 14 O 16 Na 23 Mg 24 Cl 35.5 Ca 40

一、选择题：本题共 18 小题；每小题 3 分，共 54 分。在每小题给出的四个选项中，只有一项是符合题目要求的。

1. 下列叙述错误的是

A. 天然气的主要成分是甲烷

B. 天然气是一种重要的能源

C. 天然气是一种较清洁的燃料

D. 天然气比液态碳氢化合物更便于携带

2. 下列元素的单质中，最易和氢气反应的是

A. 氯 B. 氮 C. 氟 D. 氧

3. 将新配制的氯水滴入下列物质的溶液中，不发生反应的是

A. 氢氧化钡 B. 硝酸银

C. 硫酸铁 D. 溴化钾

4. 某二价阴离子，核外有 18 个电子，质量数为 32，则其中子数为

A. 14 B. 15 C. 16 D. 17

5. 下列关于同温同压同体积的 CO_2 与 N_2O 气体的叙述：①所含分子总数相同；②所含质子总数相同；③所含电子总数相同，其中正确的是

A. ①② B. ①③ C. ②③ D. ①②③

6. 下列物质中，既能与稀盐酸反应又能与 NaOH 溶液反应的是

A. $NaHSO_4$ B. $NaHCO_3$ C. $NaNO_2$ D. NH_4NO_3

7. 下列各组化合物按其沸点由高到低的顺序排列，正确的是

A. NaCl SiO_2 CH_4 HCl HF

B. NaCl SiO_2 CH_4 HF HCl

C. SiO_2 NaCl HF HCl CH_4

D. SiO_2 NaCl HCl HF CH_4

8. 甲、乙、丙、丁 4 块相同的铁片分别镀有锌、银、铜、锡 4 种金属，如果将每块铁片的镀层刮去同样大小的面积后置于潮湿空气中，腐蚀最慢的铁片是

A. 甲 B. 乙 C. 丙 D. 丁

9. 下图是一个电解装置，a、b 是惰性电极，c、d 是铜片。通电后，c 电极质量减少。现有下列说法：①N 极是正极，②M 极是正极，③NaOH 溶液浓度增加，④$CuSO_4$ 溶液浓度增大，⑤a 极上放出的气体体积是 b 极上的 2 倍。其中正确的是

A. ①③⑤ B. ①④ C. ②③ D. ②④⑤

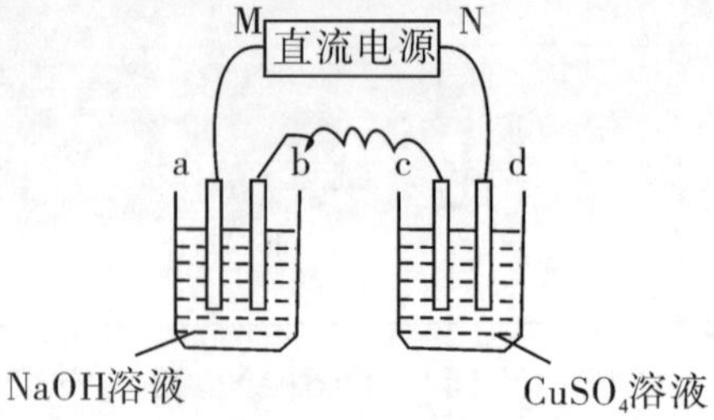

10．用0.005 mol/L HCl溶液中和50 mL pOH = 3的下列碱溶液，消耗HCl溶液体积最大的是

A．氨水　　B．氢氧化钠

C．氢氧化钡　　D．氢氧化钙

11．当反应 $Cl_2 + H_2O \rightleftharpoons HCl + HClO$ 达到平衡后，要使溶液中HClO的浓度增大，可加入

A．H_2O　　B．NaOH(s)

C．$Ca(OH)_2(s)$　　D．$CaCO_3(s)$

12．在 NaH_2PO_4 溶液中不可能大量存在的离子是

A．NH_4^+　　B．PO_4^{3-}　　C．SO_4^{2-}　　D．Ca^{2+}

13．当用加热 $(NH_4)_2SO_4$ 和碱石灰的混合物来制取和收集氨气时，下列装置中正确的是

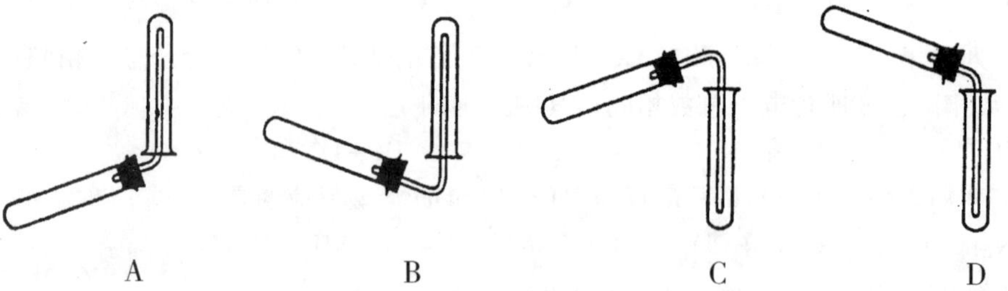

14．氮化铝具有耐高温、导热性好等优良性能，在电子工业中有广泛应用。它可通过如下反应来制得：

$Al_2O_3 + 3C + N_2 \xlongequal{高温} 2AlN + 3CO$

下列有关叙述，正确的是

A．氮化铝属于分子晶体

B．氮化铝易发生水解反应

C．反应中 Al_2O_3 是氧化剂，N_2 是还原剂

D．反应中生成1 mol AlN时，N_2 得到3 mol电子

15．为制得相同质量的硝酸铜，反应消耗硝酸的量最多的是

A．铜与浓硝酸反应

B．铜与稀硝酸反应

C. 氧化铜与浓硝酸反应

D. 碱式碳酸铜与稀硝酸反应

16. 下列各项中的两种气体，在相同的温度、压强下等体积混合，已知混合气的质量是相同条件下与其等体积的氢气质量的 10.5 倍，则该混合气是

A. 甲烷　乙炔　　B. 乙烷　乙烯

C. 乙烯　乙炔　　D. 乙烷　甲烷

17. 碳、氢的质量比为定值的烃类是

A. 烷烃　　B. 链状单烯烃

C. 链状单炔烃　　D. 单环芳烃

18. 下列物质中，不与立方烷（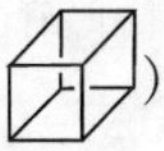）互为同分异构体的是

A. 

B. 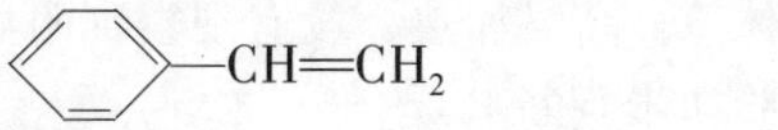

C. 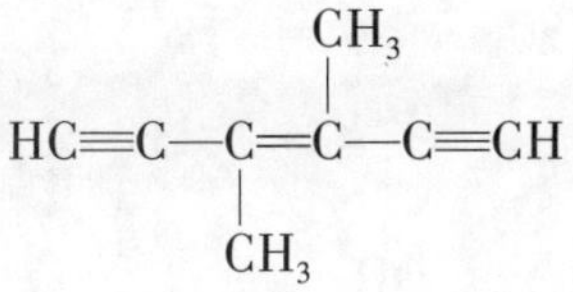

D. 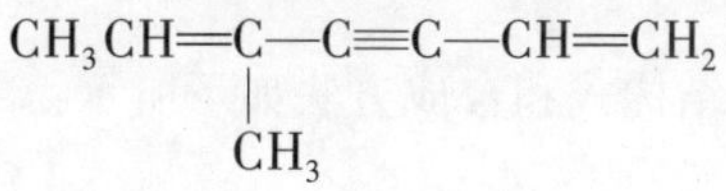

二、根据要求解答 19 ~ 25 题，将答案写在答题卡相应位置上。

19.（17 分）

由 H^+、Na^+、Cu^{2+}、Cl^-、SO_4^{2-} 等离子组成的电解质中，选择符合下列条件的电解质，进行电解。

（1）以碳为电极，电解时水量不变、电解质的量减少但成分不变。这些电解质的名称是______；

（2）以碳为电极，电解时电解质的量不变而水量减少。这些电解质的名称是______；

（3）以铂为电极，电解时电解质和水的量都发生变化，且溶液的 pH 不断减小，此电解质的名称是______，该电解反应的离子方程式是______。

20.（9 分）

明矾是一种简单易得的净水剂。它的化学式是______，它溶于水后所形成的溶液显酸性，其原因是______，而明矾可以净水的原因是______。

21.（15 分）

已知 X、Y、Z、W 四种元素是元素周期表中常见的主族元素，其原子序数依次增大。又知：①Y 的一种氢化物分子中有三个极性共价键，其水溶液显碱性；②W 元素的原子序数是 Z 元素的原子序数的 2.5 倍；③X 原子中的电子数与 W 原子的最外层电子数之和等于 Z 原子的最外层电子数的一半。

请回答：

（1）元素 X 是______，Y 是______，Z 是______，W 是______；（填元素名称）

（2）X 与 W 所形成的化合物的化学式是______，其固体属于______晶体，它跟水反应的化学方程式为______；

（3）X 与 Y 所形成的最简单化合物的化学式是______，其固体属于______晶体；

（4）由以上元素中的三种所组成的化合物中，写出两种酸、两种碱和两种盐的化学式：酸______，碱______，盐______。

22.（17 分）

某化合物 R 的阳离子可能是 K^+、Fe^{3+}、Cu^{2+}、NH_4^+ 中的一种，阴离子可能是 NO_3^-、Cl^-、HCO_3^-、SO_3^{2-} 中的一种。

（1）对 R 进行初步实验，请根据实验现象进行判断：

①在试管中加入一定量的 R 和适量蒸馏水，得到无色溶液。______

②在两支试管中分别加入部分①的溶液，向一支试管中加入适量盐酸，使溶液呈酸性，加热后没有气体逸出。向另一支试管中加入 NaOH 溶液，使其显碱性。加热该溶液，在试管口用湿润的红色石蕊试纸检验，试纸不变色。______

③取适量固体 R，高温加热，没有观察到明显变化。______

④由上述实验初步判断 R 是______。

（2）简述进一步确认 R 组成的实验方法及观察到的现象。

23.（18 分）

抗氧剂 264 的结构式和合成方法如下所示：

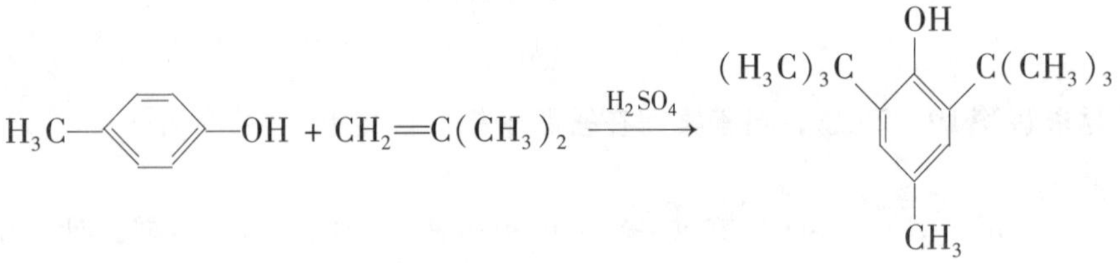

A　　　　　　B　　　　　　抗氧剂 264

（1）反应物 A 的名称是______，反应物 B 的名称是______。

（2）写出所有含有苯环的 A 的同分异构体的结构简式______。

（3）B 能使溴的四氯化碳溶液退色，该反应的化学方程式是______。

（4）已知 B 能发生如下的转换：

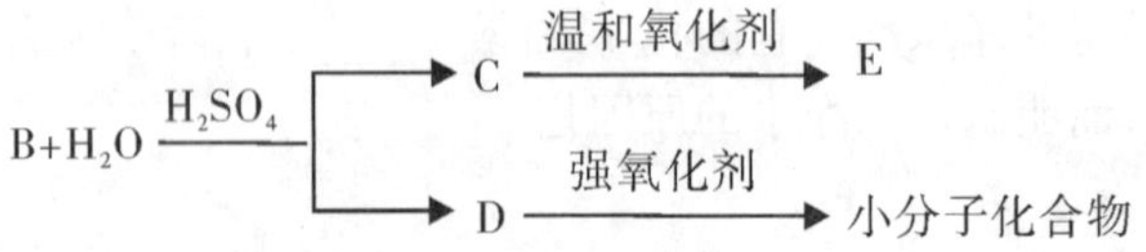

C 和 D 互为同分异构体，均能与金属钠反应放出气体。C 在温和氧化剂作用下生成 E，E 能发生银镜反应。D 在强氧化剂的作用下碳链断裂，生成小分子化合物。则 C 的结构简式是______，D 的结构简式是______，E 发生银镜反应的化学方程式是__________。

24.（10 分）

在含 7.45 g NaClO 的溶液中通入 NH_3 6.00 L（标准状况），发生如下反应：

$NaClO + 2NH_3 = NaCl + H_2O + N_2H_4$（肼）

计算反应后生成的肼的质量。

25.（10 分）

有一种石灰石样品，其中含有的杂质是二氧化硅。某学生想测定其纯度，取用 2.0 g 这种石灰石样品，把 20 mL 稀盐酸分 4 次加入，充分反应后剩余固体的质量见下表：

稀盐酸的用量（mL）	剩余固体的质量（g）
5.0	1.2
5.0	0.4
5.0	0.2
5.0	0.2

计算：

（1）此石灰石样品的纯度是多少？

（2）100.0 kg 此种石灰石充分煅烧后，得到固体多少千克？

2012 年暨南大学、华侨大学招收港、澳、台、华侨、华人及其他外籍学生入学考试题目答案

语　文

【选择题】

（本题型共 59 分）

一、基础知识（共 25 分）

（一）单项选择题（每题 2 分，共 20 分）

1. D　2. A　3. C　4. B　5. A　6. C　7. A　8. D　9. B　10. C

（二）判断题（每题 1 分，共 5 分）

11. T　12. F　13. F　14. T　15. F

二、阅读理解（共 34 分）

（一）文言文阅读（每题 3 分，共 24 分）

21. C　22. C　23. C　24. A　25. C　26. B　27. D　28. B

（二）现代文阅读（每题 2 分，共 10 分）

31. D　32. D　33. A　34. C　35. A

【非选择题】

（本题型共 91 分）

一、基础知识（共 5 分）

（三）填空题（每题 1 分，共 5 分）

16. 好之者不如乐之者。

17. 蓝田日暖玉生烟。

18. 化作春泥更护花。

19. 人声喧闹，乱成一片。

20. 借代。

二、阅读理解（共 16 分）

（一）文言文阅读（共 6 分）

29. 每当凶横的差吏来到我乡（1 分），从东头闹到西头，从南边闯到北边（1 分），吓得人们乱嚷乱叫，连鸡狗也不得安宁。(1 分)

30. 思妇。厌战、思念丈夫。(每要点 1 分)

(二) 现代文阅读 (共 10 分)

36. 多为闾巷风情、街谈巷议、逸闻轶事的记录。(大意相似即可, 2 分)

37. 单纯偏信正史 (或野史)。(大意相似即可, 2 分)

38. 一是内容广泛驳杂; 二是敢于直言不讳; 三是具有监督作用。(大意相似即可, 每要点 2 分, 共 6 分)

三、语言文字表达 (共 70 分)

39. 广州市民城隍庙前载歌载舞欢庆龙年元宵。(时间、地点、人物、事件等要素可各占 1 分, 共 4 分)

40. 与李煜的家国之愁不同, 此时此刻, 我们更多的是别绪离愁。"孔雀东南飞, 十里一徘徊", 那是怎样的一种依依不舍啊! 下面, 请大家欣赏根据古诗《孔雀东南飞》改编的舞台短剧。(能较为合理地衔接上下两个节目即可, 6 分)

41. 略

数　学

一、选择题（共 15 小题，每小题 4 分，共 60 分）

1. D　2. A　3. B　4. C　5. D　6. C　7. B　8. A　9. D　10. B　11. A　12. C　13. B　14. D　15. A

二、填空题（共 6 小题，每小题 4 分，共 24 分）

16. $2e^x+5$　17. $2x+4y+5=0$　18. $\sqrt{n+3}-\sqrt{n}>\sqrt{n+4}-\sqrt{n+1}$

19. -3　20. $\frac{3}{2}<x<4$　21. $\frac{\pi}{3}$

三、解答题（共 66 分）

22.（本小题满分 12 分）

解：（1）$\because$ 飞轮半径 $r=0.6$ m，每秒钟逆时针旋转 5 转

$\therefore$ 飞轮每秒钟转过的弧度数是 $5\times 2\pi=10\pi$（6 分）

（2）轮周上一点每秒钟经过的弧长 $l=10\pi\times 0.6=6\pi$（m）（12 分）

23.（本小题满分 12 分）

解：由 $\frac{\cos A}{\cos B}=\frac{b}{a}$，$\frac{\sin B}{\sin A}=\frac{b}{a}$，可得 $\frac{\cos A}{\cos B}=\frac{\sin B}{\sin A}$（3 分）

变形为 $\sin A\cos A=\sin B\cos B$，$\therefore \sin 2A=\sin 2B$（6 分）

又 $\because a\neq b$，$\therefore 2A=\pi-2B$，$\therefore A+B=\frac{\pi}{2}$，$\therefore \triangle ABC$ 为直角三角形．（9 分）

由 $a^2+b^2=10^2$ 和 $\frac{b}{a}=\frac{4}{3}$，解得 $a=6$，$b=8$．（12 分）

24.（本小题满分 12 分）

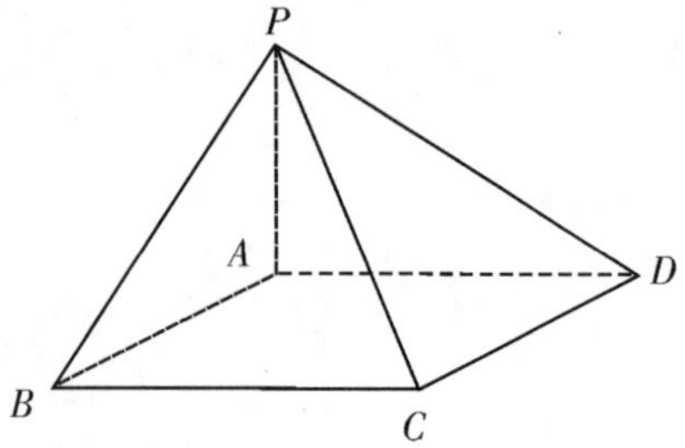

解：设底面边长 $AB=a$，$AD=b$

由 $PA\perp AB$，$PA\perp AD$ 知 $PA\perp$ 底面 $ABCD$，

于是 $BC\perp PA$，$CD\perp PA$，

而 $BC\perp AB$，$CD\perp AD$，得

$BC\perp$ 面 PAB，$CD\perp$ 面 PAD

因此 $\angle PBA=60°$，$\angle PDA=30°$（5 分）

$PA=a\tan 60°=b\tan 30°$　　（1）

$ab=4$　　（2）

由（1）（2）得

$a=\frac{2}{\sqrt{3}}$，$b=\frac{6}{\sqrt{3}}$，$PA=2$（cm）（9 分）

四棱锥 $P-ABCD$ 的体积为

$V=\frac{1}{3}a\cdot b\cdot PA=\frac{8}{3}$ （cm^3）（12分）

25.（本小题满分15分）

解：Ⅰ.（1）由于 $b_{n+1}-b_n=\frac{2}{2a_{n+1}-1}-\frac{2}{2a_n-1}$

$=\frac{4a_n}{2a_n-1}-\frac{2}{2a_n-1}=2$ （$n\in\mathbf{N}$）

从而数列 $\{b_n\}$ 是等差数列.（5分）

（2）由 $a_1=1$ 得 $b_1=\frac{2}{2a_1-1}=2$ 得

$b_n=2+(n-1)\times2=2n$（9分）

从而由 $b_n=\frac{2}{2a_n-1}$ 得，

$2a_n-1=\frac{2}{b_n}=\frac{1}{n}$

$a_n=\frac{n+1}{2n}$（15分）

Ⅱ.（1）由题意知前 n 项和为 $S_n+2=2a_n$，
则 $S_n=2a_n-2$，$S_{n-1}=2a_{n-1}-2$（$n\geqslant2$，$n\in\mathbf{N}$），两式相减得 $a_n=2a_{n-1}$
又由 $a_1=S_1=2a_1-2$ 得 $a_1=2$.
于是 $a_n=2^n$.（4分）
由于点（b_n，b_{n+1}）在直线 $x-y+2=0$ 上，则 $b_n-b_{n+1}+2=0$，
即 $b_{n+1}-b_n=2$，则数列 $\{b_n\}$ 是公差为2的等差数列，
于是 $b_n=2n-1$.（7分）
（2）由（1）得
$T_n=a_1b_1+a_2b_2+\cdots+a_nb_n=1\times2+3\times2^2+5\times2^3+\cdots+(2n-1)\times2^n$
$2T_n=1\times2^2+3\times2^3+5\times2^4+\cdots+(2n-1)\times2^{n+1}$
两式相减得
$-T_n=1\times2+2^3+2^4+\cdots+2^{n+1}-(2n-1)\times2^{n+1}$
所以 $T_n=(2n-3)\times2^{n+1}+6$.（15分）
26.（本小题满分15分）

解：Ⅰ.（1）由题意可设椭圆方程为 $\frac{x^2}{a^2}+\frac{y^2}{b^2}=1$（$a>b>0$）

$\because e=\frac{1}{2}$，即 $\frac{c}{a}=\frac{1}{2}$，$\therefore a=2c$（2分）

又 $b^2=a^2-c^2=3c^2$

$\therefore$ 椭圆方程为 $\frac{x^2}{4c^2}+\frac{y^2}{3c^2}=1$（5分）

又$\because$ 椭圆过点 A（2，3），$\therefore\frac{4}{4c^2}+\frac{9}{3c^2}=1$，解得 $c^2=4$，

$\therefore$ 椭圆方程为$\frac{x^2}{16}+\frac{y^2}{12}=1$.（8 分）

（2）由（1）知 F_1（-2，0），F_2（2，0），

$\therefore$ 直线 AF_1 的方程 $y=\frac{3}{4}$（$x+2$），即 $3x-4y+6=0$，

直线 AF_2 的方程为 $x=2$.（10 分）

设 P（x，y）为角平分线上任意一点，则点 P 到两直线的距离相等，

即$\frac{|3x-4y+6|}{5}=|x-2|$

$\therefore 3x-4y+6=5(x-2)$ 或 $3x-4y+6=5(2-x)$

即 $x+2y-8=0$ 或 $2x-y-1=0$.（13 分）

由图形知，角平分线的斜率为正数，故所求 $\angle F_1AF_2$ 的平分线所在直线方程为 $2x-y-1=0$.（15 分）

Ⅱ.（1）设椭圆 C 的方程为$\frac{x^2}{a^2}+\frac{y^2}{b^2}=1$（$a>b>0$）

由题意$\begin{cases}a^2=b^2+c^2\\ a:b=2:\sqrt{3}\\ c=2\end{cases}$，（3 分）

解得 $a^2=16$，$b^2=12$. 所以椭圆 C 的方程为$\frac{x^2}{16}+\frac{y^2}{12}=1$.（6 分）

（2）设 P（x，y）为椭圆上的动点，由于椭圆方程为$\frac{x^2}{16}+\frac{y^2}{12}=1$，故 $-4\leqslant x\leqslant 4$.（9 分）

因为$\overrightarrow{MP}=(x-m,\ y)$，

所以$|\overrightarrow{MP}|^2=(x-m)^2+y^2=(x-m)^2+12\times\left(1-\frac{x^2}{16}\right)$

$$=\frac{1}{4}x^2-2mx+m^2+12=\frac{1}{4}(x-4m)^2+12-3m^2$$

因为当$|\overrightarrow{MP}|$最小时，点 P 恰好落在椭圆的右顶点，即当 $x=4$ 时，$|\overrightarrow{MP}|^2$ 取得最小值. 而 $x\in[-4,4]$，故有 $4m\geqslant 4$，解得 $m\geqslant 1$.（12 分）

又点 M 在椭圆的长轴上，即 $-4\leqslant m\leqslant 4$. 故实数 m 的取值范围是 $m\in[1,4]$.（15 分）

英　语

Part Ⅰ　Listening Comprehension (30 points)

Section A (1 ×10)

1. W: I need to catch the bus and it leaves at 10:30.
   M: You'd better hurry. It's already 10:15.
   Q: What should the woman do?
2. W: Hmm... Let's see. Oh yes, I like this! Have they got a 14, I wonder?
   M: Can I help you at all? Hmm... Lovely skirts, aren't they? They just came in our shop this week. Would you like to try one on?
   Q: What does the woman want to buy?
3. M: Ada is a Frenchwoman, but she's worked in China for 15 years.
   W: That's right. She speaks Chinese very well.
   Q: What is Ada's nationality?
4. M: It has been snowing heavily for weeks.
   W: Yeah. That's why vegetables are so expensive these days.
   Q: What causes the prices to rise?
5. M: Morning! Five airmail stamps, please. They are going to Los Angeles.
   W: Here you are.
   Q: Where is the man?
6. M: I thought that the chair cost eighty dollars.
   W: It used to, but the price has gone up sixteen dollars.
   Q: How much does the chair cost now?
7. W: Didn't you tell Tom about this meeting?
   M: Whatever I say to him goes in one ear and out the other.
   Q: What does the man mean?
8. M: I saw a really wonderful program about children on TV last night. Did you see it?
   W: Oh, I wish I had known about it.
   Q: What is the woman's reaction to the program?
9. M: How's your job going, Diana?
   W: Great! I'm enjoying it a lot. The restaurant's really busy, so the tips are pretty good. I get free meals, too, which is nice. We have a great cook.
   Q: What can we learn from the woman?
10. M: I'd like to see Prof. Finch.
    W: I'm sorry, he's been ill since last Thursday and he'll be back next Friday.

Q: What can we learn from the conversation about Prof. Finch?

Section B (2 × 10)

Passage One

What kind of environment do you want in the future? What can you do to help make it happen? What can other people do?

Education is one way to help the environment. You can learn about the environment in school. Radio and TV can give you information. Newspapers, magazines, and books also help you learn.

Laws can also help the environment. There are laws against littering and against making the air and water dirty. Other laws help people to save resources. The law lowering the speed limit for cars helps to save fuel.

But people don't have to wait for laws to be passed. They can do things on their own. They can protest against products that hurt the environment.

Another way to help the environment is to plan for the future. We may have to find new resources. In the future, people may heat their homes with atomic power. Maybe they will use energy from the sun.

Without planning, some kinds of environment may not happen. People can act now to help make the future.

11. How many ways are there that can help the environment? What are they?
12. How does education help the environment?
13. What kind of law helps the save fuel?
14. What can people do on their own to help the environment?
15. What kinds of new resources can we find in the future?

Passage Two

In the United States, boys and girls start school when they are five years old. In some states they must stay in school until they are sixteen. Most students are seventeen or eighteen years old when they graduate from secondary school. Another name for secondary school is high school.

Most children go to public elementary and secondary schools. The parents of public school pupils do not have to pay directly for their children's education because tax money supports the public schools. If a child attends a private school, his parents pay the school for the child's education.

Today about half of the high school graduates go on to colleges and universities. Some colleges and universities receive tax money from the government. A student at a state university does not have to pay very much if his parents live in that state. Private colleges and universities are expensive, however. Almost half of the college students in the United States work while they are studying. When a student's family is not rich, he has to earn money for part of his college expenses.

16. When do the children start school in the United States?

17. How many years must most students stay in school before they go to university?

18. What kind of school do the parents have to pay for their children's education?

19. How many high school graduates go on to colleges and universities?

20. What does a college student have to do while he is studying, if his family is not rich?

1. C 2. A 3. B 4. A 5. C 6. C 7. C 8. B 9. A 10. B 11. C
12. D 13. A 14. D 15. A 16. B 17. A 18. D 19. A 20. B

Part Ⅱ Reading Comprehension (2 ×20 **points**)

21. D 22. B 23. C 24. A 25. D 26. D 27. C 28. D 29. B 30. C
31. A 32. D 33. A 34. C 35. B 36. C 37. B 38. C 39. A 40. D

Part Ⅲ Vocabulary (20 **points**)

41. D 42. A 43. B 44. D 45. C 46. D 47. B 48. A 49. B 50. C
51. A 52. C 53. D 54. B 55. A 56. B 57. A 58. D 59. B 60. C

Part Ⅳ Grammatical Structure (10 **points**)

61. B 62. B 63. A 64. D 65. A 66. D 67. A 68. D 69. A 70. A

Part Ⅴ Cloze (20 **points**)

71. C 72. B 73. D 74. B 75. D 76. A 77. A 78. C 79. D 80. A
81. D 82. C 83. A 84. B 85. D 86. A 87. C 88. D 89. B 90. C

Part Ⅵ Proof Reading (10 **points**)

91. climb 前加 to 92. one→ones 93. √ 94. picked→pick 95. them→their
96. had 97. √ 98. more 99. getting→get 100. What→How

Part Ⅶ Composition (20 **points**)

(略)

地　理

一、填空题（共 20 分，填对一空得 1 分）

1. 温带海洋性气候　欧
2. 等高线
3. 暖
4. 黄河　长江
5. 纬度位置　冬季风
6. 自然资源贫乏
7. 白种人　黄种人　黑种人　亚洲东部　东南部　南美洲　北美洲
8. 资源缺乏　市场狭小　太平洋　濑户内海

二、单项选择题（共 60 分，选对一题得 3 分）

1. C　2. B　3. A　4. D　5. A　6. B　7. A　8. A　9. C　10. D　11. C
12. C　13. D　14. A　15. D　16. B　17. C　18. B　19. A　20. D

三、是非题（本题共 10 小题，每小题 2 分，共 20 分）

1. F　2. F　3. F　4. F　5. F　6. F　7. F　8. T　9. F　10. F

四、读图及连线题（共 30 分，本题共 3 小题，填对每一空及连对一线得 1 分）

1. 河北　山东　江苏　安徽　冀　鲁　苏　皖　石家庄　济南　合肥　南京（四选三）
2. ①D　②A　③C　④B
3. （1）B　C　D
（2）少　多　冬季　地中海气候　亚热带大陆西岸
（3）夏　冬　温带季风气候　亚洲东部温带地区
（4）大　少　温带大陆性气候

五、综合题（共 20 分，每小题 10 分）

1.（第一、二个问题各 3 分，第三、四个问题各 2 分）
（1）略
（2）本区域为海拔低于 500 米，相对高度小于 200 米，坡度较缓的山区。
（3）由西南向东北　400
（4）D　河道狭窄，工程量小且安全
2.（第一个问题 4 分，第二、三个问题各 3 分）
（1）冲积扇　河流流出山口时，流速减慢，泥沙沉积而成

（2）三角洲　三角洲形成于河流入海口，而冲积扇形成于河流出山口（即山麓地带）

（3）风蚀蘑菇　干旱　风沙侵蚀

3.（第一个问题 4 分，第二、三个问题各 3 分）

（1）巴西　南赤道暖流　咖啡　大豆　伊泰普　巴西利亚

（2）2

（3）位置特点：大部分位于南回归线与赤道之间

气候特点：以热带湿润气候为主

植被特点：热带雨林、热带草原分布广泛

物　理

一、选择题（60 分，每小题 4 分）

1. C　2. B　3. B　4. A　5. A　6. D　7. D　8. B　9. C　10. A　11. C
12. A　13. D　14. C　15. D

二、填空题（30 分，16 ~ 20 题每空 3 分）

16. 0.4
17. 0.1
18. CE
19. 等于
20. 2
21. 匀变速　0.08　1.15（每空 2 分）
22.（1）ACDFH　（3 分）
（2）小（3 分）　电流增大，温度升高，电阻率增大，电阻增大　（3 分）

三、计算题（60 分）

23.（12 分）

解：（1）F 沿竖直方向的分力为

$F_1 = F\sin37° = 48\ \text{N}$

物体的重力

$G = mg = 100\ \text{N}$

由于 F 沿竖直方向的分力小于物体的重力，所以不能将物体提离地面.　（4 分）

（2）F 沿水平方向的分力为

$F_2 = F\cos37° = 64\ \text{N}$

物体沿水平方向做匀加速运动，其加速度为

$a = F_2/m = 6.4\ \text{m/s}^2$　（4 分）

（3）在 F 的作用下物体保持静止，所以物体受到一水平向左的静摩擦力的作用，大小为

$f_0 = F_2 = 64\ \text{N}$　（4 分）

24.（12 分）

解：设左管横截面积为 S，开口端水银面下降为 H，以封闭气体为研究对象：

由玻意耳定律：$p_1V_1 = p_2V_2$　（4 分）

$76 \times 20S = p_2(20 + 18)S$

$p_2 = 40\ \text{cmHg}$　（4 分）

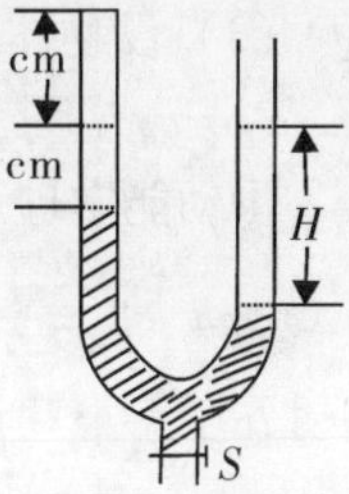

左管水银面比右管水银面高

$\Delta h = 76\ \text{cm} - 40\ \text{cm} = 36\ \text{cm}$

则开口端水银面下降 $H = 36 + 18 = 54\ \text{cm}$ (4 分)

25. (12 分)

解：(1) 小球带正电荷． (3 分)

(2) 小球由 A 到 B 的过程中，重力势能减少

$\Delta E_p = mgL\sin 60° = \sqrt{3}mgL/2$ (3 分)

(3) 小球由 A 到 B 的过程中，由动能定理得：

$mgL\sin 60° - qU_{AB} = 0$

故 $U_{AB} = \sqrt{3}mgL/2q$ (3 分)

(4) $E = \dfrac{U_{AB}}{L - L\cos 60°} = \sqrt{3}mg/q$ (3 分)

26. (12 分)

解：如图所示，光线Ⅰ和Ⅱ的距离

$l = CD = AC\cos i$ (2 分)

而

$AC = 2AE = 2d\tan r$ (2 分)

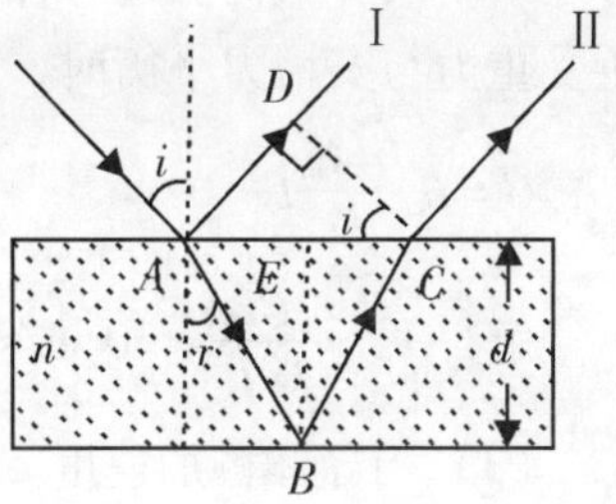

其中 r 为光从真空折射入玻璃的折射角，由折射定律得

$\dfrac{\sin i}{\sin r} = n$ (4 分)

因此

$\tan r = \dfrac{\sin r}{\cos r} = \dfrac{\sin i}{\sqrt{n^2 - \sin^2 i}}$ (2 分)

故光线Ⅰ和Ⅱ的距离

$l = \dfrac{2d\sin i\cos i}{\sqrt{n^2 - \sin^2 i}} = \dfrac{2}{7}\sqrt{7}\ \text{cm} \approx 0.76\ \text{cm}$ (2 分)

27. (12 分)

解：(1) 设物体经过 B 点时的速度大小为 v_B，由机械能守恒得：

$mg(H - h) = \dfrac{1}{2}mv_B^2$

求得：$v_B = 10\ \text{m/s}$ (4 分)

(2) 设物体经过 C 点时的速度为 v_C，对轨道的压力为 N，则轨道对物体的支持力大小也为 N，由牛顿定律得

$N - mg = m\dfrac{v_C^2}{R}$

另外，由机械能守恒得：

$mgR(1 - \cos 53°) + \dfrac{1}{2}mv_B^2 = \dfrac{1}{2}mv_C^2$

因此 $N = 43\ \text{N}$，方向竖直向下． (4 分)

（3）设物体由 D 点至 S 点的过程中阻力所做的功为 W，因为 B、D 点等高，易知

$v_D = v_B$

由动能定理可得：

$$mgh + W = \frac{1}{2}mv_S^2 - \frac{1}{2}mv_D^2$$

代入数据，解得 $W = -68\ \text{J}$ （4 分）

28. （12 分）

解：（1）当 S_1 闭合、S_2 断开时，导体棒静止，通过导体棒的电流

$$I_1 = \frac{E}{R} = 2.0\ \text{A}$$

此时导体棒所受安培力 $F_1 = BI_1L = 0.20\ \text{N}$ （4 分）

（2）当 S_1 闭合、S_2 断开时，导体棒静止，有

$G = mg = F_1 = 0.20\ \text{N}$

在 S_1 断开、S_2 闭合的情况下，导体棒做加速运动，随着速度的逐渐增大，感应电动势逐渐增大，从而流过导体棒的电流逐渐增大，导体棒所受安培力也逐渐增大，当导体棒所受重力与安培力平衡时，导体棒的速度达到最大值 v_m，有

$$G = B\frac{BLv_m}{R}L$$

解得 $v_m = \frac{GR}{B^2L^2} = 30\ \text{m/s}$ （2 分）

（3）当导体棒加速度 $a = 5.0\ \text{m/s}^2$ 时，设其所受安培力为 F_2，通过导体棒的电流为 I_2，导体棒产生的感应电动势为 E_1. 根据牛顿第二定律有

$mg - F_2 = ma$

解得 $F_2 = 0.10\ \text{N}$

由 $F_2 = BI_2L$，解得 $I_2 = 1.0\ \text{A}$ （4 分）

根据欧姆定律有 $E_1 = I_2R$，解得 $E_1 = 1.5\ \text{V}$. （2 分）

化　学

一、选择题（每题 3 分，共 60 分）

1. B　2. C　3. D　4. B　5. C　6. D　7. B　8. C　9. B　10. A　11. D
12. B　13. C　14. D　15. D　16. B　17. B　18. A　19. D　20. D

二、填空题（每空 1 分，共 28 分）

1.（1）NaCl　（2）I_2　（3）$CaCl_2$　（4）H_2SO_4　$ZnSO_4$

2.（1）A > B > C　（2）40　50　（3）80　100　100　（4）C

3.（1）CH_3COOH　C_6H_5COOH、H_2CO_3　（2）C_6H_5OH　（3）CH_3OH
（4）C_6H_5OH　（5）H_2CO_3

4. 乙醇　乙醛　乙烯　乙烷　乙酸
CH_3CH_2OH　CH_3CHO　$CH_2{=\!=}CH_2$　CH_3CH_3　CH_3COOH

三、问答题（共 32 分）

1.（本题 8 分）
（1）在 O 点醋酸未电离，无自由离子存在。
（2）$c < a < b$。
（3）c 点，因为浓度越稀，弱电解质的电离度越大。
（4）①加 NaOH 固体，②加少量的碳酸钠固体，③加入镁等金属，④加入醋酸钠固体。

2.（本题 10 分）
（1）2 mol
（2）$Cl_2 + 2Ca(OH)_2 {=\!=\!=} CaCl_2 + Ca(ClO)_2 + 2H_2O$
（3）$4Cl_2 + 8NaOH {=\!=\!=} 6NaCl + NaClO_3 + NaClO + 4H_2O$
（4）8.7 g
（5）$Cl^- + ClO^- + 2H^+ {=\!=\!=} Cl_2\uparrow + H_2O$

3.（本题 8 分）
（1）铁丝上附着一层红色固体。
（2）$Fe + CuSO_4 {=\!=\!=} FeSO_4 + Cu$
（3）$Cu + 2AgNO_3 {=\!=\!=} Cu(NO_3)_2 + 2Ag$
（4）Fe > Cu > Ag

4.（本题 6 分）
（1）用电吹风或微火慢慢加热使油类黏度降低，或熔化后用木棒轻敲塞子即可打开。
（2）氢氧化钠溶于水时放出大量的热，所以要待冷却后再注入容量瓶中，否则会因体积不准确造成配制溶液的浓度不准。

（3）用少量水洗涤两次，并把洗液注入容量瓶中，是为了保证溶液能全部移到容量瓶里。

四、计算题（任选 2 题，每题 15 分，共 30 分）

1. 解：

（1）设 +2 价金属为 M，$n(O_2)=\dfrac{224\ \text{mL}}{22\,400\ \text{mL}\cdot\text{mol}^{-1}}=0.01\ \text{mol}$ （2 分）

根据 $2M \sim O_2$ 可求出析出 M 的物质的量为 0.02 mol， （2 分）

M 的摩尔质量 $=1.28\ \text{g}/0.02\ \text{mol}=64\ \text{g}\cdot\text{mol}^{-1}$，通过推断确定该金属氧化物为 CuO。 （3 分）

（2）设有硫酸物质的量为 x

根据：$Cu \sim H_2SO_4$

64 g　1 mol

1.28 g　x

64 g∶1 mol = 1.28 g∶x

$x=0.02$ mol

$c(H_2SO_4)=\dfrac{0.02\ \text{mol}}{0.1\ \text{L}}=0.2\ \text{mol}\cdot\text{L}^{-1}$ （8 分）

2. 解：

（1）消耗 HCl 的物质的量：

$0.2\ \text{L}\times 5\ \text{mol}\cdot\text{L}^{-1}-0.2\ \text{L}\times 4.6\ \text{mol}\cdot\text{L}^{-1}=0.08\ \text{mol}$ （5 分）

（2）设 Al、Fe 的物质的量分别为 x、y

$Al \sim 3HCl$　　　$Fe \sim 2HCl$

x　$3x$　（2 分）　y　$2y$　（2 分）

$27x+56y=1.1$　（2 分）

$3x+2y=0.08$　（2 分）

得 $x=0.02$ mol（1 分）　$y=0.01$ mol　（1 分）

3. 解：

设已转化的 N_2 的量是 x mol，

$N_2+3H_2 \rightleftharpoons 2NH_3$

初始　1　4　0

转化　$-x$　$-3x$　$2x$

平衡　$1-x$　$4-3x$　$2x$ （4 分）

根据题意 $\dfrac{1-x}{4-3x}=\dfrac{1}{5}$

解得 $x=0.5$ mol （3 分）

平衡时 NH_3 的体积分数 $=\dfrac{2\times0.5}{(1-0.5)+(4-3\times0.5)+2\times0.5}\times100\%=25\%$ （4 分）

H_2 的转化率 $=\dfrac{3\times0.5}{4}\times100\%=37.5\%$ （4 分）

生　物

一、选择题（共 60 分）

1. A　2. C　3. B　4. A　5. A　6. D　7. A　8. A　9. C　10. B
11. D　12. A　13. D　14. A　15. C　16. B　17. C　18. D　19. B
20. D　21. C　22. A　23. B　24. C　25. B　26. A　27. B　28. B
29. D　30. A

二、判断题（共 20 分）

1. F　2. T　3. F　4. F　5. T　6. T　7. F　8. F　9. F　10. F

三、（共 70 分）

1.（8 分）
（1）WWDD × wwdd→WwDd　（1 分）
全部为白色盘状　（1 分）
（2）Wwdd × WwDd →1WWDd∶1WWdd∶2WwDd∶2Wwdd∶1wwDd∶1wwdd　（1 分）
3 白色盘状∶3 白色球状∶1 黄色盘状∶1 黄色球状　（1 分）
（3）WwDd × wwdd →1WwDd∶1Wwdd∶1wwDd∶1wwdd　（1 分）
1 白色盘状∶1 白色球状∶1 黄色盘状∶1 黄色球状　（1 分）
（4）Wwdd × wwDd →1WwDd∶1Wwdd∶1wwDd∶1wwdd　（1 分）
1 白色盘状∶1 白色球状∶1 黄色盘状∶1 黄色球状　（1 分）
2.（10 分，每空 1 分）
（1）脱氧核糖核酸　核糖核酸　脱氧核苷酸　核苷酸
（2）氨基酸　20
（3）复制　转录　逆转录（反转录）　翻译
3.（12 分，每空 2 分）
（1）紫
（2）Rr　RR　rr
（3）2　1∶1
4.（6 分，每空 2 分）
（1）次级　初级
（2）单
5.（8 分，每空 1 分）
（1）4　第三和第四　捕食和竞争　寄生
（2）小于　增强

（3）分解者　不能

6.（12 分）

（1）a 和 b（4 分）　c（2 分）　d（2 分）

（2）D（2 分）

（3）D（2 分）

7.（8 分）

（1）A（2 分）

（2）Mn^{2+}（1 分）

（3）活化能　不发生（2 分）

（4）蛋白质　RNA（2 分）

（5）专一性（1 分）

8.（6 分，每空 1 分）

（1）3　叶绿体

（2）1

（3）线粒体

（4）纤维素　果胶质

2012年中华人民共和国普通高等学校联合招收华侨、港澳地区、台湾省学生入学考试题目答案

语 文

第一部分（54分，每小题3分）

一、语文基础知识（30分）

1. A 2. D 3. C 4. B 5. C 6. D 7. A 8. B 9. A 10. B

二、白话文阅读（一）（12分）

11. C 12. C 13. D 14. D

三、文言文阅读（12分）

15. A 16. C 17. A 18. D

第二部分（96分）

四、文言文翻译、默写（13分）

19.（10分）

（1）（5分）梁彦光先前在岐州时，那里的风俗很质朴，他用平和的政令来安定民众。（译出大意给3分；“颇质”、“镇”两处，每译出一处给1分。）

（2）（5分）于是用薪俸等钱物，请来山东著名的儒家学者。（译出大意给3分；“秩俸”、“招致”两处，每译出一处给1分。）

20.（3分）

（1）己所不欲

（2）不尽长江滚滚来

（3）取之于蓝而青于蓝

（每答对一小题，给1分；如有错别字，该小题不给分。）

五、白话文阅读（二）（23分）

21.（5分）

要铺染的是“热”的气氛。

是为了表现父亲对儿子的爱。

（答出“热”的气氛，给 2 分；答出为了表现父亲对儿子的爱，给 3 分。意思答对即可。）

22.（6 分）

作者通过三幅画面来写“冬天”。①儿时冬夜父子围坐吃白煮豆腐的画面。②与友人冬夜泛舟静谧西湖的画面。③十年前与妻儿在寂寞的山城台州相处一室的画面。

（每答出一幅画面，给 2 分。意思答对即可。）

23.（6 分）

①白煮豆腐。“水滚着，像好些鱼眼睛，一小块一小块豆腐养在里面，嫩而滑，仿佛反穿的白狐大衣。”这儿将沸腾着的水泡比作鱼眼珠，将豆腐比作仿佛反穿的白狐大衣，十分形象生动，将水泡的翻腾，豆腐嫩而滑的特色都形容得惟妙惟肖。②荡漾在湖水中的月光。“当间那一溜儿反光，像新砑的银子。”把倒映在湖水中的月色，描摹成刚碾磨成的银子，闪耀着银色，恰到好处。

（每找出一处并能简析，给 3 分。意思答对即可。）

24.（6 分）

题目虽是“冬天”，但作者所要表现的主题却是人情的温暖，作者通过写自己与父亲、朋友、妻子之间温暖的亲情友情，将三幅画面所反映的生活片断连接了起来，形象生动地表现了亲情、友情和爱情，抒发了其暖如春的人情。

（答出表现的主题，给 2 分；答出如何表现的，给 4 分。意思答对即可。）

六、写作（60 分）

25.（60 分）

评分标准

等级分数	一等（51～60）	二等（36～50）	三等（21～35）	四等（0～20）
项目	切合题意 中心突出 内容充实 感情真挚 结构严谨 语言流畅 字迹美观 符合文体要求	符合题意 中心明确 内容较充实 感情真实 结构完整 语言通顺 字迹工整 大体符合文体要求	基本符合题意 中心基本明确 内容单薄 感情基本真实 结构基本完整 语言基本通顺 字迹清楚 基本符合文体要求	偏离题意 中心不明 内容不当 感情虚假 结构混乱 语言不通顺、语病多 字迹潦草难辨 不符合文体要求

说明：

①评分以题意、内容、语言、文体为重点，全面衡量。符合文体要求，指符合考生根据题意和内容自选的文体的要求。

②缺题目扣 1 分；每 3 个错别字扣 1 分，重复的不计；不足字数的，每少 50 个字扣 1 分。

③确认为抄袭的作文，在四等之内评分。

数　学

说明：

1. 本解答给出了一种或几种解法供参考，如果考生的解法与本解答不同，可根据试题的主要考查内容比照评分参考制定相应的评分细则.

2. 对计算题，当考生的解答在某一步出现错误时，如果后继部分的解答未改变该题的内容和难度，可视影响的程度决定后继部分的给分，但不得超过该部分正确解答应得分数的一半；如果后继部分的解答有较严重的错误，就不再给分.

3. 解答右端所注分数，表示考生正确做到这一步应得的累加分数.

4. 只给整数分数. 选择题和填空题不给中间分.

一、选择题

1. B　2. A　3. D　4. C　5. A　6. C　7. B　8. D　9. A　10. B　11. D　12. C

二、填空题

13. 182　14. $x+2y=9$　15. $9\sqrt{2}$　16. $x-y+z=1$　17. $8x-3$　18. $\frac{8}{5}\pi$

三、解答题

19. 解：由 $(\tan A+1)(\tan B+1)=2$ 得

$(\sin A+\cos A)(\sin B+\cos B)=2\cos A\cos B$,

即　$\sin A\cos B+\cos A\sin B=\cos A\cos B-\sin A\sin B$.

应用和角公式得　$\sin(A+B)=\cos(A+B)$,

即 $\tan(A+B)=1$.

因为 $0<A+B<\pi$，所以 $A+B=\frac{\pi}{4}$,

即 $C=\pi-(A+B)=\frac{3\pi}{4}$.　（5 分）

因为　$\cos 2B=\cos^2 B-\sin^2 B=1-2\sin^2 B$,

由题设可得 $\sin^2 C=\sin^2 A+2\sin^2 B$.

应用正弦定理得　$c^2=a^2+2b^2$.　（9 分）

根据余弦定理，又有

$$c^2=a^2+b^2-2ab\cos C$$

$$=a^2+b^2-2ab\cos\frac{3\pi}{4}$$

$=a^2+b^2+\sqrt{2}ab.$

所以　　$b^2=\sqrt{2}ab.$

因为　　$a=2$，$b\neq 0$，所以 $b=2\sqrt{2}.$　　（13 分）

$\triangle ABC$ 的面积 $S=\frac{1}{2}ab\sin C=2\sqrt{2}\sin\frac{3\pi}{4}=2.$　　（15 分）

20. 解：（Ⅰ）$\{a_n\}$ 的通项 $a_n=a(\frac{1}{2})^{n-1}$，即 $a_n=2a(\frac{1}{2})^n$. $b_1=S_1=4$，当 $n\geq 2$ 时，

$$b_n=S_n-S_{n-1}$$
$$=n^2-(n-1)^2+3$$
$$=2n+2.$$

$\{b_n\}$ 的通项 $b_n=2(n+1)$.　　（5 分）

（Ⅱ）由 $b_n+\log_p a_n=r$ 得 $2+\log_p(2a)+(2-\log_p 2)n=r$

该式对任意正整数 n 都成立的充要条件是

$$\begin{cases}2-\log_p 2=0\\2+\log_p(2a)=r\end{cases}$$

即 $\begin{cases}\log_p 2=2\\4+\log_p a=r\end{cases}$

解得 $p=\sqrt{2}$，$r=2(2+\log_2 a)$.　　（10 分）

这时，$r>0$ 的充要条件是 $2+\log_2 a>0$，即

$a>2^{-2}=\frac{1}{4}.$

所以，当 $a>\frac{1}{4}$ 时，存在适合题意的正数 p 和 r，$p=\sqrt{2}$，$r=2(2+\log_2 a)$；

当 $0<a\leq\frac{1}{4}$ 时，不存在适合题意的 p 和 r.　　（15 分）

21. 解：（Ⅰ）由题设知 l 不垂直于 y 轴，可设其方程为 $x=by+c$.

代入 $y^2=4x$，得方程

$y^2-4by-4c=0.$　　①

方程①有相异两实根，等价于判别式

$\Delta=16b^2+16c>0$，

即 $b^2+c>0$.　　②　　（3 分）

其次，l 与圆 $(x-1)^2+y^2=1$ 相切等价于 $\frac{|1-c|}{\sqrt{1+b^2}}=1$，

即 $b^2=c(c-2)$.　　③

由 $b^2\geq 0$ 得 $c(c-2)\geq 0$.

将 $b^2=c(c-2)$ 代入式②得 $c(c-1)>0$.

联立这两个不等式，解得截距 c 的取值范围为 $(-\infty, 0)\cup[2, +\infty)$.　　（7 分）

（Ⅱ）抛物线的焦点为 F（1，0），且可设 A（$\frac{1}{4}y_1^2$，y_1），B（$\frac{1}{4}y_2^2$，y_2），式中 y_1、y_2 是方程①的两个根，故

$y_1+y_2=4b$，$y_1y_2=-4c$.

$$\text{所以}\overrightarrow{FA}\cdot\overrightarrow{FB}=\left(\frac{1}{4}y_1^2-1\right)\left(\frac{1}{4}y_2^2-1\right)+y_1y_2$$
$$=\frac{1}{16}(y_1y_2)^2-\frac{1}{4}(y_1^2+y_2^2)+1+y_1y_2$$
$$=c^2-4c+1-\frac{1}{4}[(y_1+y_2)^2-2y_1y_2]$$
$$=c^2-6c+1-4b^2$$
$$=-3c^2+2c+1$$

由 $\overrightarrow{FA}\cdot\overrightarrow{FB}=0$ 得 $3c^2-2c-1=0$.（12 分）

解得 $c=-\frac{1}{3}$ 或 $c=1$（舍去）.

代入式③得 $b^2=\frac{7}{9}$，即 $b=\pm\frac{\sqrt{7}}{3}$.

所以 l 的方程为 $x=\pm\frac{\sqrt{7}}{3}y-\frac{1}{3}$，

即 $3x+\sqrt{7}y+1=0$ 或 $3x-\sqrt{7}y+1=0$.（15 分）

22. 解：因为 $f(x)$ 是单调增函数，所以对任意 $x\in\mathbf{R}$ 都有

$f'(x)=3ax^2+2bx+c\geqslant0$，

得 $a>0$，　①

且判别式 $\Delta=4b^2-12ac\leqslant0$，所以

$c\geqslant\frac{b^2}{3a}\geqslant0$.　②（4 分）

因为 $g(x)=f(x+x_0)-f(x_0)$

$\qquad=f(x)+3ax_0x^2+(3ax_0^2+2bx_0)x$

所以　$g(-x)=f(-x)+3ax_0x^2-(3ax_0^2+2bx_0)x$.

得 $g(x)+g(-x)=2(3ax_0+b)x^2$.

故 $g(x)+g(-x)=0(x\in\mathbf{R})$ 恒成立等价于 $3ax_0+b=0$. 因此，$g(x)$ 是奇函数的充要条件为 $x_0=-\frac{b}{3a}$.

因为对任意 $x_0\geqslant-\frac{1}{2}$，$g(x)$ 都不是奇函数，所以

$-\frac{b}{3a}<-\frac{1}{2}$，

得 $b>\frac{3a}{2}>0$.　③（8 分）

所以，由不等式①②③知

$3a+2b+c>0$，$2b-3a>0$，

从而证得 $M=\dfrac{3a+2b+c}{2b-3a}>0.$ （9 分）

其次 $M=\dfrac{1+\dfrac{2b}{3a}+\dfrac{c}{3a}}{\dfrac{2b}{3a}-1}\geqslant\dfrac{1+\dfrac{2b}{3a}+\left(\dfrac{b}{3a}\right)^2}{\dfrac{2b}{3a}-1}$

当 $c=\dfrac{b^2}{3a}$时，上式取等号. （11 分）

设 $t=\dfrac{2b}{3a}-1$，当 $t>0$ 时，则

$$M\geqslant\frac{1}{t}\left[2+t+\frac{1}{4}(t+1)^2\right]$$
$$=\frac{1}{4}\left(\frac{9}{t}+6+t\right)$$
$$\geqslant 3$$

当 $t=\dfrac{9}{t}$时，即 $b=6a$ 时，后一个不等式取等号.

综合得 $M\geqslant 3$. 同时，当 $a>0$，$b=6a$，$c=12a$ 时，既满足①②③各式，又使$M=3$. 所以 M 的最小值为 $M_{\min}=3$. （15 分）

英　语

第一卷

Ⅰ. 听力

1. D　2. B　3. A　4. A　5. B　6. B　7. C　8. B　9. C　10. C　11. C
12. C　13. D　14. B　15. D　16. A　17. A　18. B　19. A　20. D

Ⅱ. 英语运用

21. C　22. D　23. C　24. D　25. C　26. D　27. C　28. B　29. D　30. D
31. A　32. B　33. C　34. A　35. D　36. D　37. C　38. A　39. B　40. C
41. C　42. D　43. B　44. B　45. D　46. C　47. A　48. D　49. C　50. A
51. A　52. D　53. C　54. A　55. B

Ⅲ. 阅读理解

56. A　57. D　58. C　59. A　60. A　61. C　62. C　63. A　64. A　65. A
66. B　67. D　68. D　69. C　70. B　71. A　72. A　73. C　74. B　75. C

第二卷

Ⅳ. 短文改错

Dear Sally,	
It feels such a long time since last time I see you.	76. saw
So far my summer in Xiamen ∧ been great! I spent all	77. has
my weekends at the beach. I am getting a nice tan（晒黑）	78. √
and you can not longer say I am paler than you.	79. no
I've been playing lots of beach volleyballs, and just this	80. volleyball
passed weekend I got the first place in a match!	81. past
On weekdays I work in a club which I teach kids	82. where
to draw. Although the pay isn't high, ~~but~~ I love the job	83. ~~but~~
very much, because I like draw and I love kids a lot.	84. drawing
I hope the summer's been going good for you too.	85. well
There has only one month left in the summer vacation	86. is
and after that it's time to school. Would you like	87. for
to meet up some time before school starting?	88. starts

I want to share with your the photos I've taken. 89. you

I'll give you ∧ call when I return home. See you soon! 90. a

Love,

Mary

V. 书面表达

一、评分原则

1. 本题总分为 20 分，按 5 个档次给分。

2. 评分时，先根据文章的内容和语言初步确定其所属档次，然后以该档次的要求来衡量，确定或调整档次，最后给分。词数少于 80 个或多于 120 个，扣 1 分。

二、各档次的给分范围和要求

第五档：（17 ~ 20 分）能写明全部或绝大部分要点；语言基本无误；行文连贯，表达清楚。

第四档：（13 ~ 16 分）能写明全部或绝大部分要点；语言有少量错误；行文基本连贯，表达基本清楚。

第三档：（8 ~ 12 分）能写出基本要点；语言虽有较多错误，尚能达意。

第二档：（4 ~ 7 分）能写出部分要点；语言错误多，影响意思表达。

第一档：（0 ~ 3 分）白卷，或文不对题，或错误百出，不知所云。

A possible student text:

Dear friends,

We are going to have an English club which will offer you a wonderful chance of improving your English. On every Friday afternoon, you can come to our club and talk with our foreign teachers as well as foreign students. Besides, we'll teach English songs and invite you to our *Movie Tour* at weekends. What's more, We have a variety of interesting English games which will give you much fun!

If you want to join the club, please send an e-mail to *englishclub@ yahoo. cn* or just call *12345678910* to let us know! We also need your photo for making your membership card, and please send us via e-mail.

Still worrying about how to learn English well? Just come to our club! Don't miss it!

Come and Join us!

English Club

地　理

一、选择题

1. D 2. B 3. C 4. B 5. A 6. D 7. A 8. C 9. B 10. C 11. A
12. D 13. A 14. D 15. D 16. B 17. C 18. D 19. C 20. B

二、填充题

21. 原料　市场　能源（动力）　劳动力　科技
22. 霍尔木兹　直布罗陀　苏伊士　巴拿马　马六甲
23. 二氧化碳　甲烷　化石（矿物）　二氧化硫（氮氧化物等）　紫外线
24. 非洲（亚欧）　亚欧（非洲）　聚合　缩小　亚欧

三、读图、填图题

25. (1) 阿拉伯　孟加拉　(2) 印度　班加罗尔　科伦坡
26. (1) 地面（长波）　大气　大气逆　(2) 反射　增温（保温）
27. (1) 武当　(2) 神农架　(3) 十堰　(4) 丹江口　(5) 汉
28. (1) C　(2) B　(3) A　(4) E　(5) D

四、综合题

29. (15 分)

城市化起步：发达国家早，发展中国家晚。

近来城市化速度：发达国家较慢，发展中国家较快。

目前城市化水平：发达国家较高，发展中国家较低。

(每项 5 分，共 15 分。其他合理答案酌情给分。)

30. (15 分)

甲城市位于北极圈以北，乙城市位于北极圈以南。(4 分) 它们都是港口（或临海）城市。(3 分) 原因是北冰洋沿岸有来自北大西洋暖流的一个分支（或挪威暖流）经过，导致甲城市气温偏高。(8 分)

物　理

说明：

1. 第一大题为选择题，只要求写出答案，不要求说明理由或列出算式，只根据答案评分.

2. 计算题解答中只有最后答案而无演算过程的，不给分；只写出一般公式但未能与试题所给的具体条件联系的，不给分.

3. 计算题解答中因前面错误而引起后面错误的，如属单纯的运算错误，不重复扣分；属概念错误的，按评分参考规定扣分.

4. 对于计算题，答案的有效数字不作严格要求.

一、选择题：每小题4分，共52分．答错或不答的，都给0分.

1. A　2. D　3. D　4. B　5. C　6. D　7. B　8. C　9. D　10. A　11. B
12. A　13. C

二、实验题：共24分.

14. ① 1.240（4分）　② 1.682（4分，填1.683的同样给分）

15. ① 380（4分）

② $\dfrac{R_1-R_2}{2(I_1^{-1}-I_2^{-1})}$（6分）　③ $\dfrac{I_2R_2-I_1R_1}{2(I_1-I_2)}-0.25$（6分）

三、计算题：共74分.

16. 从天线 D 向接收器 A 发出的电磁波信号，一方面沿直线 DA 直接传播到 A，另一方面经过海面 E 点反射沿折线 DEA 传播到 A，前者较强，后者较弱. 由反射定律知

$\angle DEC=\angle AEB$　①

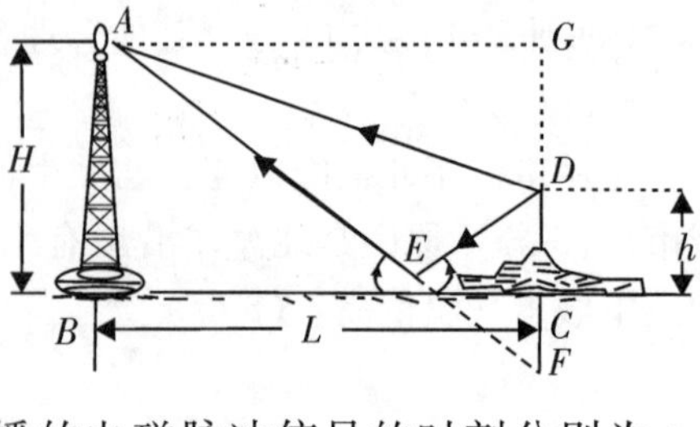

延长 AE 交 DC 的延长线于 F，过 A 作 AG 平行于 BC，交 CD 的延长线于 G，则有

$DE=EF$　②

$GD=H-h$　③

$GF=H+h$　④

设信号接收器接收到沿直线 DA 和折线 DEA 传播的电磁脉冲信号的时刻分别为 t_1 和 t_2，

$(ct_1)^2=(H-h)^2+L^2$　⑤

$(ct_2)^2=(H+h)^2+L^2$　⑥

按题意有

$t_2-t_1=\tau$　⑦

联立⑤⑥⑦式得

$4Hh = c^2\tau(2t_1 + \tau)$ ⑧

解得

$ct_1 = \frac{1}{2}\left(\frac{4Hh}{c\tau} - c\tau\right)$ ⑨

代入⑤式得

$L = \sqrt{\frac{1}{4}\left(\frac{4Hh}{c\tau} - c\tau\right)^2 - (H-h)^2}$ ⑩

评分参考：本题 16 分. ⑤⑥⑦⑩式各 4 分.

17. 设在温度为 273 K 时 A、B 压强均为 p_1（以 mmHg 为单位）. 在以后的过程中，B 中压强不变. 因 A 室体积不变，由查理定律

$\frac{p_1}{p_2} = \frac{T_1}{T_2}$ ①

得

$\frac{p_1}{p_1 + 120} = \frac{273}{373}$ ②

$\frac{p_1}{p_1 + 90} = \frac{273}{T}$ ③

式中，T 为所求温度.

联立②③式得

$T = 348\ \text{K}$ ④

评分参考：本题 18 分. ①式 3 分，②③式各 6 分，④式 3 分.

18. 设导体杆 cd 在此瞬时的滑行速度为 v_2，根据法拉第电磁感应定律，回路中感应电动势为

$\varepsilon = BL(v_1 - v_2)$ ①

设此时回路中的电流为 I，由欧姆定律有

$\varepsilon = 2RI$ ②

两杆作为一个整体，由动量定理有

$Ft = m(v_1 + v_2) - mv_0$ ③

杆 ab 和 cd 所受到的安培力的大小为

$f = BIL$ ④

设杆 ab 和 cd 在此瞬时的加速度大小分别为 a_1 和 a_2，由牛顿定律有

$F - f = ma_1$ ⑤

$f = ma_2$ ⑥

联立以上各式得

$a_1 = \frac{F}{m} - \frac{B^2L^2}{2Rm}\left(2v_1 - v_0 - \frac{Ft}{m}\right)$ ⑦

$a_2 = \frac{B^2L^2}{2Rm}\left(2v_1 - v_0 - \frac{Ft}{m}\right)$ ⑧

评分参考：本题 20 分．①式 3 分，②式 2 分，③式 3 分，④⑤⑥式各 2 分，⑦⑧式各 3 分．

19．传送带运行的速度为　．

$$v=\omega R \quad ①$$

设货物从传送带左端运动到右端的时间为 t，分三种情形讨论．

当 $v_0=v$ 时，放在传送带上的货物与传送带之间没有相互运动趋势，因而没有摩擦，故传送带上的货物在水平方向受力为零．货物从传送带左端传送到右端的时间为

$$t=\frac{L}{\omega R} \quad ②$$

当 $v_0<v$，且 $\mu mgL\leqslant\frac{1}{2}m(\omega R)^2-\frac{1}{2}mv_0^2$时，货物从传送带左端运动至右端时，一直做匀加速直线运动，货物受到传送带施加的水平向右的摩擦力

$$f=\mu N \quad ③$$

式中，N 是传送带对货物的正压力．设货物的加速度为 a，由牛顿定律有

$$f=ma \quad ④$$

$$N-mg=0 \quad ⑤$$

$$L=v_0t+\frac{1}{2}at^2 \quad ⑥$$

联立③④⑤⑥得

$$t=\frac{v_0}{\mu g}\left(\sqrt{1+\frac{2\mu gL}{v_0^2}}-1\right)\ （当 L\leqslant\frac{\omega^2R^2-v_0^2}{2\mu g}时） \quad ⑦$$

当 $v_0<v$，且 $\mu mgL>\frac{1}{2}m(\omega R)^2-\frac{1}{2}mv_0^2$ 时，货物先做匀加速直线运动，在到达传送带右端以前速度达到 v，以后做匀速直线运动，直至到达传送带右端．设货物速度从 v_0 增加到 v 所用的时间为 t_1，所走的路程为 L_1，则

$$v-v_0=at_1 \quad ⑧$$

$$v^2-{v_0}^2=2aL_1 \quad ⑨$$

$$L-L_1=v(t-t_1) \quad ⑩$$

联立①③④⑤⑧⑨⑩式得

$$t=\frac{L}{\omega R}+\frac{\omega R}{2\mu g}-\frac{v_0}{\mu g}+\frac{{v_0}^2}{2\mu g\omega R}\ （当 L>\frac{\omega^2R^2-v_0^2}{2\mu g}时） \quad ⑪$$

评分参考：本题 20 分．正确判断三种情形的物理条件各给 1 分，①②③④⑤式各 1 分，⑥⑦⑧⑨⑩⑪式各 2 分．

化　学

说明：

1. 本答案供阅卷评分使用，考生若写出其他正确答案，可参照评分参考给分。
2. 化学专用名词中出现错别字、元素符号书写错误，都要参照评分参考扣分。
3. 化学方程式、离子方程式未配平时，都不给分。
4. 在做计算题时，没有考虑有效数字的，可不扣分。

一、选择题（每题 3 分）

1. D　2. C　3. C　4. C　5. D　6. B　7. C　8. A　9. C　10. A　11. D

12. B　13. B　14. D　15. A　16. A　17. B　18. D

二、

19.（17 分）

（1）盐酸　氯化铜（6 分。写出化学式也给分）

（2）硫酸　硫酸钠（6 分。写出化学式也给分）

（3）硫酸铜　$2Cu^{2+} + 2H_2O \xlongequal{电解} 2Cu + 4H^+ + O_2\uparrow$（5 分。少“电解”扣 1 分）

20.（9 分）

$KAl(SO_4)_2 \cdot 12H_2O$（2 分）

明矾中的 Al^{3+} 离子发生水解反应，使溶液中 H^+ 离子浓度增大，显酸性（4 分）

Al^{3+} 水解过程中生成 $Al(OH)_3$ 胶体，它有很强的吸附能力，可以吸附水中悬浮的杂质并生成沉淀，使水得到净化。(3 分)

21.（15 分）

（1）氢　氮　氧　钙（4 分。写出元素符号也给分）

（2）CaH_2　离子　$CaH_2 + 2H_2O \xlongequal{} Ca(OH)_2 + 2H_2\uparrow$（3 分）

（3）NH_3　分子（2 分）

（4）HNO_3、HNO_2　$Ca(OH)_2$、$NH_3 \cdot H_2O$　$Ca(NO_3)_2$、NH_4NO_3（6 分）

22.（17 分）

（1）①说明阳离子不是 Fe^{3+} 或 Cu^{2+}，无有色离子（4 分）

②说明阴离子不是 HCO_3^- 或 SO_3^{2-}，阳离子不是 NH_4^+（6 分）

③说明 R 组成中无 NO_3^-（2 分）

④KCl（1 分）

（2）用洁净的铂丝蘸取少量 R 的溶液，在酒精灯火焰上灼烧，透过蓝色的钴玻璃片观察，火焰呈紫色，说明阳离子是 K^+。(2 分)

用试管取少量R的溶液，加入适量硝酸酸化后，向其中滴入$AgNO_3$溶液。有白色沉淀生成，说明阴离子是Cl^-。(2分)

23．(18分)

(1) 对甲基苯酚　　2—甲基丙烯（异丁烯）(2分)

(2) 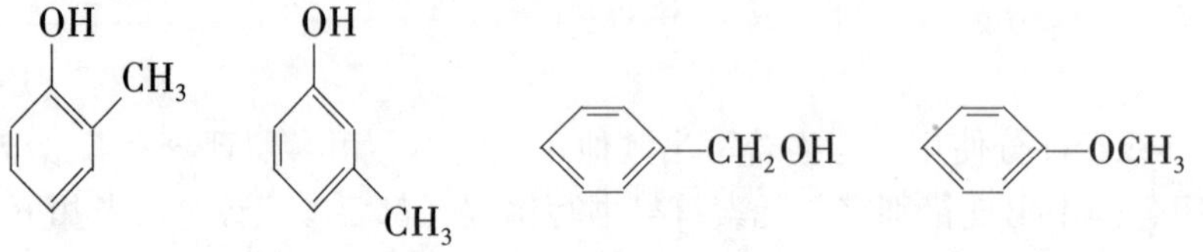 (8分)

(3) $CH_2=C(CH_3)_2+Br_2 \longrightarrow BrCH_2CBr(CH_3)_2$ (2分)

(4) $(CH_3)_2CHCH_2OH$ (2分)

$(CH_3)_3COH$ (2分)

$(CH_3)_2CHCHO+2Ag(NH_3)_2OH \longrightarrow (CH_3)_2CHCOO^-+NH_4^++2Ag\downarrow+3NH_3+H_2O$ (2分)

24．(10分)

反应物中$n(NaClO)=\dfrac{7.45\ g}{74.5\ g/mol}=0.100\ mol$ (2分)

$n(NH_3)=\dfrac{6.00\ L}{22.4\ L/mol}=0.268\ mol$ (2分)

反应物中氨过量，生成的肼$n(N_2H_4)=n(NaClO)$ (2分)

肼的质量$m(N_2H_4)=0.100\ mol\times32\ g/mol=3.20\ g$ (4分)

25．(10分)

(1) 从溶解情况知道含杂质为0.2 g (2分)，所以石灰石纯度为$\dfrac{2.0-0.2}{2.0}\times100\%=90\%$。(3分)

(2) 100.0 kg这种石灰石含$CaCO_3$的量为：$100.0\ kg\times90\%=90.0\ kg$ (2分)

设纯$CaCO_3$煅烧后得到的固体质量为x，

$CaCO_3 = CaO+CO_2\uparrow$

100　　　　56

90.0 kg　　　x

$x=\dfrac{56\times90.0\ kg}{100}=50.4\ kg$ (3分)

最终得到的固体为SiO_2与CaO，其质量为$(100.0\ kg-90.0\ kg)+50.4\ kg=60.4\ kg$。

2012 年两校联招、全国联招试题比较分析

语　文

暨南大学华文学院预科部综合教研室
袁忠群

2012 年两校联招和全国联招的中国语文考试时间都是 150 分钟，试卷满分都是 150 分，从三大方面考查考生的语文能力，内容包括基础知识部分、阅读理解部分（包括文言文和现代文）以及写作部分。两套试卷都依据考纲，“稳中有变”。

一、两校联招试卷分析

2012 年两校联招试卷分基础知识、阅读理解、语言文字表达三大部分，具体题型及分值见表 1。

表 1　两校联招语文试题类型与分值分布

试题类型		单项选择题	填空题	判断题	翻译题	简答题	写作题	合计
基础知识		10 题 20 分	5 题 5 分	5 题 5 分				30 分
阅读理解	文言文	8 题 24 分			1 题 3 分	1 题 3 分		30 分
	现代文	5 题 10 分				3 题 10 分		20 分
语言文字表达	应用写作						10 分	70 分
	作文						60 分	
合计		54 分	5 分	5 分	3 分	13 分	70 分	150 分

要特别提醒考生注意的是，两校联招考纲每 4 年会重新修订一次，题型与分值可能会有比较大的变动。2012 年与 2011 年的题型与分值相比就有很大差异。

（1）2012 年取消了多选题。多选题是考生得分率偏低的题型，近些年来，多选题在两校联招中的比重越来越小，2012 年则完全取消。多选题的分值并入了单选题。

（2）2011 年文言文阅读还是两段，而且是分开命题，但 2012 年试卷则将文言文阅读合并成一个部分，并且增加了古体诗词（2012 年出的是诗，以后也可能是词、曲或其他文体），三段文言诗文，其中依然有一段来自两校联招复习丛书。题型上变化不大，只是 2012 年翻译题只有 1 题，比 2011 年少了 1 题，分值并入了单项选择题。

（3）2012 年现代文阅读题型变化比较大，取消了判断题，增加了简答题。这对语言表达能力强的考生更为有利。

（4）语言文字表达部分没有变化。

二、全国联招试卷分析

2012 年全国联招试卷分为选择题和非选择题两大部分，主要考查基础知识、白话文阅读、文言文阅读、写作四大部分内容，具体题型和分值见表 2。

表 2　全国联招语文试题类型及分值分布

试题类型	卷一（54 分）：选择题（单选）	卷二（96 分）：非选择题				总计
		填空题	翻译题	简答题	写作	
基础知识	10 题 30 分	3 题 3 分				33 分
白话文阅读（一）	4 题 12 分					12 分
文言文阅读	4 题 12 分		2 题 10 分			22 分
白话文阅读（二）				4 题 23 分		23 分
写作					60 分	60 分
所占分值	54 分	3 分	10 分	23 分	60 分	150 分

全国联招的题型与分值稳定性非常强，多年没有变化。

三、两校联招试卷与全国联招试卷的比较

从试卷结构看，两校联招试卷包括基础知识、阅读理解、语言文字表达三部分；全国联招试卷包括选择题和非选择题两部分。从试卷内容看，两套试题都是从基础知识、文言文阅读、现代文阅读和写作这四个方面考查考生的语文能力。

（一）基础知识

两校联招的基础知识满分为 30 分，全国联招的基础知识满分为 33 分，两套试题的基础知识题分值相当，且都包括单项选择题和填空题这两种题型，两校联招除了这两种题型外，还有判断题。参见表 3。

表 3　两校联招和全国联招基础知识题型及分值比较

题型及分值	单项选择题	填空题	判断题	题量	分值总计
两校联招	10 题 20 分	5 题 5 分	5 题 5 分	20 题	30 分
全国联招	10 题 30 分	3 题 3 分		13 题	33 分

从表 3 可以看出，两校联招的基础知识题题量较大、涉及面较广，而全国联招的基础知识题题量较少，每一题的分值较大。这就要求考生在备考时根据两套试题的不同特点做出相应调整。两套试题的基础知识除了题型差异外，考点的分布也各有侧重。详见表 4。

表 4　两校联招和全国联招基础知识题考点分布

考点及分值	两校联招分值	全国联招分值	题型
字形辨识	2		单项选择题
虚词运用		3	单项选择题
成语运用	2	3	单项选择题
病句辨析	2	3	单项选择题
语义简洁辨识	2		单项选择题
语义明确辨识		3	单项选择题
语篇衔接	2		单项选择题
词义辨析	2	3	单项选择题
	1		填空题
标点符号运用	2	3	单项选择题
修辞手法辨析	2	3	单项选择题
	1		填空题
文学常识	4	3	单项选择题
	2		判断题
文化常识		3	单项选择题
	3		判断题
唐诗鉴赏	以简答题形式出现在阅读题部分	3	单项选择题
名句默写	3	3	填空题
总计	30 分	33 分	

全国联招的基础知识考查题型除了 3 分的名言名句默写外，其他均是单项选择题，而且知识点比较固定。两校联招的基础知识考查题型多，范围更广，而且知识点变动大。

2012 年考查的知识点与 2011 年相比就有一些变化，比如增加了标点符号的考查，没有了常用应用文文体知识的考查。2012 年两校联招的基础知识考查部分从题型到知识点都更偏向全国联招。

名言名句的默写部分，2012 年全国联招与两校联招都是固定为 3 题。但全国联招有时会有超过 3 题而由考生自选 3 题作答的情况。需要提醒考生注意的是，如果考生实际作答超过了 3 题，阅卷时将会只阅前 3 题。所以，考生作答如果超过了 3 题，最好只保留自己最有把握的 3 题，把其余的划去。填空题如果有错别字，该题不得分。所填的内容中如果有古今字，要求按古字写，比如"问渠那得清如许"句，不能写成"问渠哪得清如许"。"哪"字是 20 世纪才有的，在古诗文中"哪"与"那"都是用"那"。总之，名句默写要忠实于原文。但如果该句有多个版本流传，则均可。

在文化常识部分，两校联招每年都有一个关于汉字结构的题目，全国联招则很少涉及这一知识点。在文学常识部分，全国联招会涉及外国文学知识，两校联招则比较少见。

还有一点，两校联招基础知识的命题有不少题目出自两校联招复习丛书《中国语文》，这也在一定程度上降低了考试的难度。

（二）文言文阅读

2012 年两校联招的文言文阅读材料是 3 篇，包括两篇古文，一首诗词，古文中有一篇来自两校联招复习丛书《中国语文》，总分值为 30 分；全国联招的文言文阅读材料是 1 篇，总分值为 22 分。两套试题都包括单项选择题和翻译题，两校联招还有简答题。参见表 5。

表 5　两校联招和全国联招文言文阅读题型及分值比较

题型及分值	单项选择题	翻译题	简答题	分值总计
两校联招	8 题 24 分	1 题 3 分	1 题 3 分	30 分
全国联招	4 题 12 分	2 题 10 分		22 分

从表 5 可以看出，两校联招文言文阅读所占分值较高，但其难度却低于全国联招，因为其中有一段古文阅读材料出自复习丛书，包括翻译和简答在内的题目难度就大大降低了。全国联招的文言文阅读材料常是一篇中规中矩的史传类作品，作品年代多在汉代以后。两校联招 2012 年考的也是一篇史传文，这与过去的选材有比较大的区别，这是否是命题的一个新动向，还留待观察。如果考史传文被固定下来，那就是进一步向全国联招靠拢。全国联招文言文阅读考查的知识点都基本固定，这或许能为备考的考生提供导向和帮助。

（三）现代文阅读

两校联招的现代文阅读是一篇材料，总分值为 20 分；全国联招的现代文阅读是两篇材料，总分值是 35 分。两套试题都包括单项选择题和简答题，两校联招还包括判断题。参见表 6。

表 6　两校联招和全国联招现代文阅读题型及分值比较

<table>
<tr><th colspan="2">题型及分值</th><th>单项选择题</th><th>简答题</th><th>分值总计</th></tr>
<tr><td rowspan="2">全国联招</td><td>白话文（一）</td><td>4 题
12 分</td><td></td><td rowspan="2">35 分</td></tr>
<tr><td>白话文（二）</td><td></td><td>4 题
23 分</td></tr>
<tr><td colspan="2">两校联招</td><td>5 题
10 分</td><td>3 题
10 分</td><td>20 分</td></tr>
</table>

全国联招的现代文阅读所占分值较高，阅读量也大，分两篇文章考查：材料一注重考查考生的理解和分析能力，常见为学术性文章或科技类说明文；材料二注重考查考生的鉴赏和表达能力，常见为文艺性较强的文学作品。两校联招只有一篇阅读材料，一般是文学作品或学术性文章，科技类说明文较少见，2012 年两校联招增加了简答题的分量。

（四）写作

两校联招的“语言文字表达”分值为 70 分，分 3 题考查；全国联招的“写作”分值为 60 分，只有一题。参见表 7。

表 7　两校联招和全国联招写作题型及分值比较

题型及分值	新闻写作	串台词	作文	分值总计
两校联招	1 题 4 分	1 题 6 分	1 题 60 分	70 分
全国联招			1 题 60 分	60 分

从表 7 可以看出，两校联招较全国联招多了 10 分的应用写作题，这样能够更全面地考查考生实际运用语言文字的能力，显示出两校联招更重视考生的语言表达能力。应用写作题形式活泼多样，内容丰富多彩，是两校联招最有特色的题型之一。

两校联招和全国联招的作文题都是 60 分，且都是“二选一”的形式，不同之处在于：

（1）两校联招作文的两个题目一个是命题作文“放”，一个是材料作文“林书豪热”，作文材料大多与现实生活联系紧密，一般为全球，尤其是华人世界一年内的热点事件，时效性比较强；全国联招作文的两个题目都是命题作文：“当代人的追求”和“我盼望的那一天”。

（2）两校联招作文明确规定不允许诗歌创作，全国联招虽然没有明确规定，但“不少于 600 字”的字数要求也基本否定了诗歌创作的可能性。

（3）两校联招作文对字数的要求是“文言文不少于 400 字，白话文不少于 700 字”，而全国联招则统一要求为“不少于 600 字”，没有限制文言文写作。近年来不少考生尝试用文言文写作，部分考生的作文还获得高分，但用文言文写作，风险比较大，因为有些考生文言功底不深，写出来的作文是半文半白，有点四不像。不管是文言还是白话，文从字顺、表达清楚准确总是对语言的基本要求。

对作文内容和思想情感最基本的要求，也是最高的要求就是要真实。对考生来说，正确审题和认真构思都是非常重要的。

当然也需要注意作文写作的一些细节，如要在自己的文章前居中写上题目。每年都有部分考生作文不写题目。试题中有两个作文题，如果是没有题目的作文，重者可判离题，轻者也可能多扣一二十分。有些考生给自己的作文题加上书名号，这也是要扣分的。尽量减少或避免错别字。书写要工整，卷面要整洁，写的字太小、太大或太潦草，都不好。每年都发现有考生部分或全文抄袭，一旦确认抄袭，作文便会被判为零分。在作文中如果引用他人的内容，需要注明，至少要用引号标明。

两校联招作文中的材料题给考生提供的材料，考生要避免过多地引用。有些考生把试题中的材料都写到作文里去，这样，作文中自己的内容就非常少了。这样的作文显然不会得高分。类似的情况还有，有的考生写议论文，把某一个人物或故事作论据，结果把这个人物或故事写得非常具体详细，使文章看起来倒像是记叙文而不是议论文了。这些都是对文章的材料处理不当所致。

在评分标准上，两校联招与全国联招没有什么区别。

数　学

暨南大学华文学院预科部数学教研室
刘岑枫　张卓

一、两校联招试卷分析

（一）试卷基本结构

从 2012 年起，两校联招启用新的考试大纲，考试内容有所改变，但变化不大；试题结构也在原来的基础上做了改变。本试卷满分 150 分，共三道大题，26 道小题。第一大题为选择题，共 15 道小题，每小题 4 分，满分 60 分；第二大题为填空题，共 6 小题，每小题 4 分，满分 24 分；第三大题为解答题，共 7 道小题，满分 66 分，其中前三题为文理共答题，每小题 12 分，后四题分别为选考理科或文科的考生必答题，各科必做两题，每小题 15 分。具体题型及分值见表 1。

表 1　两校联招数学试题类型与分值分布

试题类型	选择题	填空题	解答题	总计
试题数	15	6	文理各 5 题	26
所占分值	60	24	66	150
所占比例（%）	40	16	44	100

两校联招数学考试一向强调对数学基础知识的考查，考查的知识重点都是考试大纲中的核心内容，考查的范围也是较全面的，难易适度，具有良好的区分度，能较好地反映出考生掌握数学知识的实际情况。从考试成绩来看，基本达到了预期的目标。从卷面看，试题大致可以分为两大类，第一类是基础知识方面的，主要是填空题、选择题；第二类是综合应用方面的，主要是解答题。试题较全面地涉及了各个知识点的数学知识，便于考查考生思维的灵活性和多角度性。

（二）试卷知识结构

（1）试题从总体上贯彻了考试大纲的基本思想，但在题目的类型上和题目的分值上与前几年不一样，主要是实行了新的考试大纲，如前几年解答题中“5 选 3”的选做题就取消了。

（2）试题覆盖的知识面广，考试大纲中要求的内容基本上都涉及了。比如代数、三角、立体几何、解析几何，概率、数列、向量等。

（3）试卷文理同卷，其中绝大部分试题相同，说明对文理科考生的基本要求相同，只是在难度上有所区别，主要体现在最后的文科必做题与理科必做题上。

（4）试卷中选择题的比例占总分值的 40%，其难度较小，考查的都是一些基本概念与基本公式，但题量较多，15 个小题几乎涉及考试大纲的各个内容，并且每题的分值较高，这就要求考生灵活运用所掌握的知识快速解题，为后面的解答留下足够的时间。

（5）试卷中填空题的比例占总分值的 16%，填空题的特点跟选择题比较类似，所考查的也是一些基本概念与基本公式，对计算能力的要求较低，应该说难度不大。

（6）解答题文理科都是必做 5 个题目，其中前 3 题是文理都必做题，第 25 与第 26 题的第一小题是文科必做，第二小题是理科必做。从考试内容来看，解答题主要考查了三角函数、数列、立体几何、解析几何等知识的综合应用，还有一题考查的是数学知识在日常生活中的应用。从难度上看，解答题的难度比前面的选择题与填空题的难度大了很多，主要体现在要求考生不但要对一些基本概念与基本公式非常熟悉，还要求能灵活应用，并且对计算能力的要求较高，所考查的是考生对所学知识的综合应用。从考试情况来看，解答题也是考生最难拿分的。

（7）两校联招数学考试的知识点的分布非常广泛，几乎涵盖了考试大纲中的每一个角落，具体情况见表 2。

表 2　两校联招数学试题知识点分布情况

内容	选择题	填空题	解答题
函数（包括不等式）	6 题（共 24 分）	3 题（共 12 分）	
三角	2 题（共 8 分）	1 题（共 4 分）	1 题（共 12 分）
数列	1 题（共 4 分）		1 题（共 15 分，文理不同题）
向量	1 题（共 4 分）		
排列组合与概率	2 题（共 8 分）		
立体几何	1 题（共 4 分）	1 题（共 4 分）	1 题（共 12 分）
解析几何	2 题（共 8 分）	1 题（共 4 分）	1 题（共 15 分，文理不同题）
数学知识应用题			1 题（共 12 分）

两校联招数学试题从整体上看，知识面较广，内容较多。从命题重点来讲，主要考查了考生对基础知识的掌握情况，符合考试大纲的要求以及港、澳、台、华侨、华人及其他外籍考生的特点。

二、全国试卷分析

（一）试卷基本结构

2012 年全国联招数学试卷分为选择题、填空题、解答题三大部分。

试卷结构具体如下：试卷共三道大题，22 道小题，满分 150 分。第一大题为选择题，共 12 小题，每小题 5 分，满分 60 分；第二大题为填空题，共 6 小题，每小题 5 分，满分

30分；第三大题为解答题，共4小题，每小题15分，满分60分。具体题型及分值见表3。

表3　全国联招数学试题类型与分值分布

试题类型	选择题	填空题	解答题	总计
试题数	12	6	4	22
所占分值	60	30	60	150
所占比例（%）	40	20	40	100

（二）试卷内容

试题紧扣考试大纲的要求，考查了考生对考试大纲所要求的数学的基础知识、基本技能和常用数学思维方法的掌握情况，考查了考生的运算能力、逻辑思维能力、抽象思维能力和空间想象能力。

表4　全国联招数学试题考查知识点与分值分布

	考查知识点	选择题（每小题5分）	填空题（每小题5分）	解答题（每小题15分）
代数	集合、子集与真子集	第1小题		
	数列求和的“裂项法”	第4小题		
	等差数列的运算	第5小题		
	等差数列、等比数列公式及性质			第20小题
	复数的运算性质	第6小题		
	排列组合及概率	第7小题		
	代数的基本公式及运算能力	第12小题		
	多项式		第17小题	
	二次函数的性质及求值域的方法			第22小题
三角	三角函数的二倍角公式及性质	第11小题		
	三角函数的化简及解三角形			第19小题
立体几何	线面角及二面角	第10小题		
	正四棱柱的对角线及侧面积公式		第15小题	
	圆锥的性质		第18小题	

（续上表）

	考查知识点	选择题 （每小题 5 分）	填空题 （每小题 5 分）	解答题 （每小题 15 分）
解析几何	几种直线方程的互化	第 3 小题		
	双曲线的基本概念及几何性质	第 8 小题		
	椭圆的基本概念及几何性质	第 9 小题		
	直线与抛物线相交问题			第 21 小题
	点的对称		第 14 小题	
	空间直线与平面方程		第 16 小题	
微积分	常见函数的导数	第 2 小题		
	三次函数的导数			第 22 小题
概率与统计	分层抽样		第 13 小题	

试题覆盖的知识面广，涉及了代数、三角、立体几何、解析几何、微积分和概率诸多方面，较全面地考查了考生的知识结构。代数部分仍然是考试的重点。

解答题所涉及的内容分别为函数、三角、平面解析几何和数列，这也是各年试卷中解答题所涉及的典型内容。解答题难度较大，不仅要求考生具有综合运用知识的能力，而且还要具有较高的解题技巧。从考试结果看，考生普遍在解答题上得分不高。当然，四道解答题的难度也是不一样的，相对而言，第 19 题难度较小，第 22 题难度较大，是整份试卷的压轴题。值得注意的是，2011 年和 2012 年连续两年都没有出现立体几何的解答题。

2012 年全国联招数学试卷保持了一贯风格，题型稳定，难度较高，计算量大，综合性强。这就要求考生灵活运用自己所掌握的知识，仔细审题，把握关键字句，巧妙使用估算法、排除法、特殊法等答题技巧，以较快的速度解题。

三、复习建议

1. 加强基础知识、基本方法的复习

基础知识、基本方法在全国联招的试卷中占很大比重，也是解答综合题的基础。

2. 加强运算能力的训练

运算能力是全国联招数学考试的一个重点，题目的运算量都比较大。

3. 适当关注一下近几年国内各地高考题型

全国联招数学试卷有一些题型与国内高考的题型非常相似，因此，适当关注一下国内各地高考题型是非常必要的。

附：学习建议

读书要咬文嚼字，要自己嚼出味道来，要把知识当作一把钥匙，掌握在自己手中，去开启取之不尽的形形色色的东西。课前应通读教材，了解本节课要学习的内容。课堂上适当地做笔记，不要盲目地照抄老师的板书。应该结合书本的内容，记下老师补充的知识点、一些关键的语句及自己预习时不懂的地方即可；也可以不记在笔记本上，直接记在书中恰当的位置上，这也是一个不错的办法。对于老师提出的问题，不要急于看书本，满足于现成的答案，应勇于发表自己的见解。应先自己主动思考，再细听老师的讲解，逐字推敲，认真钻研，多问为什么，比较两者的方法有什么异同，琢磨每一题的切入点和每一步的原理。所谓“学起于思，思起于疑”、“小疑则小进，大疑则大进”，就是这个道理。经常有学生说“我上课都听懂了，可做作业时就不知如何下手了”，这主要是因为盲目地看书、听课，欠缺思考。也有程度较好的学生认为自己已经会了，不必再听，但解题时往往灵活性、创造性不够，这主要是没有仔细比较老师的方法和自己的方法之间的优劣，取长补短所致。殊不知，老师之所以能百发百中，是因为认真钻研了教材，备了课，老师在备课的过程中经历了思维受阻、碰壁。认真聆听老师讲方法、讲思路就可以避免走弯路。课后先自己回忆一下所学内容，回忆例题的解答要领和解题格式，再有目的地看书和笔记，弄清概念及公式、定理的来龙去脉，然后认真做作业，最后再次看书和笔记，查漏补缺。

多数人都认为要学好数学，一定要多做题，不能“减负”。其实不然，数学成绩的高低与做题的多少是没有必然联系的。关键是在做题的过程中，要认真对待每一题，要有主动的意识，多思，善问，不断总结，促进理解，提高自己的认知水平。这样既减轻了学习负担，又提高了学习效率。

在学习数学的过程中，要根据自己的情况，不要盲目地做难题，特别对选择题、填空题要“小题大做”，应该把每一个选择题、每一个填空题都当成解答题去做。当然做选择题的方法是最灵活的，比如特殊值法、比较法、排除法、数型结合法等等，但是做选择题即便有很多种好方法、巧方法，平时还是要尽量减少猜的成分，也要像做解答题一样，每一个环节、每一个步骤、运用的每一个原理都搞清楚。这样就从选择题里吸取了解题的经验，增加了解题的方法。再进一步扩展到填空题，如果能够提高填空题的正确率，说明这是一个比较大的进步。当你的选择题和填空题的成功率比较高的时候，对知识的灵活运用能力自然就提高了，解决比较简单的解答题的能力也相应地提高了。俗话说“万丈高楼平地起”，选择、填空题就像地基，只有地基打稳了，高楼才坚固耐用；只重视解答题，就像高楼暂时盖起来了，却是危楼。所以说做选择题是提高成绩的关键，就看你怎么做了。经常“小题大做”，基础知识掌握得牢固了，对做大题特别有帮助，大题也就可以“小做”了。

英　语

暨南大学华文学院英语教研室
陈芳

一、全国联招试卷分析

试卷包括5个大题：

（一）听力

共20小题，每小题1.5分，满分30分。考生根据所听到的简短对话或独白，从所给选项中选出最佳答案。所有录音仅读一遍。

设问形式如下：

（1）问原因，如第11、15、18小题等。

（2）问动作或对象，如第2、3、4、5、9、12、13、16、17、19小题等。

（3）问观点，如第20小题。

（4）问地点，如第1、14小题等。

（5）问时间，如第6、7、10小题等。

（6）问方式，如第8小题。

（二）英语运用

共35小题，每小题1分，满分35分。共分两节：

1. 单项填空

共15小题。所考知识点如下：

题号	考点	题号	考点
21	动名词用法	29	不定式
22	冠词用法	30	定语从句关系词的省略
23	词义辨析	31	状语从句连词选择
24	情态动词	32	情态动词及不定式用法
25	过去进行时用法	33	状语从句连词选择
26	短语辨析	34	虚拟语气用法
27	过去分词用法	35	定语从句关系词选择
28	关系代词		

2. 完形填空

共20小题。

本文主要记述了笑脸图像的由来。考查的主要形式如下：

（1）在分析语境的过程中对逻辑意义和考生理解能力的考查，如第 37、38、39、43、46 小题等。

（2）对常用的习惯用语和搭配用法的考查，如第 40、42、51、52 小题等。

（3）对词义辨析的考查，如第 36、37、54 小题等。

（4）对考生整体思维能力的考查，如第 41 小题。

（三）阅读理解

共 20 小题，每小题 2.5 分，满分 50 分。

（1）共 5 篇短文，其内容分别如下：

短文一讲述了泰德和迪娜因环保而结识，并喜结良缘，一同进行环保的宣传之旅。

短文二分析了女性不愿从事计算机行业工作的原因。

短文三简要介绍了消费者产品安全委员会给出的购物小贴士。

短文四简要介绍了面部表情的作用。

短文五简要介绍了塞浦路斯的几种博物馆的情况。

（2）考查的主要形式：

①主旨大意题，如第 63、71 小题等。

②事实细节题，如第 56、57、60、61 小题等。

③判断推理题，如第 62 小题。

④词义猜测题，如第 68 小题。

⑤文体判断题，如第 64 小题。

（四）短文改错

共 15 小题，每小题 1 分，满分 15 分。

该短文比较简单，主要讲述了一个年轻人在暑假期间的经历。

主要考点如下：

（1）时态一致，如第 76、77 小题等。

（2）冠词用法，如第 90 小题。

（3）主谓一致，如第 88 小题。

（4）词类是否恰当，如第 81、85 小题等。

（5）关系词，如第 82 小题。

（6）固定搭配，如第 79、80、86 小题等。

（7）上下文的逻辑联系，如第 83 小题。

（8）动名词，如第 84 小题。

（9）介词，如第 87 小题。

（10）代词，如第 89 小题。

（五）书面表达

共 1 小题，满分 20 分。

假如你是李华，与几位同学一起成立了一个英语俱乐部。为了号召同学们积极报名参加，你需要在校刊“英语园地”上写一篇英文“致同学信”。信的要点已经列出，词数为 100 个左右。考生需要根据给出的要点，适当增减细节，完成这封信件。

二、两校联招试卷分析

试卷包括 7 个大题：

（一）听力

共 20 小题，满分 30 分。

今年本大题出现了较大变动，删减了前面的听辨数字和回答问题两个部分，只留下了后面的两大块，即对话和短文独白，而且对话由以前的 5 段增加至 10 段，短文独白由以前的 1 篇增加至 2 篇。具体如下：

A 节：对话。要求考生在听到对话后，再根据所提问题选出正确答案。共 10 小题，每小题 1 分，共 10 分。每段对话仅读 1 遍。

B 节：短文独白。要求考生在听到短文后，再根据所提问题选出正确答案。共 10 小题，每小题 2 分，共 20 分。每段独白会读 2 遍。

1. 对话部分设问形式

（1）问原因，如第 4 小题。

（2）问动作或对象，如第 2、3 小题等。

（3）问地点，如第 5 小题。

（4）问数字，如第 6 小题。

（5）推测意图或行为，如第 1、7、8、9、10 小题等。

2. 短文独白部分的设问形式

（1）问数字，如第 11、17、19 小题等。

（2）问方式，如第 12 小题。

（3）问对象或行为，如第 13、14、15、18、20 小题等。

（4）问时间，如第 16 小题。

（二）阅读理解

共 20 小题，每小题 2 分，满分 40 分。

（1）4 篇短文的内容分别如下：

短文一介绍了美国东北部地区的意义。

短文二论述了网上购物的利弊。

短文三介绍了有关布莱克夫妇的一个幽默小故事。

短文四记叙了布兰森先生的意外发现：不带薪轮流休假的好处。

（2）考查的主要形式：

①主旨大意或段落大意题，如第 21、30 小题等。

②事实细节题，如第 22、23、24 小题等。

③判断推理题，如第 25 小题。

④词义猜测题，如第 27、36、40 小题等。

（三）词汇

共 20 小题，满分 20 分。

（1）本题由两部分构成：

A 节：每题在一或两句话中留出空白，要求考生根据所给情景选出合适的词或短语。

共 10 小题，每小题 1 分，共 10 分。

B 节：要求考生从给定的四个选项中选出与题干画线部分的词或短语意义和用法最接近的选项。共 10 小题，每小题 1 分，共 10 分。

（2）考点如下：

A 节题号	考点	A 节题号	考点
41	keep	46	look after
42	raise	47	few
43	promote	48	soon
44	go off	49	sense
45	confident	50	shelter

B 节题号	考点	B 节题号	考点
51	sharp – dramatic	56	leading – major
52	request – ask	57	count – matter
53	in no time – immediately	58	competence – ability
54	turn down – reject	59	isolate – cut off
55	drive – make	60	set – establish

（四）语法结构

共 10 小题，每小题 1 分，满分 10 分。考点如下：

题号	考点	题号	考点
61	不定式	66	it 用法及不定式
62	主谓一致	67	情态动词
63	定语从句的关系代词	68	反意疑问句
64	虚拟语气	69	宾语从句的语序
65	虚拟语气	70	形容词的比较级

（五）完形填空

共 20 小题，每小题 1 分，满分 20 分。

这篇短文讲述了苏珊·克夫威兰接替父亲执掌糖果厂后如何振兴糖果厂的故事。

考点如下：

（1）在分析语境的过程中对逻辑意义和考生理解能力的考查，如第 71、73、74、77、79、82 小题等。

（2）短语辨析，如第 72 小题。

（3）词语辨析，如第 76、85、89 小题。

（4）对常用习惯用语或搭配的考查，如第86小题。

（5）对句子的结构或句型的语言分析能力的考查，如第80小题。

（6）对考生整体思维能力的考查，如第84小题。

（六）短文改错

共10小题，每小题1分，满分10分。

这篇短文讲述了坏习惯如何养成的过程。

考点如下：

（1）不定式，如第91小题。

（2）替代词，如第92小题。

（3）一般现在时，如第94、96小题。

（4）物主代词，如第95小题。

（5）形容词的比较级，如第98小题。

（6）情态动词，如第99小题。

（7）感叹句，如第100小题。

（七）书面表达

共1小题，满分20分。

要求考生从看图或命题作文中任选一题写一篇200～250字的短文。

选项一为命题作文，题目是“Living in School Dormitories or Living off Campus”。全文由三段构成，每段的主旨句已经在段首给出，考生只需依据主旨句扩展每段的内容。

选项二为看图作文。题中没有给出具体的标题，但通过文字和四幅图画给出了相关的要点，要求考生以学生会的名义给校长写一封信。

作文二选一为考生提供了更多的选择，两个选题都紧贴学生的生活实际，没有出现偏题怪题，学生对话题十分熟悉，主要考查考生的英语应用能力。

三、全国联招和两校联招试卷的比较

（一）听力部分

（1）全国卷和两校卷的考查形式都为对话或短文独白。

（2）全国卷的所有问题均显示在卷面上，有助于考生对所听材料的理解；而两校卷的所有问题均没有标示在试卷上，要求考生自己从录音材料中听取，因而加大了理解的难度。

（3）全国卷的所有材料均只读一遍，而两校卷的对话部分只读一遍，但是短文独白部分会读两遍。

（4）全国卷的对话部分含单层对话和多层对话，短文独白一篇；两校卷的对话部分均为单层对话，短文独白则为两篇。

（5）全国卷的提问多集中于what、which、where、when、why等问题；两校卷的设问除了上述要点外，还有少量听辨数字和听辨发音相似词的题。如两校卷第2题，文中提到的是skirts，而在备选答案中就出现了shirt这样的干扰项。

（二）阅读理解

从分值和题量看，全国卷由五篇材料构成，共20小题，每小题2.5分，满分50分；

两校卷由四篇材料构成，共20小题，每小题2分，满分40分。

从材料类型看，全国卷第五篇材料为旅游指南，重在考查考生的快速阅读能力；两校卷的四篇材料均为400字左右的短文，暂没出现应用文体。

从设问形式看，全国卷除了以往的细节题、主旨大意题以及判断推理题外，还出现了一道体裁判断题；两校卷除了上述题型外，还包括词义猜测题。

（三）词汇

两校卷的词汇题占20分，每题1分，由两部分构成，第一部分是选词填空，主要考查词的搭配、词义辨析等，第二部分是释义题，主要考查单词或短语在具体语境中的含义。其中考查动词及动词短语11题，形容词3题，不定代词1题，副词2题，名词3题。而全国卷并没有单独列出词汇题部分，只是和语法填空一起组成单项填空，在这部分中，词汇题仅2题，每题1分。它主要考查了固定搭配和词义辨析。显然，两份卷在词汇这一部分的分差较明显，考生应引起注意。

诚然，不论词汇题在试卷中所占的比例是多少，词汇对于英语学习而言犹如建造房屋的砖石，砖石不够是无论如何也建造不了宏伟的大厦的，因此，考生在平时的学习中一定要注意识记单词并反复使用，尤其是大纲词汇。2012年考试中，两校卷和全国卷的测试词汇均没有超出大纲范围。考生在识记单词时应学会利用词根、词缀来牢牢记住其意义，同时还应注意词的搭配和用法，以及相似词的辨析等。

（四）语法结构

两套试题都涉及的考点有不定式、定语从句、情态动词、虚拟语气等。除此之外，全国卷还涉及的考点有动名词、冠词、过去进行时、名词从句、状语从句等；两校卷还涉及的考点有主谓一致、it的用法、反意疑问句、宾语从句的语序、形容词的比较级等。纵观近几年的考题，不定式、定语从句、情态动词、虚拟语气等一直是两校和全国联招考试所考查的热点所在，因此考生仍应引起足够的重视。

此外，虽然在此次考试中，全国联招试卷没有涉及强调句、反意疑问句、形容词的级、倒装句等考点，但今后仍是考查的重点。同样，对于两校联招试卷而言，虽然此次考试没有涉及动名词、动词的时态、强调句、倒装句等考点，但考生也需对以上考点加以重视。

（五）完形填空

两套试卷考查名词7题，主要考查考生根据语境选择适当的名词；考查动词6题，主要考查词义辨析、主谓一致等；考查形容词和副词5题，主要考查形容词的级，形容词和副词的搭配等；考查介词和连词各1题，主要考查上下文的逻辑语义关系等。全国卷考查名词9题，主要考查考生根据语境选择适当的名词；考查动词5题，主要考查词义辨析、时态、结合词的搭配及上下文来选词等；考查形容词和副词4题，以及固定搭配1题。显然，在完形填空中，名词、动词、形容词和副词仍是考查的重点，除了要考虑它们的搭配之外，更要考虑它们在具体语境中的灵活运用。

（六）短文改错

全国卷共15小题，每小题1分，共15分；两校卷共10小题，每小题1分，共10分。

热点考点如下：时态一致、主谓一致、代词、情态动词、形容词的级、不定式、词类是否恰当、介词、冠词、关系词、连词等。

（七）书面表达

（1）字数上，全国卷要求100字左右，两校卷要求200~250字。

（2）形式上，全国卷仅给定一题给考生，而两校卷提供了两种选择：看图作文或命题作文。

（3）题目要求上，全国卷用中文给出了部分要点，而两校卷则用英文直接给出了要点或每段的主题句。

（4）两套试卷的主题均贴近学生的生活实际，每个考生基本上都有话可说，得分高低关键在于以下几点：

①题中列出的所有要点必须齐备，评分时，会先根据文章的内容和语言初步确定其所属档次，然后以该档次的要求来衡量，确定或调整档次，最后给出分数。

②用词恰当，尽量选用简洁、标准的大众化词语，尽量使用自己熟悉的词、短语或句型，慎用把握性不大的短语、复合句或长句，避免句子结构混乱。

③适当使用一些表示递进、因果等关系的过渡词，使文章连贯流畅。

④注意词数范围，如全国卷规定词数如果少于80个或多于120个，则扣1分。

地 理

暨南大学华文学院预科部综合教研室
蔡贤榜

2012 年全国联招、两校联招考试地理试卷延续了近几年的命题传统，试题内容在保持相对稳定的情况下有所突破，尤其是考查内容更具有时代性，体现了地理学科特点。试卷在结构设计、考试知识点方面基本上没有超出考试大纲基本内容，现就试卷题型结构、学科知识结构及各细化知识点分布等进行探讨。

一、试卷基本结构分析

1. 题型结构

表 1　2011、2012 年两校联招试卷题型结构比较分析

年份	2011				2012			
试卷结构	题型	题量	分值	比例（%）	题型	题量	分值	比例（%）
	填空题	20	20	13.3	填空题	20	20	13.3
	单项选择题	20	60	40	单项选择题	20	60	40
	判断改正题	5	10	6.7	是非题	10	20	13.3
	填表与连线题	3	40	26.7	读图及连线题	30	30	20
	读图分析题	2	20	13.3	综合题	2	20	13.4
合计		50	150	100		82	150	100

表 2　2011、2012 年全国联招试卷题型结构比较分析

年份	2011				2012			
试卷结构	题型	题量	分值	比例（%）	题型	题量	分值	比例（%）
	选择题	20	60	40	选择题	20	60	40
	填充题	20	20	13.3	填充题	20	20	13.3
	读图、填图题	4	40	26.7	读图、填图题	20	40	26.7
	综合题	2	30	20	综合题	2	30	20
合计		46	150	100		62	150	100

由表 1 可见，2012 年两校联招地理试卷题型结构与 2011 年基本一致，试题由选择题（单项），填空题，判断改正题，读图、填图题或连线题，读图分析题等五大模块构成。2012 年题量有所增加，主要是增加了读图类的知识，目的是加强对考生读图识图能力的考查，有利于较全面反映考生对基础地理空间区位和空间概念掌握的实际能力；增加了是非判断题量及分值，此类题目着眼考查考生的识别能力和运用地理知识的基本技能，体现了地理教学大纲的精神，符合考试大纲的要求。

表 2 中反映出 2012 年全国联招地理试卷题型结构与 2011 年试卷保持一致，这是近几年来全国联招地理试卷的共性，体现了试卷风格趋于成熟定型。这一方面有利于较全面考查考生对地理基础知识的掌握程度、对基本技能的运用能力；另一方面也有利于考生备考，保持考试的连续性。2012 年试卷在题量方面较 2011 年略有增加，扩大了知识面，这种低分值、大题量的结构特点是选拔性考试的发展趋势。

两校联招与全国联招试卷题型结构均保持了各自多年的传统，两校联招较全国联招在题型方面更多一些，在分值上更分散一些，其权重较均匀，减少考试的偶然性，更有利于考生备考。

2．知识结构

表 3　2011、2012 年两校联招试卷知识结构比较分析

	地球与地图		中国地理		世界地理		自然地理		人文地理	
年份	2011	2012	2011	2012	2011	2012	2011	2012	2011	2012
填空题	9	1	2	4	9	14		1		0
单项选择题	9	18	24	9	27	24		6		3
判断改正题/是非题	0	2	2	6	8	0		12		0
填表与连线题/读图及连线题	12	0	12	11	16	4		15		0
读图分析题/综合题	10	10	0		10			10		
分值	40	31	40	30	70	42		44		3
比例（%）	26.7	20.67	26.7	20	46.6	28		29.3		2

注：（1）2012 年两校联招的综合题 3 道选做 2 道即可，本分析就按顺序取前 2 道题目作为统计对象。

（2）2011 年两校联招试卷将知识有机融合，本分析根据考查知识合并为中国地理、世界地理及地球与地图知识三部分。

表 4　2011、2012 年全国联招试卷知识结构比较分析

	地球与地图		中国地理		世界地理		自然地理		人文地理	
年份	2011	2012	2011	2012	2011	2012	2011	2012	2011	2012
选择题	9	9	21	24	15	12	9	6	6	9
填充题	0	0	20	0	20	5	0	10	0	5
读图、填图题	0	0	10	10	10	20	0	10	0	

（续上表）

	地球与地图		中国地理		世界地理		自然地理		人文地理	
年份	2011	2012	2011	2012	2011	2012	2011	2012	2011	2012
综合题	0	0	15	0	15	15	0	0	0	15
分值	9	9	66	34	60	52	9	26	6	29
比例（%）	6	6	44	22.67	40	34.67	6	17.3	4	19.3

表3反映了2012年两校联招考试地理卷中各部分内容相对较平衡，就部门知识结构而言，地球与地图知识占20.67%，中国地理占20%，世界地理占28%，自然地理占29.3%，人文地理占2%。其中区域地理（中国地理和世界地理）部分知识量占48%，综合地理（地球与地图和自然地理）部分占49.97%，这既有利于港澳台、华侨及外籍青年学生更好地了解中国地理知识，又能结合生源地教材实际情况进行有效的备考，体现了两校联招考试的特点。

表4反映了2012年全国联招试卷各部门地理知识的分值分布特点。就部门知识结构而言，地球与地图知识占6%，中国地理占22.67%，世界地理占34.67%，自然地理占17.3%，人文地理占19.3%。其中区域地理（中国地理和世界地理）部分知识量占57.27%，综合地理（地球与地图和自然地理）部分占23.3%。这说明命题侧重于考查区域地理知识，同时人文地理知识考查内容也较多，而地球与地图部分内容相对较少，这也是考虑到天体地理是中学地理教学的难点。同时，我们还发现2012年试卷中各部门地理知识分值较2011年有较大的调整，如将2011年试卷中中国地理、世界地理分值分别由44%、40%调整为22.6%和34.67%，而自然地理、人文地理部分知识点的分值由6%与4%调整到17.3%与19.3%。试卷分值调整幅度较大，使试卷覆盖面更广，信度更高。

两类考试均侧重于考查中国地理和世界地理的知识，说明它们是每次考试的重点内容。此外，全国联招考试也关注到人文地理内容，且考查量正在不断增加，而两校联招考试仍然更关注自然地理方面知识点的考查。

二、试卷知识点分析

两校联招和全国联招考试试题基本符合考纲内容，覆盖面广，重视基础知识、基本技能的考查，但两者也有不同之处。

1．两校联招

表5　2012年两校联招知识点分析

考点＼题型	填空题	单项选择题	是非题	读图及连线题	综合题
地球与地图	等高线	经纬线特点	地方时		等高线地图上地形的读判
		八大行星			
		地球公转			
		太阳直射点移动规律			

（续上表）

题型 考点	填空题	单项选择题	是非题	读图及连线题	综合题
地球与地图		地球公转轨道			
		日期变化规律			
		时区计算			
中国地理	中国河流	长江水文特点	影响中国气候的因素	中国高速公路网	
	影响中国气候的因素	中国经纬度位置	中国典型区气候类型形成		
		世界河流	中国降水分布		
			中国自然环境整体性		
世界地理	世界气候类型分布		太阳辐射及分布	典型气候类型	
	瑞士的工业特点			气温曲线与降水量线读判	
	世界人种分布				
	日本工业布局				
自然地理	世界洋流	全球降水带分布	世界地震带分布	南美洲地形	地球外力作用形成的地貌
		发达工业国家工业布局	水资源的概念		
		世界农业类型	大气能量、河水补给的概念		
		世界重要水上通道	外力作用形成的地貌		
		澳大利亚的人口与工业分布	影响太阳高度角的因素		
		影响工业布局的因素			
		大气分层			
人文地理		中国农业			

由表5可见，两校联招考试强调对地理学科主干知识和基础知识的考查，试卷中与气候相关的考点占22%，共计33分；具体题型分别是：填空题、单项选择题和读图及连线题，主要考查影响中国气候的因素、中国典型区气候类型形成、中国降水分布、由等温线和降水量线判断典型气候类型、全球降水带分布和判断世界特色气候类型等。工业地理内容也是今年两校联招考试的另一个重点，重点考查考生对主要工业国家工业地域和工业区位的了解情况，如瑞士工业特点、日本工业布局、澳大利亚人口与工业分布和影响工业布局的因素等。

从考查的形式看，试题难度系数较小。地球与地图部分内容较少，基本是选择题，而区域地理部分也是一些常识性的知识，没有出现背离教材或考试大纲的内容，综合性题目也仅仅是基础性地理知识的转移，仍未出现多重抽象性的知识点，无论是选择题还是非选择题，都具有针对性强的特点，有利于考生准确解答问题。

因此，考生只要根据考试大纲的内容，在全面认真复习的基础上，重视基本知识和原理的记忆，掌握基础知识并具有一定分析能力，相信能考出较理想的成绩。

2. 全国联招

表6　2012年全国联招知识点分析

题型 考点	选择题	填充题	读图、填图题	综合题
地球与地图	比例尺 相对位置 昼夜长短变化			
中国地理	中国南水北调 西气东输		中国区域 （汉中盆地）	
	中国河流 水文特点			
	影响中国天 气的因素			
	判断天气与气候			
	中国典型地形区			
	中国海洋			
世界地理	世界主要工业区	世界重要海上通道	南亚位置图	温带海洋性气候对西 欧北欧的影响
	热带物种		美国东北 工业区图	
	气候类型			
	非洲河流			
自然地理	世界洋流	大气污染因子	大气热力 作用循环图	
	板块与地形区	板块构造与 火山地震带		

（续上表）

考点＼题型	选择题	填充题	读图、填图题	综合题
人文地理	世界农业地域类型	影响工业布局的因素		两类国家城市化差异
	各洲人口增长特点			
	环境问题			
	影响工业布局的因素			

由表 6 可见，与两校联招考试比较而言，2012 年全国联招考试所考查知识点覆盖面更广，难度系数更大。2012 年在传统考点（工业区位、世界工业布局和气候类型的判断等）基础上增加一些新内容，如加强考查考生地理计算技能，出现两道地理计算题，增加考试的难度，这在往年极少出现；加大考查环境地理的内容，如大气污染因子、大气热力作用循环图、环境问题；更加关注全球性问题，如选择题中的环境问题，填充题中的生态问题、世界人口问题以及世界城市化问题。这既是地理基本知识，又是全球性社会经济问题，因此，2012 年地理试卷的时代性特别明显，应引起考生们重视，这是今后地理学科考试的新趋势。

总之，2012 年两校联招、全国联招考试地理试卷充分体现了地理学科的综合性特点，弱化纯知识性和记忆性题目，强化考查考生的地理知识运用能力，社会热点问题分析能力成为考生必备的地理素养之一。另外，强化地理图表考查，重点考查考生从图表中获取和运用地理信息的能力。无论是两校联招还是全国联招地理考试，考查以地理图表为信息载体的地理空间想象力将成为常态。

物　理

暨南大学华文学院预科部综合教研室
姚　蓓

一、全国联招试卷分析

1. 试题结构

全国联招从 2011 年开始电脑阅卷，试卷结构做了必要的调整，调整后，有效地降低了考生的阅读量，考生一目了然，将答案写到答题卡上，便于电脑阅卷的操作。2012 年全国联招物理试题遵循考试大纲的要求，试题结构与 2011 年的试题结构保持一致，总题数为 19 题，约 4 500 字。全面考查考生对所学物理基础知识、基本技能的掌握程度和运用这些基础知识分析解决问题的能力。

表 1　2011 年与 2012 年全国联招试题结构比较

	力学		热学		电磁学		光学		原子物理	
年份	2011	2012	2011	2012	2011	2012	2011	2012	2011	2012
选择题（52 分）	24	20	4	4	12	12	4	4	8	12
填空题（24 分）	10	8			14	16				
计算题（74 分）	20	20	20	18	18	20	16	16		
分值	54	48	24	22	44	48	20	20	8	12
占试题比例（%）	36	32	16	15	29	32	13	13	5	8
占考纲比例（%）	34		12		34		10		10	

近两年的试题结构对比见表 1。总体来看，2012 年试题一如既往突出力学和电磁学，其分值相同，都是 48 分，所占比例为 32%，略低于考纲要求的 34%；2011 年力学题明显过多，共 54 分，2012 年力学减少一道选择题，并减少实验题的分值；电磁学加大实验题和计算题的分值。热学、光学保持“1 + 1”的模式，即一道选择题和一道计算题，热学 22 分，占 15%，高于考纲要求的 12%；光学 20 分，占 13%，高于考纲要求的 10%。原子物理较 2011 年增加了一道选择题，分值增加至 12 分，占 8%，低于考纲要求的 10%。总而言之，经过调整的 2012 年全国联招物理试题结构更趋于科学合理。

2. 试题内容

表2　2012年全国联招试题主要知识点分布

内容	选择题（13题）	填空题（实验题2题）	计算题（4题）
力学	自由落体运动	游标卡尺、螺旋测微器的读数	匀速圆周运动、动能定理、机械能综合应用题
	动量守恒、牛顿运动定律		
	斜面、动能、牛顿运动定律		
	斜面、物体的平衡		
	多普勒效应		
热学	玻意耳—马略特定律		理想气体的状态变化
电磁学	理想变压器、有效值	测电池的电动势和内阻实验	法拉第电磁感应定律、全电路欧姆定律和安培力综合题
	带电粒子在匀强电场中的运动		
	感应电动势		
光学	光的折射		电磁波的接收与反射测距离
原子物理	原子核的实验		
	原子核的衰变		
	氢原子光谱和能级		

表2列出了2012年全国联招的主要知识点。全卷涉及知识点75个，约占大纲的65%。试卷明显突出了力学和电磁学等核心知识的考核，强调了力和运动的关系、对牛顿运动定律的应用、功和能的关系和综合处理应用、带点粒子在电磁场的运动、基本仪器的使用、电路连接、电磁感应定律与电路和力学综合运用等主干知识的考查。热学的知识点集中在理想气体性质；光学主要考查光的折射和反射；原子物理的知识点依旧是关于探讨原子核内部结构的实验、衰变、氢原子光谱等，但是个别题目超纲，如第10题氢原子光谱中的巴耳末线系，超出考纲要求，未给出相关对应的能级的具体数据；又如第12题多普勒效应也属此种情况。

3. 试题特点

试题重点关注试题与科学技术、社会生活等主题的结合，注重体现物理思想和理念，把考查知识与能力、过程与方法、科学态度渗透在试题中。

试题的单选题共13题，考查的知识点分布较广，有力学、静电学、直流电、交变电流、热学、光学、原子物理。在思维和分析能力的要求上也略高于2011年。而填空题的难度略低于2011年，共2题5空。2012年的实验填空题仍然注重对规定实验的考查，且重点考查了基本的仪器仪表如游标卡尺、螺旋测微器、电流表的读数。计算题4题，依旧是光学、热学、电磁学综合、力学综合的组合。考题设计进一步突出物理知识的灵活实用性，第16题利用光学中光的反射原理，推理出用电磁波的反射测量距离，且有对几何数学知识的灵活运用，使得本题成为试卷中难度系数最大的题。第17题是比较经典的关于理想气体性质的题，要求考生掌握经典的物理模型、物理过程、物理规律，并能简单、直观、正确地展现出来。第18题注意考查考生的综合处理能力，注重将电磁感应、电路和相应的力学知识有机地结合起来；第 19 题有针对性地考核考生的物理思维能力和分析能力。试题的设计做到科学严谨、自然完整，正确体现物理学科内部联系，把物理各部分内容有机结合起来，能够较好地考查考生运用基础知识和基本技能，综合分析和解决问题的能力，测试目标明确。试题的叙述规范合理，稳中有新，稳中有变。试题有鲜明的物理学特点，既有常规题（如第 15、17、18 题），也有比较新颖的试题（如第 16 题），易、中、难的比例大约为 1∶6∶3，试题与 2011 年相比总体难度持平。试题有效地突出考查主干知识，灵活控制试题难度，确保区分度。

二、两校联招试卷分析

1. 试题结构

2012 年两校联招物理试题结构与新大纲要求保持了高度的一致性，题型与样卷高度吻合，满分 150 分，其中选择题 60 分，填空题 30 分，计算题 60 分。

表 3　2011 年与 2012 年两校联招试题结构比较

	力学		热学		电磁学		光学		原子物理		实验	
年份	2011	2012	2011	2012	2011	2012	2011	2012	2011	2012	2011	2012
选择题（60 分）	16	20	4	4	24	20	8	4	8	12		
填空题（30 分）	12	6			6	6	6		3	3		15
计算题（必做每题 12 分）	12	12	12	12	12	12		12				
计算题（选做每题 12 分）	12	12			12	12	12				12	
分值	52	50	16	16	54	50	26	16	11	15	12	15
占试题比例（%）	30	31	10	10	31	31	15	10	7	9	7	9
占考纲比例（%）	30		10		30		10		10		10	
备注	力学和电磁学的百分比计算中，2011 年的总分值是按 174 分，2012 年的总分值是按 162 分。（总分值包含选做题）											

从试题结构看（见表 3），选择题和填空题保持稳定，分值和题量没有太多的变化，但内容进行了合理优化。力、电的选择题由原来的 4 题增加到 5 题，可形成阶梯式难易题，有利于考查考生的思辨能力；将实验题从选做题变成必做题，分值由 12 分增至 15 分，内容由原来只考力、电其中一个实验，变化为考力、电两个实验，加强对考生实验技能的考核。基于有利于电脑阅卷的操作，计算题变化较大。计算题的必做题由原来的 3 题变为 4 题，力、电、光、热各一题，突出对基础知识的掌握与应用的考查，题型较之前更加经典，充分体现出两校联招注重考核基础知识的全面性和掌握基本解题能力的特色。计

算题的选做题由原来的四选二变为二选一，有效地减少了考生的阅读量，考题内容是难度大的力学和电磁学的综合题，提高区分度，更有利于学校选拔新生。

2. 试题内容

从知识结构来看，2012 年试卷考查了物理学科的主体内容：力、电、光、热、原子物理，全卷考查的知识点覆盖了考试大纲的全部，覆盖率为 100%。在考查考生物理基础知识和基本技能的基础上，重点考查了考生的物理思维能力、物理实验能力、综合分析和应用能力。

试卷特别注重对牛顿运动定律、力和运动、功和能的关系、电路与电磁感应等主干知识的考查，具体考查的知识点如表 4 所示。试题易、中、难的比例大约为 4∶5∶1，试题与 2011 年相比总体难度降低。这些知识点都是中学物理的核心内容，也是大学理工类学生所必须掌握的与大学学习密切相关的内容。这种重点考查学科的重点内容和主干知识的命题思路，对考生复习有良好的导向作用。

表 4　2012 年两校联招试题主要知识点分布

<table>
<tr><th>内容</th><th>选择题</th><th>填空题</th><th>计算题</th></tr>
<tr><td rowspan="5">力学</td><td>匀变速直线运动，相遇</td><td rowspan="2">摩擦力</td><td rowspan="5">牛顿运动定律的运用
匀速圆周运动、动能定理
机械能守恒综合应用题</td></tr>
<tr><td>弹力概念</td></tr>
<tr><td>动量、冲量</td><td rowspan="3">简谐振动的周期</td></tr>
<tr><td>匀速圆周运动，地球自转</td></tr>
<tr><td>简谐振动</td></tr>
<tr><td>热学</td><td>理想气体性质的微观解释</td><td></td><td>理想气体的状态方程</td></tr>
<tr><td rowspan="5">电磁学</td><td>输出功率</td><td>电容器</td><td>电场强度、电场力做功、电势差</td></tr>
<tr><td>安培定则判断电流方向</td><td rowspan="4">电磁波传播速度</td><td rowspan="4">法拉第电磁感应定律、全电路欧姆定律和安培力综合题</td></tr>
<tr><td>洛伦兹力</td></tr>
<tr><td>电场强度概念</td></tr>
<tr><td>交流电的有效值和频率</td></tr>
<tr><td>光学</td><td>光的波粒二相性</td><td></td><td>光的折射、全反射</td></tr>
<tr><td>原子物理</td><td>同位素的应用
原子内部电场力做功
氢原子光谱和能级</td><td>放射性元素的衰变</td><td></td></tr>
<tr><td rowspan="2">实验</td><td rowspan="2"></td><td>电磁式打点计时器的使用</td><td rowspan="2"></td></tr>
<tr><td>用电压表和电流表测电阻</td></tr>
</table>

3. 试题特点

试题重点关注物理基础知识与科学、技术、社会、生活等主题的结合，把考查物理知识与能力、物理实验过程与方法、科学态度、价值观渗透在试卷中。

试卷的单选题共 15 题，考查的知识点分布较广，有力学、静电学、直流电、热学、光学、原子物理。在思维和分析能力的要求上略高于 2011 年。填空题分为两部分，前 5 空 15 分，主要考查考生对摩擦力、简谐振动、电容器、电磁波的传播和核反应方程式的掌握，后 5 空为实验题共 15 分，仍然注重对规定实验的考查，并且重点考查了考生是否亲手做过相应的实验，如第 21 题电磁式打点计时器实验中，对纸带上一系列点的处理；第 22 题是电路常规实验“用电压表和电流表测电阻”，难度略低于 2011 年。必做计算题 4 题，考查牛顿运动定律、理想气体状态方程、静电场、光线的折射等经典基础题。选做的力学和电磁学的综合试题体现了对考生物理思维能力和分析、推理能力的考查，如第 27、28 题，要求考生把物理模型、物理过程、物理规律以推理的形式，简单、直观、正确地展现出来，命制这些试题的目的，旨在引导考生重视物理知识形成和发展的过程。

三、复习建议

2012 年联招考试均用电脑阅卷，考题的阅读量较之前明显下降，考核的知识点保持稳定，题型也没有太多的变化，对于备考的考生来说非常有利。由于全国联招与两校联招的侧重面不同，全国联招试题的难度系数大于两校联招，考生的复习策略也应不同。全国联招复习要求掌握各部分知识网络，正确理解物理各部分知识之间物理量的联系，将变化过程中的物理量的变化与物理公式、定理有机地结合起来，并有灵活使用数学知识解决问题的能力。两校联招要求对基础知识的理解要深入全面，特别注意细节处理；重点掌握经典的物理题，特别是在物体变化过程中能对基本公式定理熟练运用。下面根据 2012 年联招的物理试题分析启示，提出复习的有效策略，有助于备考。

1. 选择题

选择题具有考查对象覆盖面大，涉及知识点多，信息量丰富，评卷客观、准确、迅速等优点。这是联招考试必有的题型，两校联招有 15 题，全国联招有 13 题，比重相当大。联招考试中均采用单选的方式，适当地增加考生得分的几率。有计算型、判断型、图线分析型等经典形式。全国联招试题较侧重计算型，如第 3、4、8、10、11、13 题等 6 题；根据状态变化发展推理判断题型，如第 2、5、6、7、9 题等；直观的知识辨认题型，如第 1、12 题等。两校联招判断题型较多，如第 2、4、9、11、12、14 等 6 题；分析推理推断结论题型有第 1、3、5、7、8、13 题等；计算型只有 3 题，图线分析型只有第 10 题，推理判断题最为重要。所以，复习基础知识时，要概念清晰，对于定理、定律要明白其来由，明确定理、定律的使用范围和条件等。做题时明确题意，正确分析物理过程是关键，最好以不同角度确认或排除备选答案，以提高准确率。

2. 填空题

填空题是联招考试必有的题型，在两校联招中占有 30 分的分值，在全国联招中占有 24 分的分值，比重最小。两校联招的填空题，前 5 空一般是简单的计算题和判断题，主要是检验对基本物理原理和物理概念的理解，考查简单运用计算能力。后 5 空与全国联招相同，都是考查实验能力，考查内容一般是实验步骤和实验结果的计算与推导；考查频率最高的知识点是电路的连接，以测量电阻、电动势、内阻等形式出现，通过电路已知量、可直接测量的电流、电压值推出测量物理量的推导结果。所以，复习方法是亲自动手做实验，将考纲要求的实验认真地做一遍，搞清实验仪器和实验步骤，电阻的串联、并联关系等。此外，基本的仪器读数，如游标卡尺、螺旋测微器、电流表、电压表也是常考的知识点。

3. 计算题

计算题是联招考试中分值最高的题型，尤其是综合性的计算题，能对考生的思辨能力、推理判断能力、综合运用知识能力进行全面的考查，具有较高的区分度和信度。在两校联招中占有 60 分的分值，在全国联招中占有 74 分的分值，比重非常大。2012 年，全国联招和两校联招在力学、电磁学综合题的题型上高度相似，均回归经典的物理模型。因此，在联招考试复习过程中一定要重视对计算题的练习，特别要注重解题规范化的训练，也要留意联招考试与生源地物理教材中物理量符号的异同。参加全国联招考试的考生应注意提高数学计算能力。

计算题的主要训练步骤是：①认真审题，建立相应的物理情景；②确立研究对象，进行细致的物理运动过程分析和状态变化分析；③选用正确的物理公式；④列出方程求解；⑤检验结果。

只要考生认真解读联招考纲，掌握考纲要求的知识点，认真复习常考的基础知识，多做经典题型，灵活运用常考的公式、定理和定律解答推算物理过程，提高运算能力，就能有效地解决物理问题，考出理想的成绩。

化 学

暨南大学华文学院预科部综合教研室
李志红

2012 年内地普通高校联合招收港澳台侨生入学考试已经结束了，为了利于今后港澳台侨生有针对性地进行复习应考，我们对联招考试化学试题进行了比较和分析，希望能对考生有所帮助和启发。

一、全国联招试卷分析

1. 试卷结构

2011 年和 2012 年全国联招考试实施网上阅卷，由此引起了试卷结构的一些改变，如取消了计算题的选做部分、总题量由 27 题减少到 25 题、题型只设选择题和解答题两类，原有的二至六题的长题目合为一题等。

2012 年化学试卷结构：选择题（共 18 题，54 分）；解答题（共 7 题，96 分）。解答题中包括填空题、问答题、实验题和计算题等。

2. 考试内容

2011 年和 2012 年全国联招考试化学试题考点分布列于表 1 中。考点是以试题中涉及的知识点进行统计的，有重复。如化学实验与元素化合物、化学计算与化学概念、化学计算与基本原理等。

表 1　2011、2012 年全国联招试题考点分布及比较

	2011 年	2012 年
化学基本概念	物质的熔沸点与纯净物和混合物的关系；化学反应方程式；物质的量、摩尔质量、气体摩尔体积；溶质的质量分数、物质的量浓度 （共 33 分）	化学反应方程式；物质的量、摩尔质量、气体的相对密度、气体摩尔体积、物质的量浓度等 （共 35 分）
原子结构和元素周期律	碱金属的性质递变规律；原子结构和元素的化学性质；化学键的概念、共价键的特点、分子的结构式和电子式；晶体类型、结构和性质 （共 33 分）	原子序数、元素周期律、元素周期表、化学键；卤素性质的递变规律；原子的组成，质量数、中子数、电子数、质子数及其关系；晶体类型、物质的熔沸点与晶体结构的关系 （共 25 分）
化学反应速率和化学平衡	反应热、热化学方程式；化学反应速率及影响因素；化学平衡及反应物转化率的计算 （共 9 分）	化学平衡及其影响因素 （共 3 分）

(续上表)

	2011年	2012年
电解质溶液	酸、碱、盐溶解性及之间的反应，离子方程式，盐类水解反应及应用，水溶液中离子共存及溶液中离子浓度的计算；pH的意义 (共19分)	酸碱中和反应、水溶液中离子的共存、盐类水解的意义及应用，pH和pOH的意义和计算 (共18分)
氧化还原反应和电化学基础	氧化剂、还原剂的概念；根据氧化还原反应方程式的计算；电解原理及电解方程式 (9分)	氧化、还原的概念；电解质、电解原理、电解水、离子的放电顺序；电解池、电极(正负极)的判断、电极反应式 (共20分)
元素及其化合物	常见阳离子和阴离子的性质及检验方法；氯气及含氯化合物的性质；钠及其化合物的性质，碱金属的性质 (共25分)	常见酸、碱和盐的性质；金属活动性顺序，金属单质与盐溶液的置换反应；碳酸的正盐和酸式盐的性质 (共33分)
有机化学	同分异构和官能团的概念；常见的烃类及其衍生物的主要性质；有机物分子式的计算 (共33分)	天然气的性质；同分异构和官能团的概念；烯烃、酚类的命名；醛类的银镜反应；烃类组成中碳氢个数比，气态有机物平均摩尔质量的计算 (共30分)
化学实验	分离和提纯物质的方法；物质的检验方法；酸、碱、盐在水中的溶解性；物质除杂质的方法和实验现象；氯气及其化合物的性质等 (共43分)	实验室制备气体的发生装置和收集气体的装置；离子的性质和检验；电解原理及应用 (共40分)
化学计算	物质的质量、物质的量、气体摩尔体积之间的计算；物质的量浓度、溶质的质量分数和离子浓度的计算；根据方程式的计算；有机物分子式的计算；混合物的计算 (共33分)	气体的微粒数、物质的质量、物质的量、气体摩尔体积的计算；根据方程式的计算、物质的纯度计算、反应物过量的计算；pH的计算 (共32分)

3. 试题特点

(1) 全国联招试题严格遵守考试大纲的要求，试卷形式、试卷结构、考点分布、难易程度等均保持平稳；

(2) 重点考查考生的观察能力、理解能力、实验能力、文字表达能力、灵活运用所学知识进行分析问题和解答问题的能力；

(3) 基本概念和基础理论知识的考点增加，共101分，占总分的67%；

(4) 综合计算题的考点主要是根据化学反应方程式进行物质的质量、物质的量、气体摩尔体积的计算，反应物过量问题的计算，混合物的计算，气体平均摩尔质量的计算等；

(5) 实验题目重点考查考生对知识的应用能力，主要是物质(离子)的检验和物质(离子)的鉴别；

(6) 2012年化学试题增加了电化学知识，如原电池、电解原理及其应用的考点，共

23 分；

（7）增加了解答题的难度，特别是用文字表达和叙述实验过程、结论及解析的考题难度更大。

二、两校联招试卷分析

1. 试卷结构

表 2　2011、2012 年两校联招试卷结构比较

	2011 年	2012 年
选择题	20 题，每题 3 分，共 60 分，占 40.0%	20 题，每题 3 分，共 60 分，占 40.0%
填空题	3 题，共 15 分，占 10.0%	4 题，共 28 分，占 18.7%
问答题	4 题，共 45 分，占 30.0%	4 题，共 32 分，占 21.3%
计算题	3 选 2 题，共 30 分，占 20.0%	3 选 2 题，共 30 分，占 20.0%
总分	150	150

2. 考试内容

2011 年和 2012 年两校联招考试化学试题考点分布列于表 3 中。考点分布是以试题中涉及的知识点进行统计的，有重复。如化学实验与元素化合物、化学计算与化学概念、化学计算与基本原理等。

表 3　2011、2012 年两校联招试题考点分布及比较

	2011 年	2012 年
化学基本概念	化合价的概念、质量守恒定律、分子、原子、离子的书写；溶液、溶解度、溶质的质量分数、物质的量浓度；离子浓度的计算（共 38 分）	元素、原子、离子和分子的概念与区别；物质的量、物质的质量、摩尔质量、气体摩尔体积的概念及相互关系；溶液的概念及组成，溶解度及溶解度曲线的意义，溶质的质量分数和物质的量浓度（共 51 分）
原子结构和元素周期律	元素的概念，原子的组成、结构、电子排布（原子结构示意图）；元素周期表的结构和周期律；氢化物的稳定性、最高价氧化物的水化物的酸碱性；化学键、分子的极性（共 17 分）	元素的性质及元素性质的周期性变化规律；化学键的概念及化学键的类型（共 9 分）
化学反应速率和化学平衡	反应热的概念、热化学方程式的写法和意义；化学反应速率的概念及计算；化学平衡及平衡浓度计算（共 21 分）	化学反应速率及化学平衡，平衡浓度、反应物的转化率、平衡混合物中各种成分的百分数，影响化学平衡移动的因素（共 21 分）

（续上表）

	2011 年	2012 年
电解质溶液	酸碱中和反应、离子方程式；pH 的意义和计算；盐类水解原理及应用 （共 7 分）	电解质的概念、电解质在水中的电离；水的电离、水的离子积；电离度、氢离子浓度及溶液浓度的关系 （共 14 分）
氧化还原反应和电化学基础	氧化剂、还原剂的概念，氧化还原反应化学方程式的配平；电解原理及电解方程式、电解后离子浓度的计算 （共 18 分）	氧化还原反应原理及应用，原电池的原理、电解原理、电极反应式；电解过程中两极反应及生成物的量的计算 （共 18 分）
元素及其化合物	氢气、氧气、一氧化碳、二氧化碳等气体的性质和用途；碳酸的正盐和酸式盐的性质及相互转化；亚硫酸盐的还原性；铝离子的水解、氢氧化铝受热分解 （共 29 分）	重要元素及化合物（氯气、氮气）的性质、制法、用途等；金属活动顺序、金属还原性强弱的比较；物质（离子）的检验 （共 24 分）
有机化学	同分异构体的概念；甲烷、乙烯、乙炔、苯、乙醇、乙醛、乙酸、乙酸乙酯、苯酚等基本有机物的性质；有机物的鉴别 （共 43 分）	有机物、同系物、同分异构体的概念；有机物与无机物的区别与联系；有机物的检验；有机反应的基本类型；官能团的概念、官能团与化合物性质的关系；醇、醛、酸、酮的性质及转化 （共 40 分）
化学实验	分离和提纯物质的方法；常用仪器的使用；一氧化碳还原氧化铁的实验，包括制备纯净、干燥的气体，气体检验及尾气处理，仪器（药品）的连接顺序等 （共 27 分）	基本的实验操作；常用仪器的使用；金属之间的置换反应；物质的检验；一定物质的量浓度溶液的配制；物质的分离方法 （共 23 分）
化学计算	物质的质量、物质的量、物质的量浓度、溶质的质量分数，稀释定律；化学反应速率与化学平衡的各种反应物浓度的计算；根据电解方程式和氧化还原反应方程式的计算 （共 33 分）	物质的质量、物质的量、气体摩尔体积的计算、平均摩尔质量的计算；物质的量浓度、离子浓度的计算；根据电解方程式的计算；化学反应速率的计算；化学平衡浓度、反应物转化率的计算；混合物的计算 （共 44 分）

3．试题特点

（1）2012 年起两校联招采用新考试复习大纲，试题内容严格遵守考试大纲的要求，试卷结构、题型、题量保持平稳；

（2）重点考查考生的记忆能力、观察能力、理解能力、实验能力和运用知识分析解答问题的能力；

（3）2011 年与 2012 年化学试卷结构、题型、题量等都基本相同（见表 2）；

（4）考点涉及的知识覆盖面比较广，难易程度适中；

（5）试卷中有关基本概念和基础理论知识的考点增加，共 113 分，占总分的 75.3%，其中化学基本概念占总分的 34%；

（6）计算题难度提高，近两年的计算题主要是化学平衡、电解平衡、氧化还原反应等有关的计算；

（7）问答题所占比重增加，灵活性增强，有一定难度；

（8）实验题主要考查基本实验仪器的使用方法，气体的制备、检验、收集、除杂质、性质，离子的检验等。

三、复习建议

近年的联招考试化学试题更注重对基础知识和基本技能的考查，2012 年联招考试化学试题有关基本概念和基础理论的考点占总分的 70% 以上，化学实验的考题与概念、理论、元素化合物知识结合紧密，化学计算题的难度、题量和考点基本保持稳定。根据近年的考试特点，对今后的复习应考提出以下几点建议：

1. 注重基本概念和基础理论知识的学习，夯实基础

联招考试化学试题的考点以考查基础知识和基本技能为主。这就要求考生在复习过程中，熟练掌握所学的化学概念和理论知识，注意知识之间的联系和区别，并能应用知识解答问题。在考试答题中，有的考生在化学式、结构简式、元素符号、化学方程式、离子方程式的书写等问题上失分比较严重。例如，2012 年全国联招试题：第 19 题关于电解原理的应用，这一题几乎没有得满分的，化学式、电解离子方程式书写错误的特别多，盐酸多写成氯化氢（HCl）；第 20 题对水解和电离的概念分不清楚，水解方程式没有配平；第 21 题中的氧元素（O）错写成氧气（O_2），方程式不配平，化学式写错，晶体类型判断错误等。这表明考生对化学基本概念和原理等知识的理解和掌握还不到位，应用所学知识解答问题的能力也有待提高，所以，考生在复习时应强化基本概念和基础原理学习，特别是要强化文字叙述化学原理、实验过程、实验结果、化学现象分析等方面的能力训练。要时时刻刻抓规范的落实，不能只停留在口头表达，要具体落实在书写上，打好基础是取得优秀成绩的根本。

2. 力争做到认真细致，准确解答，避免出错失分

联招考试化学试题的难度和题量都比较适中，考点均在考纲要求范围之内，但知识覆盖面大，考点分散又细微。这就要求考生在解答题目时，一定要认真审题，仔细书写，避免出现笔误。在考试中，经常有考生拿到试卷急于答题，有时没有读完题目就动笔写答案，没有认真审题，出现错漏就不奇怪了。例如 2012 年全国联招试题：第 20 题的明矾化学式，有一大批考生就漏写了结晶水或结晶水个数写错；第 21 题出现元素判断错误，推断元素是钙（Ca）错写成镁（Mg）、氨气化学式错写成 NH_4 或 $NH_4 \cdot H_2O$；第 23 题，有机物的名称写错的比较多，如甲基误写成甲烷（2－甲烷丙烯、4－甲烷苯酚）、加成反应错写成取代反应、同分异构体漏写苯甲醚（$CH_3—O—C_6H_5$）、银镜反应错写成与氢氧化铜的反应等；第 25 题，计算单位写错、剩余固体的质量没有考虑二氧化硅、计算错误等。2012 年两校联招试题：第二题中的第 4 小题，乙醛和乙酸的结构简式多写一个碳原子，误写成 CH_3CH_2CHO 和 CH_3CH_2COOH；第三题中的第 2 小题，被氧化的氯化氢（HCl）错答为 4 mol，离子方程式写错等。在两份试卷中都有考生写错化学式，如氯化钙（CaCl）、硫酸钠（$NaSO_4$）、硝酸铵（NH_3NO_3）等等。希望考生能引以为戒，平时认真对待每一次的测验、模拟考是大考发挥如常的保证。在考试答卷时做到情绪稳定，不急躁；细心审题，不大意；准确解答，不出错，就会取得优异成绩。

生　物

暨南大学华文学院预科部综合教研室
何红卫

两校联招生物试题是为了考查考生在基础学习和专题复习过程中对生物学基础知识、基本技能的掌握情况，选拔优秀学生进入暨南大学、华侨大学进一步深造。2012 年的两校联招考试已经完成，为了有利于港、澳、台、华侨、华人及其他外籍考生参加 2013 年的两校联合招生考试，使考生能够有针对性地进行复习应考，我们对 2011 和 2012 年两年的两校联招考试试题在试卷结构、考点分布、试题特点等方面做了比较和分析。

一、试题保持稳定

2012 年两校联招考试体现了考试大纲中“以能力测试为主，考查考生基本知识、基本技能的掌握程度，以及运用这些知识分析和解决实际问题的能力”的指导思想。全卷分为三道大题，第一道大题为选择题，共 30 个小题，每小题 2 分，共 60 分；第二道大题为判断题，共 10 个小题，每小题 2 分，共 20 分；第三道大题为综合简答题，共 7 个小题，共 70 分。总分为 150 分。考试时间为 120 分钟，闭卷独立完成。

表 1　2011、2012 年两校联招试卷结构

	2011 年	2012 年
选择题	30 题，每题 2 分，共 60 分，占 40.0%	30 题，每题 2 分，共 60 分，占 40.0%
判断题	10 题，每题 2 分，共 20 分，占 13.3%	10 题，每题 2 分，共 20 分，占 13.3%
综合简答题	7 题，共 70 分，占 46.7%	8 题，共 70 分，占 46.7%
总分	150	150

二、试题覆盖章节及分值

2011 年两校联招生物试题全部考查的是考试大纲中的主干知识，命题围绕着生物学科的主干知识、核心知识做文章，每道题都有一定的综合性，但又不超出考试大纲所规定的考试范围和考试要求，引导教学回归教材。试题中知识点的分布、所占分数和比重如表 2 所示：

表2　　2011、2012年两校联招试题覆盖章节及分值、比值

相关章节	选择题		判断题		综合简答题		分值		比值（%）	
	2012	2011	2012	2011	2012	2011	2012	2011	2012	2011
第一章　细胞学	7	14	1	3	3	3	40	62	26.7	41.3
第二章　遗传和变异	7	6	1	2	3	2	46	40	30.7	26.7
第三章　生物与环境	3	2	0	1	1	1	14	16	9.3	10.7
第四章　人体生理	7	8	7	4	0	1	28	32	18.7	21.3
第五章　生物起源进化与微生物	2	0	1	0	0	0	6	0	4	0
实验	2	0	0	0	1	0	12	0	8	0
其他	2	0	0	0	0	0	4	0	2.7	0

三、命题特点

2011年和2012年的两校联招生物试题严格遵守考试大纲的要求，试卷结构和考点分布基本保持不变，试题难度也相当。2012年的试题保持了2011年的风格，注重基础知识的考查，知识覆盖面较广，同时又具有以下特点：

1. *以考查主干知识为主*

2011年的两校联招生物试题出题的范围、内容靠近预科部编写的《暨南大学、华侨大学联合招收港澳台、海外华侨、华人及其他外籍学生考试复习丛书·生物》，从试题在各章节中所占的比重可以看出，试题以考查学科主干知识为主，其中以细胞学、遗传和变异、生物与环境、人体生理所占比重较大。由于细胞学、遗传和变异、生物与环境、人体生理是生物学的重要内容，因此这些章节比重较大是符合大纲要求的。从表2可以看出，在题量和分值上，试卷侧重第二章“遗传和变异”的内容。另外第一章“细胞学”和第四章“人体生理”所占分值也较重。第五章出了两道选择题和一道判断题，所占分值为4%。另外，在选择题中出了一道植物各部分染色体数的题（第26题）和一道有关单性生殖的题（第19题）。生物实验方面，在选择题出了两道实验方法的题（第29、30题）和一道大题（综合简答题第7题）。

对比2011年和2012年各相关章节分值及比重（见表2）可以看出，与2011年相比较，2012年第一章的比值下降，而第二章的比值上升，第三章和第四章比值基本持平，第五章从零上升为4%，增加了实验和课本外一些其他内容的考查。但这不能作为判断2013年两校联招试题出题规律的依据，只能说明第一章、第二章和第四章在出题时占有比较重要的分量，且实验内容也是未来复习要特别留意的一个方面。

2. *充分体现考试大纲的能力要求*

具体包括以下几方面：

（1）能应用学过的知识和专业术语，正确阐述基本的生物学现象、概念、方法和原理。

（2）正确理解、分析生物学中以图表、图解等表达的内容和意义，并能用图表等多种表达形式准确地描述生物学现象。理解生物体的结构和功能、部分与整体及生物与环境

的关系。

2012 年考图表的题目较多，共有 8 道题。要求考生结合图表，回答出相应的问题。这就要求考生会看图表，明白图表中所给的信息，结合所学知识点，作出正确的回答。

从以上的特点可以看出，2012 年两校联招生物试卷仍然坚持了注重基础知识，强调考查灵活运用所学知识的能力，说明生物学教学应该让学生牢固掌握基础知识，在此基础上培养学生对基础知识灵活运用的能力；还要求对图表能正确理解并表述。

四、复习建议

根据 2012 年两校联招生物试题的特点以及多年的高考复习教学经验，提出以下 2013 年两校联招生物科备考策略：

1. 紧扣教材，夯实基础

夯实基础是提高综合能力的前提，没有扎实深厚的基础知识，解题效率、综合能力就不可能提高。从前两年两校联招生物试题来看，考试内容紧扣教材，注重基础，没有超纲题、偏题、怪题，没超出现行教材范围，基础性强，试题面貌比较熟悉，难度降低。因此，从试题命题导向给出的信息看，复习必须以教材为本，不脱离教材，步步夯实教材基础知识是关键。另外，在夯实基础的同时，注意扩大知识面，增强对生物实验内容的学习。

2. 挖掘内在联系，形成知识网络

多层次多角度地理解和把握基础知识点，构建知识体系，是贯穿整个复习过程的主线。对知识体系的构建要通过师生共同努力，做到网络化、立体开放化和学生自身化。教师以每节考点知识为起点或平台，联系穿插相关章节的内容，使知识结构合理化，让学生在消化记忆中构建知识框架。这种通过教师的引导，由个人融会各章节内容而完成的知识网络，便于迅速准确地提取信息、处理信息，科学地解决问题。近几年来，两校联招试题注重考查考生对基本知识的掌握和理解，基本上没有偏题和难题。也就是说考生只要熟练掌握好考纲所要求的知识，就应该可以取得比较理想的成绩，而不需要去钻难题和怪题。但考生在考试的时候往往由于紧张，或本身对知识的掌握不够牢固，对于哪怕是比较基础的题都不知道如何下笔，遇到多个知识点相联系的题目就更不知所措。所以，建议考生在复习时应把所学知识构成网络图，不但要注意每一章节内知识之间的网络联系，还要建立不同章节之间的知识网络联系。这样既有助于考生快速、准确地提取相关知识，又有助于考生建立起知识之间的联系，在考试中就可以应对自如。

3. 加强训练，注重理科素养的培养

生物作为一门理科课程，考生在学习时要有意识地培养自己的抽象思维能力，培养自己获得新知识的能力，图文信息转换的能力，运用所学知识解决实际问题的能力，语言、图表表达能力，逻辑思维能力。另外，生物学是一门实验科学，加强实验方面的学习，可以更好地提高生物实验技能。这些能力都是理科考生必备的素养。2012 年两校联招生物试题就体现了对考生这些能力的要求。所以考生在备考中应加强这方面的训练，以便提高解题能力和解题效率，取得更好的成绩。